FEMINISM and RECENT INDIAN LITERATURE

FEMINISM and RECENT INDIAN LITERATURE

Edited by
R.K. Dhawan

Prestige
an international publishing house

Published by
Prestige Books
3/28, East Patel Nagar
New Delhi 110 008
Ph. 9818755529
email: prestigebooks@gmail.com
website: asiabookclub.com

Printed at Chaman Offset Press, New Delhi 110 002

Contents

Mistresses and Sisters: Creating a Female Universe: The Novels of Chitra Banerjee Divakaruni

VEENA SELVAM
Anna University, Chennai

Sometimes you want to talk

about love and despair
and the ungratefulness of children
A man is no use whatever then
You want then your mother
or sister
or the girl with whom you went through school,
and your first love, and
first child—a girl—
and your second
You sit with them and talk
She sews and you sit and sip
and speak of the rate of rice
and the price of tea
and the scarcity of cheese
You know both that you've spoken
of love and despair and ungrateful children.

Gauri Deshpande, "The Female of the Species"

The cliched complaint that it's a man's world has more to it than catches the eye. It is an aphorism that captures the androcentric nature of the world we inhabit. The historic, geographic, social, political, intellectual and even mythological definitions of our world are all male, to the complete exclusion of one half of humanity. And yet it is the male version of the world that has traditionally passed for the "truth."

The postmodern spirit challenges, among other things, the solidity of traditional "truths." Truth now is a hollow construct, made possible by language that is itself hollow and can, therefore, accommodate many more such constructs each of which may claim for itself the virtue of veracity. Each edifice of truth has no stronger foundation than a house of cards for it is constructed on ground whose apparent solidity only conceals a vacuous shallowness beneath.

Chitra Banerjee Divakaruni is a product of this postmodern spirit. Her fundamental preoccupation, revealed in her two novels *The Mistress of Spices* and *Sister of My Heart*, is to create a female universe out of (though not outside of) the conventional male world. The male universe is not altogether shut out. There is the obvious effort to bridge the two. But there is a definite attempt at defining them as distinctive domains.

In both her novels conventional geography is rejected. The rejection of other male definitions of the world automatically follow. Tilo, the protagonist of *The Mistress of Spices*, learns to be a mistress on a faraway island that cannot be located on a regular globe.

> 'The island has been there forever,' said the snakes, 'the Old One also. Even we who saw the mountains grow from buds of rock on the ocean bed, who were there when Samudra Puri, the perfect city, sank in the aftermath of the great flood, do not know their beginning.'
>
> . . . 'The island . . . what does it look like? And she?'
>
> 'We have only seen it from far: green slumbering volcano, red sand of beaches, granite outcrops like grey teeth. Nights when the Old One climbs the highest point, she is a pillar of burning. Her hands send the thunder writing across the sky.' (23)

It is a world in which everything is inverted—the dormant but dangerous volcano is painted a life-sustaining green, while the normally pleasant beaches take on a dangerous red hue. The nights are bright with the "pillar of burning" which is the Old One. (That itself is an inversion of sorts for in traditional Hindu mythology that is extensively used in this novel, it is Shiva, the quintessentially male deity, who is depicted as the pillar of fire.)

That the island has always been there, though undiscovered, situates the female universe outside traditional geographic locations. Conventional geography is represented by the various real cities to which Tilo and the other mistresses who have undergone training along with her on the island are sent. These cities are seen as misty images that the Old One shows the mistresses before they can decide where each one wants to go.

> 'Look,' she said.
>
> Cleaving through the milk-thick fog the images piled one on another, their edges hard and glittering.
>
> Skyscrapers of silver glass by a lake wide as ocean, furcoated men and women, white like the snow that lines the pavements, crossing the street to avoid dark skin. Brownsugar girls in flimsy bright dresses, leaning lipsticked on shantytown porches, waiting for customers. Marble mansion walls embedded with glass shards to tear a man's palms to strips. Pothole roads lined with beggars whose skin can't hold in their jagged bones. A woman watching through her barred window a world beyond her reach, while on her forehead the marriage sindur presses down like a coin of blood. Narrow cobble streets, shuttered houses, men in fez eating mejdool dates and spitting out infidel dog as an Indian passes.
>
> All around us, overpowering like singed flesh, the odour of hate which is also the odour of fear.
>
> 'Toronto,' said the Old One. 'Calcutta Rawalpindi Kuala Lumpur Dar es Salaam.' (53-54)

The images are harsh and ugly. The male universe is full of the "odour of hate." The island itself is a world where men are excluded and where, as a result, there is neither hate nor fear.

> We had known it would be hard to leave this island of women where on our skin the warm rain fell like pomegranate seeds, where we woke to birdcall and slept to the First Mother's singing, where we swam naked without shame in lakes of blue lotus. To exchange it for the human world whose harshness we remembered. But *this*? (54)

It is explicitly stated that it is an "island of women." Ironically the phrase "human world" is contrasted, not with a supernatural world, but with the "island of women." The exchange for the island of women is the human world. This indicates that the world as we know it, though inhabited by both halves of humanity, is actually a male world.

That the female universe is an island is also significant. It is cut off from the male universe and the only way in which contact between the two worlds can be established is when the mistresses of their own volition reach out to the other world.

Even when the spice mistresses enter the human world they live isolated within their spice shops.

> when I woke in this land the store was already around me, its hard, protective shell. The spices too surrounded me, a shell of smells and voices. And that other shell, my aged body pressing its wrinkles into me. Shell within shell within shell, and inmost of all my heart beating like a bird. (125)

Tilo is not permitted to leave the store. Within the male universe the store is an isolated female world by itself. Men may enter it but they do not belong there. It is filled with spices that are associated with the kitchen, the traditional female domain. It is evident that Divakaruni does not step out of the sphere of conventional feminine territory. She attempts only to recreate the female world out of existing stereotypes.

In *Sister of My Heart*, once again the protagonists Sudha and Anju live in a female universe. In this novel the male and the female worlds are more symbolic than real.

> the sun hangs low on the horizon, half hidden by the pipal trees which line our compound walls all the way down the long driveway to the bolted wrought-iron gates. Our great grandfather had them planted 100 years ago to keep the women of his house safe from the gaze of strangers. Abha Pishi, one of our three mothers has told us this.
>
> Yes, we have three mothers—perhaps to make up for the fact that we have no fathers. (16)

The girls live in a matriarchal home in which there is absolutely no male control. The only male alive in the family is disguised as Singhji, the driver and exerts no authority over the household. What was originally conceived of as a restrictive boundary for the women is recreated into a female universe just like Tilo's store. But the difference is that the rules that are upheld in this world are those laid down by the patriarchal society. It is only later that the world of the Chatterjee women is completely transformed into a feminine one.

The male world only creates trouble for the protagonists. Marriage tears them apart and Anju moves to America while Sudha to rural Bengal. Men separate them effectively in terms of geography. Their lives are shattered when they attempt to conform to the rules of the masculine society. Anju almost loses her mental stability and Sudha her freedom. It is only when they decide to migrate to a female universe quite removed from male geographic definitions, albeit symbolic, that they begin to find solutions to their problems. When Anju is upset by her miscarriage Sudha calls her over the telephone and tells her a story.

> Once there was a princess who spent her girlhood in a crumbling marble palace set around with guards. They told her what was proper and what was not, and held up their poison spears before her face if she attempted to stray outside the boundaries they had drawn for her. (308-9)

The crumbling marble palace is symbolic of the confined space which men have allocated to women in their universe. The princess (mythic representation of Sudha, the narrator of the story) tries to live by the rules of the male world. She marries the King chosen for her and conceives. But when it is known that the foetus is female, the men decide to destroy the baby. It is then that the queen rebels to protect her baby. She leaves the kingdom and reaches the ocean's edge. (Here Sudha pauses in her story and Anju, slowly recovering from her depression, continues the tale.)

> Then, very softly, I hear Anju's voice. 'But suddenly the queen heard someone say, "Don't worry, dear one. Reach for my hand." And looking up she saw a rainbow that extended all the way from the other side of the earth to her. You see in all this turmoil, the queen had forgotten that she had a twin sister who lived in the land across the ocean. The sister was sending her all her love in the form of this rainbow.

> Anju's voice falters, but I take up the story. 'The queen held her daughter with one hand and with the other she grasped the rainbow. And her sister pulled her across the ocean, over the gaping jaws of sea monsters to safety.' (310)

It is only beyond the male world that the protagonists find safety. Although the female universe, unlike Tilo's island and store, are only symbolic and not material realities, it is still the only refuge for the women.

The female world though cannot be made up of isolated women. They need to bond with one another in order to create a safe refuge for themselves. Divakaruni has expressed her ideas about female bonding in her article for *Bold Type*:

> In the best friendships . . . with women, there is a closeness that is unique, a sympathy that comes from somewhere deep and primal in our bodies and does not need explanation, perhaps because of the life-changing experiences we share—menstruation, childbirth, menopause. The same tragedies, physical or emotional, threaten us. . . . We take joy in the same small, good things of life. . . . Oh, we fight too. We're sometimes furiously competitive and bitchy and exasperated. But ultimately we can be ourselves with each other. Ourselves with all our imperfections. Ourselves uncomplicated by all the emotions that complicate our other relationships: duty, lust, romance, the need to impress or control. We can be women and that, as women, we are understood.

In both novels the idea of female bonding is explored, though there is a greater focus on the theme in *Sister of My Heart*. Divakaruni speaks of her particular concern with this topic while speaking of her second novel.

> My latest novel, *Sister of My Heart*, explores the particular nature of women's friendships, what makes them special and different. The two main characters, Sudha and Anju, grow up in the same household, love each other fiercely and completely, and know each other so well that they believe no one else will ever know them this way.

Female bonding is definitely different from male bonding. Also women relate to each other in a manner quite unlike the way they relate to men. As in Gauri Deshpande's poem, cited as the epigraph of this article, women bond with each other in a circumlocutory manner.

Tilo bonds with the Old One and the other women who were on the island training to be mistresses. There on the island she feels safe and secure. When once she lands in America in her spice store she is able to empathise with her women customers better than with her male customers.

> But here is another image. A woman in a kitchen, cooking my rice. She is fragrant as the grains she rolls between her fingers to see if they are done. Rice steam has softened her skin, has loosened hair tied back taut all day. Has gentled the smudges under her eyes. Payday today, so she can begin the frying, mustard seeds sputtering in the pan, brinjal and bitter gourd turning yellow-red. Into a curry of cauliflowers like white fists, she mixes *garam masala* to bring patience and hope. Is she one, is she many, is she not the woman in a hundred Indian homes who is sprinkling, over sweet *kheer* that has simmered all afternoon, cardamom seeds from my shop for the dreams that keep us from going mad? (61)

Although she helps all who come to her store irrespective of their sex, she can feel the pain of the women like Lalita Ahuja and Geeta as her own. Her understanding of the women is expressed through the typically feminine metaphor of spices. Although she does reach out to male characters like Raven, Haroun, Geeta's grandfather and Jagjit, she cannot relate to them in the same way. When Tilo talks about the lessons she learnt on the island she says:

> Most of all we learned to feel without words the sorrows of our sisters, and without words to console them. In this way our lives were not so different from those of the girls we had left behind in our home villages. (52)

They learn this lesson of bonding with other women by doing ordinary everyday chores like sweeping and stitching. When she says that their life on the island of spices was no different from that of the village girls, the implication is that women for generations have learnt to bond with one another while learning household chores. Female bonding, therefore, has always been indirect and Tilo learns it in the same indirect way as women all over the world.

In *Sister of My Heart*, the bond between the two characters, Anju and Sudha, is examined. The title itself speaks of the emotional ties between the two women. Divakaruni's use of the word "sister" in both her novels reflects her specific concern. Sister here is used in the sense of a universal sisterhood, a female universe by itself. Sudha and Anju live in a world of their own removed from the others around them.

> I could never hate Sudha. Because she is my other half. The sister of my heart.
>
> I can tell Sudha everything I feel and not have to explain any of it. She'll look at me with those big unblinking eyes and smile a tiny smile, and I know she understands me perfectly. (24)

Their particular manner of relating to each other is through the myths, legends and fairytales of their childhood. Even in adulthood they continue to communicate through tales. (The story of the queen who fought to keep her female foetus alive has already been cited above.)

Their own life has a mythic quality about it. Sudha and Anju are close because it was Anju who called Sudha out into the world. When Nalini, Sudha's mother, tells the story of Sudha's birth, she remembers how she had trouble in labour. Then Anju's mother, Gouri, who had delivered only a few hours before,

> walked all the way across the hall with Anju in her arms and put her face down on my stomach. Anju lay there for a moment, draped over my huge belly . . . all at once she gave a loud cry, and right then I felt a contraction so strong it was as if my backbone was snapping in two. Next thing I knew, the midwife was handing Sudha to me, saying, "It's another girl." '
>
> 'That's why Anju is my twin, don't you see,' Sudha said. (29-30)

There is more myth and mystery surrounding the girls' fathers. One part of the story is told by Pishi to Sudha. Sudha's father had lured Anju's father to the cave of rubies with a story about how a friend of his had inherited a ruby brought from the cave.

Later, towards the end of the novel, Sudha gets to know the real story of what happened after the two men went to the cave. She also gets to know the incredible truth that the man who has for so many years served in their house as the driver Singhji is really her father. But in the end neither the myths nor the truths of the male world have any use for the girls. They do not affect the relationship between them in any way.

The mythic framework of both these novels contributes to the creation of a female universe. The world of myth is essentially feminine in nature as opposed to the cerebral world which is masculine. In both novels there is an attempt to create fresh myths or at least give new interpretations to existing ones.

Tilo, the mistress of spices takes her name from Tilottama, the divine danseuse in Indra's court. But she also brings another meaning to the name. She associates herself with *til*, the sesame seed. In this sense, the divine and the earthly are united in Tilo. When she decides to give up the divine and restrict herself only to the human, she takes another name—Maya, a name with profound mythological and philosophical associations. Maya, in Hindu philosophy is feminine and is the principle behind the entire material universe. The material universe is considered an illusion. When Tilo assumes the name Maya, she once again reasserts her earthly and feminine character.

Tilo's friends are serpents. All her mythic knowledge has been imparted to her by serpents. The serpent is usually a chthonic manifestation of the Mother Goddess and is therefore a symbol of fertility. By association it is also a symbol of the feminine. Divakaruni uses conventional myth and symbolism whenever it serves her purpose of creating a female world.

But in *Sister of My Heart*, Divakaruni rejects conventional myths and creates new ones. The first book in the novel is titled *The Princess in the Palace of Snakes*. In this part both the protagonists attempt to conform to the traditional feminine roles allocated by the male hegemonic society. This is symbolised by the traditional fairytale of the princess in the palace of snakes waiting for her Prince Charming to rescue her. The second book is titled The Queen of Swords. This is not a traditional fairytale.

(The tale has already been cited earlier in this essay.) When Anju is upset over her miscarriage, Sudha tells her this tale and Anju recovers. Then she relates what happened to the three mothers. Then Pishi, the usual teller of tales, asks her about the story she told Anju.

> 'I told her a story.'
>
> 'Ah, a story,' nods Pishi. More than any of us, she knows the power stories hold at their centre, like a mango holds its seed. It is a power that dissipates with questioning, so she merely asks, with an odd, wistful look, 'Was it a story I had told you, Sudha?'
>
> I am sorry to disappoint her. 'It's a new story. One I made up, sort of, on the spot.'
>
> 'Does it have a name?' asks Gouri Ma.
>
> I start to shake my head. Then it comes to me.
>
> 'The Queen of Swords,' I say. (312)

This new myth symbolises the new feminine world that Divakaruni envisages. It is a world across the rainbow (ironically a conventional symbol of hope) where women rescue other women and do not wait helplessly for the men.

This change is seen not only in the story that Sudha narrates but also in her attitude and her actions. During their childhood, the girls used to enact the fairytales that Pishi told them. Sudha always played the princess in danger and Anju the prince who rescued her. Even while they were playacting, Sudha would never reach out to the prince and help him help her. She always said that it was the duty of the prince to do all the hard work and rescue her. Later when she falls in love with Ashok and the mothers decide to get her married elsewhere, she waits for Ashok to make all the moves and rescue her. But after her marriage to Ramesh, she enters a household ruled by her tyrannical mother-in-law. She puts up with the ill-treatment there for a long time, still the conventional princess of the fairytale, waiting for her husband, the prince, to rescue her. When she conceives and it is established by tests that her baby is a girl, her mother-in-law tries to force her into an abortion. But now Sudha decides that she should do something to protect her baby. She leaves her husband's home and returns to her parental home in Calcutta. She transforms herself, from the princess in the palace of snakes to the queen of swords. She refuses to return to Ramesh. She also turns down the conditional offers of Ashok to marry her. The rejection of male-allotted stereotypical roles is complete. Sudha's journey to America is really the beginning of her journey to a new world of women.

The mothers also enter this new world of women. This is symbolically shown when they sell their dilapidated, ancestral house and move to a new flat. The change in them after they move to their new home is amazing.

> Along with the old house, the mothers seem to have shrugged off a great burden of tradition. Perhaps, ironically, I helped it happen. For now that I have come back neither wife nor widow, now that I have let go of all that society considers valuable, what is left for them to fear? Away from those ancient halls echoing with patriarchal voices which insisted that foremost of all they must be widows of the Chatterjee family, for the first time they can learn to live their lives with a girlish lightness. (296)

The mothers begin to lead a fulfilling life with a social purpose. They listen to the music that they like and take walks where they please. They no longer worry about the social stigma attached to a divorcee and keep Sudha with them. They lovingly take care of her daughter. The final gesture of the rejection of patriarchal norms and the acceptance of the rules of the new female universe is the gifting of the ruby left to them by Sudha's father to Dayita, Sudha's daughter.

Much of Divakaruni's writing is inspired by her experiences and encounters with suffering women in the organisation Maitri, which she has established to help battered women in America.

> My work with Maitri has been at once valuable and harrowing. I have seen things I would never have believed could happen. I have heard of acts of cruelty beyond imagining. The lives of many of the women I have met through this organization have touched me deeply.
>
> It is their hidden story that I try to tell in many of the tales in my short story collection, *Arranged Marriage* and my subsequent books. It is their courage and humanity that I celebrate and honor.

It is Divakaruni's professed manifesto to celebrate the courage and humanity of suffering women who have rebelled against oppressive patriarchy and have joined a universal sisterhood. Both Maitri and her writings are efforts in the direction of creating a world of women. The effort is certainly rewarding both for the author and for her readers. Both the novels, despite defects and discrepancies, ring a fervent note of sincerity and that is where their appeal lies.

Works Cited

Divakaruni, Chitra Banerjee. *Mistress of Spices*. London: Black Swan, 1997.

______ . *Sister of My Heart*. London: Penguin, 1999.

______ . *Bold Type*. (1998). n.p. Online Internet. 20 Aug. 2000.

______ . *'Do South Asian Women Need Separate Shelter Homes?'* Rediff on the Net (6 July 1999) n.p. Online. Internet. 20 Aug.2000.

Lucy, Niall. *Postmodern Literary Theory*. Oxford: Blackwell, 1997.

Chitra Banerjee Divakaruni: A Rising Star in the Diasporic Literature

R. LALITHA
Aurora Engineering College, Bhongir

There are innumerable Indian authors who have written in English. Some have reached incredible heights of literary firmament and are shining stars. To name a few—Raja Rao, R.K. Narayan, Mulk Raj Anand, Salman Rushdie. They are in no way less compared to any of the British authors. The new generation of Indian authors is a far cry from the senior ambassadors of yesteryears. Maxine Hong Kingston who won the National Book critics award for *The Woman-Warrior* (1976) has paved the way for a radical transformation in the Asian-American literature. Women writers in India have captured the multiple natures of the domestic spaces in a changing world. In *Diaspora and Multiculturalism*, Ramraj reflects: "Though diasporic writing is about or by peoples who are linked with common histories of uprooting and dispersal, it develops different cultural and historical identities depending on the political and cultural particularities of the dominant society" (229).

Chitra Banerjee Divakaruni is an award-winning author, born in Calcutta, who spent the first nineteen years of her life in India. Immigrant writers are nostalgic of their homeland and make creativity an important medium. They are "imaginary homelands, Indias of the mind" (Rushdie 10). Divakaruni has won a readership for her poetry and fiction of immigrant life in the US that takes us into the female psyche and its disruptions through real forms of violence. *A Chronicle of South Asian Woman, A Patchwork of Shawl* highlights the significant contribution made by South Asian women in discussing ideological assimilation and resistance to marginalisation. Divakaruni strongly believes that writers have a social responsibility and she focuses on the life of immigrants as she confesses, "the idea of diaspora is very important to me" (Seshachari 12). Indian experiences are viewed from the diasporic women's lens that facilitates the empathetic understanding of the plight of the immigrants to the U.S. An immigrant writer "is obliged to deal in broken mirrors" (Rushdie 11). But its validity need not be questioned because "the broken mirror may actually be as valuable as the one which is supposedly unflawed" (Rushdie 11). Divakaruni's works flaunt the romanticism of the female body captured in the close ups of rituals and ceremonies from birth to death, constantly brutalised by greed and patriarchal power. The Indian woman is depicted as a passive victim suffering in silence at home and abroad. She attempts to weave "the elements of myth, magic and ancient culture alongside contemporary culture" (Ismat 2).

The Diasporic woman becomes the nucleus for stories of dislocations—geographic and emotional, recollected narratives of grandmothers, mothers, and old daughters and narratives of the women as writers. As Uma Parameswaran writes in "Home is where your feet are, and may your heart be there too!": "Chitra Divakaruni, the most recent star in the Diaspora sky, delves into the darker dreams and nightmares of womanscape and has an appreciative readership among feminists, but since her women characters are mainly Indo-American, there is a tendency to see them not as individuals so much as representative of the Diaspora, and we are back on square one perpetuation of negative stereotypes that the average north American reader has of Indian life and culture" (34).

Immigration carries an infinitely greater responsibility for a woman being the one to maintain her cultural identity in the middle of the evolution of a new being. "Such schisms generate personal crisis for many immigrant women," and is integral to Divakaruni's writings (Uhland 2). In an interview with Gowri Ramnarayan, Divakaruni says: "I think writing is a great tool to create empathy" (*The Hindu*, 5 November 2006: 3). As a child she took a vow that when she gets older, she would search the epics for herself and find the female-female relationships. But when she read the epics and other classic texts of Indian culture, she was surprised to find few portrayals of friendships among women. This was the-thought provoking angle which she highlighted in most of her works. In a conversation with Gowri Ramnarayan, she states: "I think literature is a wonderful way in which people can dissolve their differences and find common ground" (*The Hindu*, 5 November 2006: 3). She focused her writing on friendships with women and trying to balance them with the conflicting passions and demands that come to women as daughters and wives, lovers and mothers. She believed that friendship with women is a unique one because of life-changing experiences that they share—menstruation, childbirth, and menopause. In an interview she states that the force behind her writing "is the desire to put women in the centre of stories, to have their voices be the voices of interpretation, their eyes the ones that we see through. There just hasn't been enough of that in the world, if you look back at literary history." Somdatta Mandal in her article on Bengali Diasporic women writers reiterates: "Chitra has broken away from the 'Footnote School' and the culture specific Indian associations have become passé for the western readers, invoking exoticism in its newer form in a deliberate attempt on the part of the writer to eroticize her own motherland" (136).

Divakaruni approaches the themes of disillusionment and exile in innovative ways. She projects varied themes in her works like inter-racial marriages, mobile parents or preference for alternative sexualities, home and family, ethnicity and identity, body and sexuality through which she articulates a perspective of women's experience of exile in particular and women's alienation in general. She brings her ideas into the story, which makes us feel about the character, and the reality with which she interweaves the story is really appreciable. The characters are very close to reality and we find a balance between old treasured beliefs and surprising new desires. The heroines in Divakaruni's novels lead an imperfect life which shows how women struggle hard for their personal identity. Divakaruni comments that her protagonists may be Bengalis, but her 'Desh' is now America (Roy 1). In an interview, she has reiterated, "My hope is that books will build bridges" (Ismat 4).

There is a remarkable significance of the cultural conflict in most of her novels and short stories. The Indianness in her novels is stunning. She gives prominence to her native culture in which she was born and brought up. The sufferings of women in silent agony are depicted in most of her stories. In spite of the suffering, how a woman in India longs to stay with her husband shows the significance of the tradition of marriages which are not easily broken here. In the collection of stories *Arranged Marriage*, Divakaruni writes about the transformed lives of the women both liberated and trapped by cultural changes. The heroines in almost all the stories lead imperfect lives. In the story "The Bats," the main character is vexed with the domestic violence in the hands of her husband and runs away to her distant uncle in a village. Social norms play a key role in this story, as she is unable to listen to the words, which women often say. She is optimistic about her family life even after repeated blows she faces from her husband. This clearly shows the demarcation between the cultures of America and India. Living together, dating and staying as unwed mothers are common things in a liberated society like America, but in India at least some sections of people still value social norms, customs and traditions. So, even if they have an unhappy marriage they cannot take a decision of breaking it. In another story "Silver Pavements Golden Roofs," the young girl Jayanthi in order to pursue her studies reaches America and stays with her aunt and uncle. Divakaruni writes about how it is not that easy to settle down in an alien land. "Things here aren't as perfect as people at home like to think. We'd thought we'd become millionaires. But it's not so easy" (43). Divakaruni speaks about racial discrimination: "The Americans hate us. They're always putting us down because we're dark-skinned foreigners, kala admi" (43). Crime, which is at a higher rate and the risks that are included in running a business, are presented to us in a very lucid manner. "This damn country, like a dain, a witch—it pretends to give and then snatches everything back" (54). The protagonist of "clothes" rather poetically sums up her predicament in the "land of freedom" thus: "Caught in a world where everything is frozen [. . .] like a scene inside a glass paperweight. It is a world so small [. . .] I stand inside this glass world, watching helplessly [. . .] wanting to scream" (26). These lines depict the entangled web of the Asian immigrant women that involves the twin processes of "migration" and "relocation" and it ultimately ends up in a "Trishanku" existence (Parameswaran 292).

The young girl Jayanthi fancies in her dreams: "will I marry a prince from a far-off magic land?"(54) The enthusiasm which the child shows in looking at the simple things like the well in the story "The Bats" shows how in modern society children brought up in cities watch the simplest things of life with fascination. On seeing the simple things like the well and the chicken, the child feels as if she had entered into a fantasy world because she had known about them only in picture books. "A real well! I clapped my hands in delight. I'd only seen wells in picture books" (4). In the story "The Word Love" the heroine starts living with a man. Love is magical and mysterious word which cannot be defined easily. Americanization has been accepted in totality when the young woman decides to live with her boyfriend outside the institution of marriage. She recollects how her mother had taken pains to bring her up after her father's death. Mother-daughter relationship, which is something special, can be seen at its best in this story. She makes a self-introspection in living with a man even before marriage and repents for hiding this from her mother. She wants to confess and finally faces the wrath of her mother after her confession. She cannot bear the thought of losing total correspondence with her mother. This made him say: "it was never me, was it? Never love. It was always you and her, her and you" (70). Thus parental love makes her take a decision to live alone. Even though one lives thousands of kilometres away from their native lands, their native cultures and traditions make them nostalgic. As against the regular themes of women's sufferings in the earlier stories, "The Disappearance" tells something about a man's feelings. Divakaruni highlights the relationship between husband and wife that should run smoothly like two wheels of a cart. He was badly affected with the absence of his wife as the crime rate is high in that area. She was not a quarrelsome one and it never appeared that she was dissatisfied. Later he realised that she intentionally eloped by taking the jewellery with her. He was very much surprised on knowing this and couldn't forget her even after remarriage.

The dissatisfaction of women is the major theme in most of the stories. If they live in a liberated society like America, they break the marriage easily, but if they stay in a close knitted society like India where every act of women is watched with a microscopic view they suffer in silent agony. The story "Doors" is a perfect blend of the two cultures—western and Indian. Preeti, the protagonist, brought up in America, settles to marry Deepak who is from India. In spite of her mother's warning, she marries Deepak. Preeti being a lonely child is a private person and always wants the doors closed. Hospitality has its own definitions and parameters in these two societies. This is the view which brings clashes between the couple. Preeti realises how in insisting to shut the doors, she is shutting herself even from her husband. "Ultra Sound" presents a sensitive portrayal of the treatment which an expecting mother meets after knowing about the arrival of a girl child. The mother-to-be Runu is castigated for decimating the masculine bastion by giving birth to a daughter. Runu's friend Anju invites her to America in order to give her reprieve from her ill-fated life. Yet she worries about her friend's future. "Had I taken all that away from her by my misplaced American notions of feminism and justice?" (227) Meera had a live-in relationship with Richard in "A Perfect Life." The feeling of motherhood upsurges when she suddenly discovers a six-year old boy one morning in a rose garden. She names the child as Krishna which brings in the image of the mythical Krishna in the Brindavan. "Mother love, that tidal wave, swept everything else away. Friendship. Romantic fulfilment. Even the need for sex" (98-99). With the disappearance of the child life which once appeared "civilised, as much in control, as perfect" (77) suddenly turns imbalanced. She settles to marry Richard as an antidote to the child's disappearance, on the condition that she is never burdened with biological maternity.

She not only shows us how contemporary society makes an individual but also portrays how man's greed has wreaked havoc and horror in the world we live. She enlarges the enormity of consequences. She recognizes the social, economical and psychological forces behind colonialism and strives to show how they dehumanize both the colonizer and the colonized. These worlds are also imbued with a moral vision that emphasizes social interaction, growth and carrying out of responsibilities. Divakaruni expresses her own idiosyncrasy, one that is composed of facts and fancy where a vision of life and love is revalued. She has forged a new identity in the process of cultural variation, in which the translated self has lost much more than it has gained. Most of her stories shuttle back and forth between Bengal (mostly Calcutta) and the U.S. because those are the places and cultures in which she is most at home and can write about with great confidence. In her works, Divakaruni continues to explore such contentious social issues as abortion, the failure of family life, single parenthood, childlessness, loneliness, illness, age and death. Her stories are full of isolated and eccentric people, a little unhinged but with deep human sensitivity. If they appear to inhabit a crazy world, it is our world and she draws them with compassion and artistry.

Works Cited

Brah, Avtar. "Diaspora, Border, Transnational Identities." *Feminist Postcolonial Theory:* A Reader. Ed. Reinia Louis and Sara Mills. New York: Routledge, 2003. http://www.ebstudios.com/homespun /poetry/divakaruni.html

Gibson, Margaret. "Accommodation without Assimilation: Sikh Immigrants in an American High School." Qtd. Richard Albee and Victor Nee. *Remaking the American Mainstream.* London: Harvard University Press, 2003.

Ismat, Mangla. "Review of *The Queen of Dreams* by Chitra Divakaruni," *Nirali Magazine*, 2 October 2004.

Mandal, Somdatta. "The City of the Mind or Return to Roots, Representations of Calcutta in the Fiction of Diasporic Bengali Women Writers," ed. Rajender Chetty and Pier Paolo Piciucco, *Indias Abroad: The Diaspora Writes Back*. Johannesburg: S.T.E, 2004.

Mathur, Suchitra. "Ethnic or Postcolonial? Gender and Diaspora Politics." Review of *A Patchwork of Shawl: Chronicles of South Asian Women in America*, ed. Shamali Dasgupta, 2000: 1-4.

Mycak, Sonia. "Theorising Ethnicity: Ukrainian Emigre Literature!" *New Literature Review*, ed. Efi Hatzimanolis and Brigitta Olubag. New South Wales: University of Wollongong, 24, 1992 79-90.

Parameswaran, Uma. "Contextualizing Diasporic Locations." *Diaspora: Theories, Histories, Texts*, ed. Makarand Paranjape. 290-300.

___. "Home is where your feet are and may your heart be there too!," *Writers of Indian Diaspora: Theory and Practice*, ed. Jasbir Jain. Jaipur: Rawat, 1998.

Rai, Sudha. "Re-Mythologies: The Dialectical Aesthetics of the Female Self in Diasporic Poetry." *Expatriate Indian Writing in English* ed. T. Vinoda, P. Sailaja. vol. I. New Delhi: Prestige, 2006.

Ramraj, V. "Diasporas and Multiculturalism." *National and Postcolonial Literatures*, ed. Bruce King. Oxford: Clarendon Press, 1998.

Rushdie, Salman. *Imaginary Homelands*. London: Granta, 1991. <sasià lit-owner@mailman.rice.edu> <http://www.saja.org/divakaruni.html> <www.Sawnet.com>

Seshachari, Neila C. "Writing as Spiritual Experience: A Conversation with Chitra Banerjee Divakaruni." *Weber Studies* 18.2, Winter 2001: 1-16. *The Hindu*, 5 November, 2006, 3. <http://www.time.com/time/daily/special/india/chitra.html

Uhland, Mary. "Paroxysms of Desire: Visions of Psycho-Social Schemes in the Immigrant Literature of Chitra Divakaruni and Gita Mehta." Paroxysms.html.1-14.

Immigrant Dilemma and Feminist Sensibilities in Chitra Divakaruni's *Arranged Marriage*

REENA SANASAM
DEVASHREE BHATTACHARJEE
NIT, Silchar

In Divakaruni's short stories entitled, *Arranged Marriage*, we can explore the psychological conflicts playing in the minds of her protagonists, as they venture into the western way of life and culture. The protagonists of her stories struggle between the irony of past memory and new situation. Her characters struggle between these two diverse worlds, and crave to assimilate these two extremes for a new future. They are so entangled in their root and origin that every step they take in their newfound land is approached with a half-hearted will. The protagonists linger in their past life with nostalgia, amidst the claims of an exotic and coveted culture, gradually sucking up and consuming them completely. Somewhere in the deepest terrain of their memories, they can feel the scars of those long forgotten memories and make them conscious that they still persist. These memories of the past make the characters hesitant to move away freely with their newfound life in America.

The author explores India and America as two different worlds epitomizing two different cultures, and for the immigrant Indians, new life in America was like 'being thrown into the sea' even before learning how to swim. It is really a new and a very different setting. For the immigrant Indians, it is a mixed experience too, at one time it acts as a boon that shatters the inhibitions and taboos, with which they have long been associated, and at other time they experience the void and nothingness of a superficial culture. This is typical to all the immigrant Indians where freedom does not come without a price. It places all the protagonists on the same plane with Sita in the *Ramyana*, who becomes more vulnerable after crossing the *Lakshman Rekha*.

Divakaruni's stories deal mainly with the clash of a primitive way of life with the western ideals of high culture. Her protagonists, mainly immigrant Indians, dream of walking past their lived experiences and practices to experience exotic land, and explore unknown realms. Even though her protagonists aspire to adapt to their newfound world, Divakaruni's female characters, as they are firmly rooted in tradition, find it hard to break the bounds set by patriarchy, to experience what has so far been restricted in their life, and resolve the psychological conflict that is accompanied with the new situation. Other than the problems of immigrant Indians in American society, she also presents very vividly the dilemmas of Indian women in traditional society. Her women characters represent the sentiments of women within traditional bounds and outside traditional bounds. Divakaruni's stories are also replete with vivid and lively images of Calcutta dwellings and surroundings, which we can experience through the longings of the nostalgic minds of the protagonists. Her characters are so emotionally attached to their past, that they cannot revel and rejoice at their newfound freedom without scrutiny and a sense of scepticism. This dilemma is basically the result of these two lived experiences, which develop conflicting ideologies in the minds of the protagonists.

The expectation of a different culture, and the pull towards the unknown realm, is altogether a new experience, and this aspect is well substantiated when we come across these lines where the protagonist craves to assimilate in her speech certain English words as a sign of westernization:

> "Sorry," I say, "So very sorry," like the nuns had taught me in those old, high-ceilinged classrooms cooled by the breeze from the convent neem trees. ("Silver Pavement," 35)

For the immigrant Indians, the past and its associated traditions have their own beauty and assurance, in spite of their limitations. This realization, which comes with the experience of freedom, makes one sympathetic towards one's own prejudices against one's own culture and tradition. This awareness gives the protagonists of Divakaruni's stories, a sense of new judgement and understanding of their own culture and traditions. Culture changes according to the demands and needs of the protagonists, but to detach old memories and old past from their psyche, as they move further away to suit expectations of the present and future, becomes a conflicting task. In Divakaruni's writings, we see the struggle of the protagonists as they progress to assimilate their past and their newfound situation, and feel the unfulfilled longings of the characters who, finding themselves stranded in the middle of nowhere, desperately try for a way out and suffer in the process. This dilemma is the core of Divakaruni's writings. "The Americans hate us. They're always putting us down because we're dark-skinned foreigners, kala admi. Blaming us for the damn economy, for taking away their jobs. You'll see it for yourself soon enough." (43)

The domination of a superior culture or race hindering the local culture, hypnotizing us with their outward superficiality, whose theme ultimately is hollow and void, is quite obvious as we explore her writings. Her protagonists struggle to find solace, assimilating the two worlds, her past and the present, but the conflict that arose makes the protagonists, at times, schizophrenic and disillusioned. This phenomenon gulps down the minds of the protagonists in their aspiration to achieve something in life. "But here my imagination, conditioned by a lifetime of maternal censorship, shuts itself down." (45)

The hungry yearning for "homehomehome" (55) when disillusioned by the stark reality of the coveted American culture, makes evident the realization of a lost essence of the past. Then the ultimate realization that "the beauty and pain should be part of each other." (56)

In the story, "The Word Love," we find the dilemma of the protagonist in the middle of two cultures, one represented by her mother and the other by her boyfriend. The protagonist struggles to make a choice between her mother and her boyfriend, which ultimately lands her in the middle of nowhere. In this story, the protagonist experiences ideological conflict as she struggles to leave behind her mother's ideals and continues a live-in relation with her foreign boy friend. Her respect for her tradition and her past makes it hard to lie to her mother about her affair, and also at the same time she is unable to come out of her relationship. This situation is best explained when we come across the boy-friend advising her to forget her mother, alluding to the need of cutting the umbilical chord.

> "So don't tell her," he said, "that you are living in sin with a foreigner, no less. . . . You don't want to hear the question, which might be how did you get yourself into this mess, or perhaps why, so you leap in with that magic word." (59)

Something in her urges her to coax those past memories out of their dark recesses. But it persists giving her solace, and tries to bring back a newer option, to recuperate the mistakes she had committed by living with a foreigner outside the sanctity of marriage. "What will you remember of him when it is all over." (63) The warring experiences, ultimately, gives her new strategy to deal with her dilemma and chalk out ways of surviving with the old past and the present cosmopolitan culture. The past, in spite of its failings, gives the protagonist strength to move forward with a new hope.

Looking from another angle, we find that there are some of Divakaruni's protagonists who are so much stuck in the web of social stigmas and prejudices that they find it unable to shed off those bindings and move towards a renewed life and vision. The opening story of Divakaruni's enthralling collection of short stories *Arranged Marriage*, "The Bats," projects such a situation. It is a touching and heart-rending tale of a young girl caught between an abusive and cruel father and a torn and helpless mother. It is the story of a girl who is yet on the verge of being initiated into the life of experience and the first thing which she notices as the initial stirrings of realizations dawn upon her is that her "mother cried a lot." For anyone of us, being gifted with such a pathetic awareness on the occasion of initiation into life is nothing less than a trauma. Amidst the incomprehensive darkness of a hot Calcutta night, she wakes up startled, to watch her mother crying. "the sound of her weeping would be all around me, pressing in, wave upon wave, until I could no longer tell where it was coming from." The child initially fails to understand why her mother has started sharing her narrow child's bed with her, and also the cause of her mother's agony.

As time flows by, the child grows up with an ever-increasing apprehension of the man whom she knows to be her father, but hardly gets any fatherly affection from him. "I didn't see him much. I heard him, though, shouts that shook the walls of my bedroom like they were paper, the sounds of falling dishes." For a child who is presented with such a draconian image of the figure called father, it is not very hard to discern a foggy silhouette of the painful truth of her mother's life when one day she notices a yellow blotch on her mother's cheek, its edges turning purple. The perturbed child inquires about the mark, and reaches out her hand to touch it. But the mother jerks her head not allowing the child to reach the spot, a symbolic gesture of her denial to give anyone admittance to her pain and shame. However, the truth is no longer really hidden from the young girl.

The next time when the child notices another mark on her mother's face, reddish blue, and even bigger, she is agonized with shock, the shock being more severe for now she no longer needs to guess the cause. In some hidden corner of her heart, she is well aware of that poignant truth of her mother's life to which no one is given access. However, when the mother suggests that they go to grandpa's house, she becomes overtly thrilled. So begins their escapade, their journey from a torturous and confined life to a life of newness, freedom, and liberty from bondage. Life in grandpa's house in the very heart of nature seems no less than a paradise. It is a life of unended bliss; all sorrows forgotten, all wounds healed. "Grandpa-uncle soon became my best friend. All day I would follow him around as he went about his job, which was taking care of the Zamindar's orchard. He taught me the names of all the trees—mango, lichee, kul—and let me taste the first ripe fruits. He pointed out hares and squirrels and girgits that hid in the grass, their shiny greenish bodies pulsing in the sun. On his off-days he took me fishing and taught me how to hold the rod right." (7) Yet, this paradisiacal realm proves to be a very short recluse. It proves to be just a temporary shelter where one may be given enough time to lick one's wounds, but is never allowed to be made a permanent refuge. Unable to stand "the stares and whispers of the women, down in the market place," the wife decides to go back to her battering husband, once again to flee away from something which she now considers the greater of the two evils. The life of adventure and freedom which she had envisioned so broadly seems to betray her pathetically with its negative and darker aspects. So, she goes back to the life which she had left behind, even with its tortures, hassles, heart-breaks. Life once again becomes an infernal experience and the mother and the child's life gets reduced to a never-ending cycle of escapes and returns, as they move out, and move in, always back to the world of batterings, thrashings, crashing agonies.

The dilemma faced by the woman in the story is not dissimilar to the postmodern dilemma faced by all those souls stuck between the crossroads of tradition and modernity, unable to find solace in either. When certain aspects of the conventional pattern of life become morbid and tormenting, one wishes to tear apart all boundaries and escape into a world where everything is replete with novelty, glory and adventure. However, this allure of a magical world proves illusory as soon as one is confronted with its bitter, not-so-open facts. The new kind of claustrophobia which comes with this new world shatters all dreams to smithereens and convinces one that what one had been visualizing so long was no concrete form but an insubstantial mirage. In this story, the journey of the wife and the child from a suffocating environment in an urban setting to a natural and rural backdrop symbolizes the flight from the inadequacies of modern life, which is but a floating essence, to the recesses of the past heritage in quest of a solid foothold. However, it soon dawns on her that even the customary past is not a solid ball but a mere handful of sand which can provide solace only so long we are able to hold the sand-grain in the palm of our hands. The moment we allow our courage, patience and endurance to slacken, the grains start flowing out from between our fingers even before we know it, and what we are left with is nothing but an empty hand, forlorn, forsaken. The wife reverts to the past in search of peace, but when the buried past resurrects itself with its same old troubles, the prejudices of blind and orthodox customs, the irony of culture, the social stigma, the unbearable tauntings, the wife finds herself stranded once more on the shores of loneliness. She is in a precarious position, on the fringes of a shore from which she can witness the ebbing waves of the past securities, and at the same time feel the trembling and slackening of the present ground beneath her. Janus-like, she faces two opposite directions, but none seem to offer any relief.

The story, "The Bats," is also a hallmark of feminist sensibility. Here we find a woman whose life is an unhappy cauldron of untold miseries, unsung agonies, unheard dirges, a deep ocean of betrayals, those very betrayals which she prefers to keep buried within the impenetrable domain of her sepulchral heart, lest they blurt out into the open and expose the vanities of those conventional footholds to which she strives to keep herself glued. The readers' hearts tear with painful empathies as they follow the sorrowful journey of the mother who runs away from the endless beatings of her husband in the hope of discovering a life of quietude for her child and herself, but agonizedly recoils to the same intolerable situation when she realizes that conventional society has no place for a woman who has crossed the determining bounds of her home, the Lakshman Rekha to which she is bound. The greatest irony for a woman lies in the fact that there is no 'coming back.' Every step taken by her, whether voluntarily or involuntarily, is a *Lakshman Rekha*, and the steps can never be retraced because the mythical *Lakshman Rekha* is always a one-way crossover. The condition of the wife becomes akin to that of the bats who are hunted down by grandpa in the village home because they prove to be a nuisance to the solace of the house. However, the strangest part is that the multitudes of bats haunting their house do not seem to decrease. Grandpa says, "I guess they just don't realize what's happening. They don't realize that by flying somewhere else they'll be safe. Or maybe they do, but there's something that keeps pulling them back here." (8)

The wife, like the bats, attempts initially to fly away to a safer place, but the pull of a fake sense of honour which can at least shield her from the pricking taunts of the world keeps pulling her back to the same claustrophobic atmosphere, the batterings, the thrashings, the unending schedule of tormentings.

The story "Clothes" provide another perspective to Divakaruni's awareness of feminist sensibility and immigrant dilemma. Here, we follow the story of Sumita, a simple, homely girl from an Indian village, who grows up amidst the ecstasies of rural life, "visiting the charak fair," "raiding the neighbours' guava tree" (18), taking long swims in the waters of the women's lake, dallying with other maidens on a hot summer afternoon, even as they braid each other's hair in long, elaborate patterns and tell fairy-tales: "And she married the handsome prince who took her to his kingdom beyond the seven seas." (18) Amidst the charming abode of heavenly happiness the golden days of her childhood pass, slowly, undisturbed, couched within the romantic tower of fairy tales where innumerable maiden desires get born and nourished—mysterious dreams of a prince who would come someday and take her, far, far away, to the kingdom of the skies, where everything would be so tempting, so marvellous, so magical.

Time flies along, in its own leisurely pace, and finally, one day, the prince of her heart indeed comes, "all the way from California" (18), to marry her and carry her to his kingdom beyond the oceans. On one hand, she is thrilled by the expectations of a new phase in her life, losing herself in the alluring beckonings of the exotic world of America, hypnotized by its magnetism even as she touches it on the metal globe on her father's desk: "California . . . a chunky pink wedge on the side of a multicolored slab marked Untd. Sts. of America. I touched it and felt the excitement leap all the way up my arm like an electric shock." But then, "it died away, leaving only a beaten metal coldness against my fingertips." (18) Even within the aura of scintillating dreams and aspirations she remembers, with a tinge of pain, the doors of her girlhood which had forever closed behind her: "But already the activities of our girlhood seem to be far in my past, the colours leached out often, like old sepia photographs." (18) All of a sudden, the magical world of newness, for which she had longed so ardently, becomes frightening, as she realizes that she would never see her parents again. "Don't send me so far away" (18), the dirges of longing flow out from her heart. A peculiar sensation runs up her spine, even as she whispers to herself her new name 'Sumita Sen.' It seems to her as if she has been transformed anew, into another radical being, and has taken on a new identity that is quite unknown, "like a stiff satin that's never been worn." (20) She finds herself stuck in the tug of war between the enchanting prospects of a bold future and the cold fears of losing the past. However, interestingly, that very past and its norms which she apprehends to lose give her the inspiration of diving into the future, as she remembers the age-old Indian dictum: "A married woman belongs to her husband, her in-laws." (19) Tears swell up her eyes as she gauges the unfairness of such a norm, yet she dutifully succumbs to the lessons of her culture.

Life in California with husband Somesh Sen would be a garden of bliss and fruitfulness, thinks Sumita, for Somesh is the type of husband any maiden may desire to have, an ideal prince of the fairytales. All the same, America too has its own wonders to unfold, America, the vivid, vibrant, vivacious land of the fairy tales. And so, Sumita becomes strangely surprised when she sees the violent spouts of anger in her husband's heart, when one day he spits up "The bastard!" while speaking of his disloyal and arrogant partner. She becomes surprised on learning that the name of her husband's store is '7-Eleven,' which seems quite a strange, exotic and risky name to her, because back in her home, she knows people always named their shops piously "after gods and goddesses—Ganesh Sweet House, Lakshmi Vastralaya for Fine Saris" (21), as a signal of good luck. She is also surprised when Somesh tells her that for the Americans, drinking is a normal routine. "It's a part of their culture, not considered immoral . . . there's nothing wrong with it" (21). Sumita remembers what her father used to tell about those "village toddy shops" where alcohol was sold, "dark, stinking dens of vice." (21) Caught in the web of immigrant dilemmas, she indeed begins to wonder what America really is.

At this stage, Sumita is totally unaware of how America is to betray her. And when the trembling and frightening part does arrive, we all are made to shiver at the perception of a fate we may well imagine but seldom dare to encounter. An unidentified gunman breaks into Somesh's store one night when he is alone, and after stealing his money, shoots him dead. One moment of crisis, and the silvery world of marriage, the arbour of love, the dreams of conjugal bliss, the fountains of expectations, all fall and crumble before Sumita's eyes like a house of cards left exposed in the storm. All hopes, all colours vanish, and what is left open before her is a solitary, painful life of widowhood. Standing in the middle of the empty bedroom, she ponders upon what America the alluring new world, had offered her. "Great America, a place where people go to have fun" (31). Hair still wet from the purification bath, she stares at the white sari which she is to wear now: "White. Widow's colour, colour of endings." (29)

When she had come to America, she was dressed in a blue and red sari, blue being the colour of possibility, red being the signifier of marriage. All these colours were lost to her now. Her bangles had been broken, the red marriage mark had been wiped off her forehead. Someone had wanted her hair to be cut off, but her in-laws were good people, kind. They did not allow this humiliation, nor did they ever say, like the people in the village would have done, that it was her bad luck and evil steps which had brought her husband to such a fate. Where did this kindness come from? Was it also a legacy of America? If it was so, what greater irony could be than this that the lessons of kindness and consideration should be taught by a land which, on the other hand, had been so cruel so as to snatch her husband away? The readers too, like the protagonist, get trapped in the maze of dilemmas.

Sumita's in-laws want to take her back to India. Sumita trembles with fearful anticipation of what lay before her days as a widow, neglected, pitied, denigrated, insulted. Horrible imaginings shape themselves inside her eyelids. She feels dizzy. Fragments fly about her head, "multicoloured and piercing sharp like bits of bangle glass." (31) Memories of Somesh come back to her: "I want you to go to college. Choose a career." The words of her husband thunder inside her head like the poundings of a thousand hammers. She remembers how once, as a young girl, while swimming in the women's lake, she had let loose her body, allowing it to go down. As it had started to sink, she had suddenly awakened to her senses. The desire for survival had given her an alarmingly strong impetus, and with "desperate flailing of arms and legs," (32) she had fought her way upward. The press of water had been terribly heavy, but when she had finally returned to the open, she had felt that she had been resurrected to a fresh life, and she had drawn the air of that new life with so much vigour that it seemed she would never let go off that life again. As soon as she remembers this, she realizes that we are lost only when we ourselves let go off our lives.

Life may be heartless, merciless, despairing yet we have to survive. Isn't that also what a woman stands for—a manifestation of strength? Sumita thinks of the faces of all those smiling American children whom she had dreamt of teaching. She dreams of herself in the cream blouse and long brown American skirt which Somesh had bought for her. She imagines the faces of all those customers she had anticipated to meet at the store. Once again, she stares at the mirror. This time, a new woman holds her gaze, "eyes apprehensive yet steady" (33). The woman in the mirror is none other than she herself, but in a novel manifestation. She is that woman who has emerged victorious over all dilemmas, all oppositions, all crushing sensibilities, and is as bright and radiant as a bird, ready to fly into the exotic skies. She refuses to go back to a tormenting past, she is ignorant of what the future holds for her, yet her eyes look forward, and the spirit of fire burning within her convinces everyone that none can now dare to stop her in her upward and onward journey. She indeed, emerges as a triumphant woman. "I know I cannot go back. I don't know yet how I'll manage here in this new, dangerous land. I only know I must. Because all over India, at this very moment, widows in white saris are bowing their veiled heads, serving tea to in-laws. Doves with cut off wings." (33)

The cause of Sumita's emergence as a bold and victorious woman is clearly due to the fact that as a woman, as well as an immigrant and member of high culture, she knows how to make all ends meet. She knows how to delve into the past in order to overcome its torturous bondages, at the same time she knows not to disown the positive aspects of the past heritage. As an immigrant, she embraces the promoting feature of both cultures and as a woman, she strikes a remarkably admirable balance between the various roles and norms assigned to her.

The dilemma presented by Chitra Bannerjee is relevant to the sensibilities of human beings in the age of globalization. The clash of cultures associated with myriad options of lifestyles in different geographical settings, and the trauma of rootlessness in the process of hybridization, are some of the problems she delves with in her writings. Her protagonists lurk at the threshold of two worlds of myth and reality, probing for authenticity and perfection, which ultimately disable them to shiver the root of their heritage and localism.

"The Maidservant's Story" also gives a vivid picture of the change in ideology of two generations, from mother to daughter. The protagonist, Manisha, grows up in America and enjoys the liberty of choosing her own life partner, a privilege which her mother and aunty were deprived of. But she remains attuned to her past, in spite of her changed outlook and ideology, and this is evident when she intermittently lingers around "Kadam trees," "strains of Rabindra Sangeet," "Ami chini go chini tomare, I know you well, women from a distant land beyond the ocean." (110)

Manisha's mother has no objection to her newfound right and lifestyle. Even if she hardly praises her daughter for her achievements like winning debates, standing first in exams and drama competitions, it is an open truth that she has been an inspiration behind these feats: "You know I want the best for you." (113) Manisha is aware of the fact that her mother is watching her everytime, seeing to her needs and aspiration but never allowing her to explore the wounds that lie hidden in the deep ocean of her heart, "what made her cry in her dreams" (113).

Manisha wonders why her mother has built a thin, transparent wall around herself, not even letting her own daughter to break the silence. This makes her feel that her relation with her fiancée is far better and liberated than her relation with her own mother. She dreams of a relation with no strings attached, sailing into uncharted and amazing areas of experience that someone like her mother couldn't imagine. She is so fascinated by her new American experience that she decides never to come back to India after getting married. But an argument with her aunt regarding the choice of saffron colour for her wedding dress, changes her attitude towards her mother.

Mashi tells her a story of a young educated wife, who was occupied with household work and who was a proud possession of her husband, an assistant manager of a British bank. The wife used to read books which the husband brought from the library for her on his way back from the office and practised her singing. And, when she was pregnant for the second baby, she asked her younger sister, who was unmarried to stay with her until her delivery. It was then that the maidservant, who was good-looking enough in a primitive adivasi way, came to look for work. The wife took pity on her and employed her as a servant in the house. Seeing her obedient and dutiful nature, the wife loved her all the more and she even started teaching her. She wanted to teach her because it was the only way to liberate the likes of her. But the sister could not help having a prick of apprehension—where will this lead? (125) The wife had even dared to gift the maidservant a saffron saree from her own almirah. She had indeed taken up bold steps to uplift the downtrodden maidservant by defying her husband and her husband's aunt in many ways. The maidservant's life was taking a complete turn towards new possibilities and new status until one morning when her wicked mother came and declared her identity as a prostitute to the family. Even if the husband and his aunt were against her staying in the house, none of them could do anything since the wife was unconditionally on the side of keeping the maidservant. This revelation makes the maidservant vulnerable from within and outside, and her only saviour was the wife, who herself was burdened and weakened with pregnancy. This was the dilemma where she was stuck. She had two options, either to stay in or walk out. In this way, she becomes a victim of the husband's lust, who swore to throw her out of the house when she refused to entertain him. To show his might on the powerless, helpless maidservant, he had thrown her out to perdition, where darkness prevails so that she was eternally damned and could never recover from that nightmare.

This ironical situation shows the might of the husband who was watching for weak spots to defile a loyal servant, just to take revenge upon her for non-conforming to his lust. Had the wife not been hospitalized, not biologically destined to bondage, the maid servant would have had a better future. Who is victimized? Is it the maid servant alone? Isn't the wife victimized too? Thus we can witness the predicament of women in a male-dominated society where women are victimized either as wife or as the other woman. After narrating the story, Deepa Mashi, the protagonist's aunt cautions Manisha against taking all things for granted and emphasizes: "Oh, you Americanized girls! The really important things never change." (111)

Deepa Mashi's story gives her a new insight and understanding of her own culture. After listening to the story, she realizes that she is also a part of that tradition, which she so much wants to get rid of. That her mother and aunt were the forerunners of the freedom and liberty she now enjoys freely without inhibitions and taboos. Even if the story has myth like aspects, the protagonist feels that the maidservant, the high class family members, the servants, the prostitutes, the slum dwellers etc. are part of her own family.

The story appeals to her as if she is very much a part of it. She can visualize the people in the story as her near and dear ones. She is enlightened to the fact that her own family members are at one level responsible for the degradation as well as emancipation of womenfolk in her society. The maidservant's predicament was partly a result of her own father's lust and greed, and her own position, a consequence of a long and patient struggle of her mother and her aunt. None of the problems and issues is new; it was all part of their existence, rooted in their own values and systems.

In the story, "Ultra Sound," we are presented with two different situations of women in two different cultural settings. We see the different situations of Anju and Runu, who are cousins but world apart in terms of space and experience. Runu's husband belongs to a rich traditional brahmin family in India, whereas Anju lives in America with her husband. In spite of their meagre saving, after sending money to her in-laws, Anju enjoys more liberty than her cousin Runu, who lives in India with the big family of her husband. Even if international calls are expensive, with their slender budget Anju takes up initiative everytime, to ring up Runu and share the experiences of their pregnancy. Anju knows that her husband can never feel the way the two cousins do. Their memories go so far back to the time when they were both seven. The two cousins share the same past even if their economic backgrounds differ. They symbolize the experience of women in different cultural settings.

The writer through Anju gives us a clear picture of the need of economic stability for emancipating women. Runu's father left nothing other than debts. This has been one of the reasons for her inability to perform academically well even if she is as intelligent as Anju. On the other hand, Anju gets a lot of encouragement from her mother and she goes on to win spelling bees and debate contests and good academic achievements in college. Runu, nevertheless, also does well with her cooking, knitting even if she can't excel like Anju. She chooses to be traditional which also demands a lot of courage and tolerance. We see the difference in the attitude of the two cousins when Anju describes: "When I carelessly tore my sari borders, she would mend them with stitches so tiny they were almost invisible. And she made the best mango chutney I ever tasted." (207)

These differences in their outlook and attitude, instead of making them apart, pull them together to help each other in their times of need. For Anju, talking with Runu on the phone is one of the most special times. The two cousins are so much in love that they have even fixed the date of getting amniocentesis test results together. Anju, being an educated and sensible woman, knows much about Runu's life, even if she hardly tells her anything about the situation in her in-laws' place. Anju had already sensed the disturbing and unusual aura that prevails in Runu's place when she visited there during her visit to India. Anju doesn't ask Runu anything because she knows that Runu is a proud woman and asking her about her condition may hurt her ego. This aspect of Runu is quite evident to Anju, as they grew up together in the same environment sharing a good measure of experience together. Anju exhibits a nature of defiance and this is evident when we see her ringing up Runu, in spite of her husband's rebuke every time when she does it. She has inherited this nature from her mother who had the courage to look after the family business and surprised everyone by managing it with shrewd efficiency. Runu, on the other hand, imbibes the traditional and subservient nature of her mother. She enjoys knitting, crocheting and cooking, which Anju dislikes. She, like a mild and tolerant Indian woman, bears everything until the ultra sound result comes and makes her defy her husband and her in-laws' decision.

Amidst the different settings and ideologies, the writer brings home the similarities of the psychological and physiological changes accompanied with the experience of pregnancy of the two cousins. Runu, who was bearing everything, now wants to stand up to defend the life of the child inside her. She is forced to run away from her husband's house but she knows that nobody will entertain her and bear the stigma she carries. Even her mother will not understand her predicament as she has more to worry about her society than her daughter's plight. Moreover, she can never come out of the belief that a married woman should always live under the shelter of her husband, no matter what the condition is.

Even the fortunate Anju cannot stop musing "Does Sunil love me, or only the mother-to-be of his son? Would he have cared for me as much if we had been in India and the baby had turned out to be a girl? What if I hadn't been able to have a baby at all? Would he be asking his parents to look for another wife for him?" (228)

NOTE

1. Chitra Banerjee Divakaruni, *Arranged Marriage,* Black Swan, Great Britain, 1997

"Tilotamma and the Bougainvillea girls": Creating identities in *The Mistress of Spices*

SANDHYA RAO MEHTA

In an early episode in Chitra Divakaruni's novel *The Mistress of Spices*, the narrator, Nayan Tara, later Tilo, finds herself washed to the shores of a magical island inhabited by an Old Mother. She is asked, "Who are you, child?" Nayan Tara can only speculate her reply and answers it with another question: "Who was I? I could not say. Already my name had faded in the rising island sun, like a star from a night that had passed away."[1] Of the numerous discourses of diaspora in the postcolonial context, the question of emerging identities assumes centrality and import, not only for the characters created in the narrative but the narrator whose function it becomes to voice these tensions in their varying manifestations. Much of Indian expatriate literature grapples with the predicament of what it means to be an Indian living in America or in other parts of the first world. An important consideration, therefore, for writers like Salman Rushdie, Bharati Mukherjee and Rohinton Mistry, among many others, is the way the expatriate writers, acutely conscious of their own status of being marginal, at times ostracized and at best tolerated, fill the creative works with the longings of the outsider. In most novels, the central consciousness inhabits the threshold of two worlds, a real, vibrant, often painful, changing one and another one in the process of being created, identified, named and understood.

The outsider thus becomes a metaphor, even a spokesperson helping to etch out a picture of contemporary reality. The marginal point of view, so often used by Rushdie as the figure of the narrator in *Midnight's Children*, *Shame* and *The Moor's Last*

Sigh, privileges the character with inner knowledge, with sympathy, pity and understanding, making possible a strategy of narrative and perspective unavailable to a mortal, human narrator. Chitra Divakaruni's *The Mistress of Spices* assumes an identical strategy of narration to evoke a world of dislocations and non-belonging. The double-edged narrative in Divakaruni's fiction succeeds in exploring the changing face of diaspora, its inherent pain and subsequent rewards. There is a way, however, that the central narrative at times falls in this novel under the weight of its own imagination, a fantasy gone awry. Tilotamma, in quest of her own identity unlike Sufiya Zinobia in *Shame* who renders the experience of a nation without being self-involved, becomes ensnared in the many layers of her own expatriation from many worlds, a series of multiple journeys each of which brings her close to catastrophe. The parallel quest for emerging identities on the part of the other characters involved in the central narrative structure coupled with the narrator's own increasingly desperate search for meaning and identity creates a fiction which is successful only in parts. The novel reads a complex experience of emigration but the quest for identity often falls under the sheer weight of overstatement, repetition and exaggeration.

The characters in *The Mistress of Spices* are almost always more real and their predicament more immediate and more sensitively portrayed than the narrator's long-winded struggle to break free from the clutches of the spices. More importantly, however, if grappling with one's sense of the self and the repercussions of what it means to be off-centred and create meanings in those margins defines the role of the expatriate Indian writer, *The Mistress of Spices* fulfils the purpose which it gives itself, creating a narrative capable of responding to the predicament of the postcolonial diaspora. Its heady mix of exotica and urbanity, myth and reality, fact and fantasy along with its unabashed intermingling of native and English phrases makes for a challenging experience of migrancy.

Tilotamma's beginnings are as uncertain as her future as seer and mistress of the spices. Named Nayan Tara, she is at once gifted with special qualities, of being able to foresee the future, a gift which brings followers and believers to her and makes her rich. The face of luxury, however, can be ever so dangerous as Nayan Tara discovers when the Pirates come looking for her and she begins her initially reluctant travels to a distant world which she neither understands nor desires. In her travels with the pirates, she finds herself swept into the island of spices, a travel which demands of her the stripping of her every existing identity. Of the sea serpents she says, "They were the first among all that the spices were to take from me." (24) With her mentor, the First Mother, the initiation on fire strips her of her past, of everything she remembers until she even falsifies her own being by hiding within the body of an old woman. The stripping of identity thus seems to be an essential pre-requisite for the discovery of a new, perhaps true one. Tilo learns on the island even before she reaches the shores of America that the self is itself fluid, always moving toward a higher meaning, a bigger role and that no final answers are ever possible. The question "Who are you, child" cannot be answered with the certainty of the insensitive as the self is a creation, a process and never a confirmed finality.

Her being catapulted into American society at Oakland, running a grocery store in a dilapidated part of the town at once merges myth and reality. Tilo's gifts make it now possible for her to peer into the lives of the migrants—lives of hope, suffering, loneliness and pain. The merging of Tilo's gifted sense of understanding and possible cure not only provides an immediate insight into contemporary American society but also creates a perspective from which such a predicament could be solved. Her gift of the spices endows her with an inner eye through which the sufferings of the alienated, the persecuted and the damned find a voice. There is Jaggi, the little Sikh boy, teased in school for wearing a turban, Geeta the Bengali girl whose affair with her American friend is almost doomed to failure as her parents desperately cling to an Indian past they hope can be passed on to the future generations in America. There is also Ahuja's wife, caught in the trap of an arranged marriage with a balding, ageing man, restlessly seeking alternatives to her suffering and discovering, much to her horror and disappointment, that the voices of tradition and social expectation are not different for Indians in America, for "we carried them all the way inside our heads." (103) There is also Haroon the taxi driver who is suspicious of anything American and whose fears are finally justified one dark night as he is struck down in a racial assault by frustrated white American boys.

The layers of emigrant angst and suffering in *The Mistress of Spices* is evocative, complex and enduring. As tale after tale of migrant narratives unfold before Tilo, the voices entwined, confused and frightened, the collective experience of marginalisation assumes urgency. As each character confronts the possible meanings of being an outsider, the complexity of their solutions becomes more apparent. There is a way in which the predicament of the marginal assumes a tremendously human perspective in this narrative as the confrontation between past and present, Indian and American seeks out possible meanings, synthesis and a viable framework within which contentment, if not happiness, could be affected. It is a weary, almost dangerous process for the creation of identities is neither facile nor prompt. The many experiences of diaspora and the divergent tales spinned in the store of the spices underline the struggle for each individual as they undergo their own passage by fire, stripping the meanings of their collective and distinct individualities in a desperate attempt to create new ones which may better serve to express their new selves, only to find that such finalities are often allusive and imaginary.

Jagjit responds to his sense of alienation and racial abuse by resorting to gang wars as he is initiated into a group which makes him feel protected, "And in return, so little. Carry this packet here, drop off this box there." (112) Geeta blames her grandfather for having pitted her parents against her, for having forced her to confess her love for an American, suddenly and viciously without preparation. Out of love, perhaps respect for a memory of traditions, Geeta refuses to live with her boyfriend, a fact she would like her parents to know as a gesture of compromise, loyalty and love. Lalita, Ahuja's wife, looks longingly at the stitched clothes inside the store as she remembers the fondness with which she could stitch and embroider for a baby she does not have and for a life gone waste in the shadow of a violent husband. Haroun's joy at his new taxi, his sense of new-found confidence and dignity, Tilo knows would be short-lived but she can find no cure for it. And then there are the bougainvillea girls, rich and self-assured, but almost always hiding a secret fear, a discomfort with the way events unfold in their luxurious lives, often underlining the emptiness within, hidden under the layers of success:

> And right now in front of me a woman in oversize Bill Blass jeans and Gucci shoes is buying stacks and stacks of naans for a party tonight, is drumming rubyflash fingers on the counter as I ring up the flat brown bread, is saying shrill as tin 'Come *on* I'm in a hurry.' But inside she is thinking of teenage son. He's been acting so strange lately, hanging out with boys who frighten her with their razor earrings and biker jackets and heavy boots as though for war, their cold, cold eyes and slits of mouths that are becoming *his* eyes, *his* mouth. (77)

What emerges in these varying narratives is the urgency with which the Indian expatriates attempt to create identities in the American landscape by retaining, to the extent possible, a sense of Indianness as the final arbiter of emotional relationships and a way in which to forge a viable relationship with the external environment which is so often hostile. Thus the leather-jacketed Jagjit instinctively responds to Tilo's use of his childhood's "Jaggu Raja Beta" and takes the syrup she makes for him; Geeta works towards an affirmation of relationships which would involve the various people she loved and tie them into a common bond of family, Haroun ultimately finds love, meaning and a purpose beyond the cruel racial incident which could have left him embittered and alone. The past, in the form of traditions and memories leave an impression in the mind of the expatriate and it is to this past that they turn in moments of loneliness and emptiness. For all their faith in the past, for their pain of non-belonging, however, there is a way in which Divakaruni's migrants are forced to live in a vacuum, almost without a past. The idea of 'home,' of a land left behind, so eulogized and often mythologized in much of diasporic writing, is almost non-existent for most of the emigrants in this fiction. If anything, home is conservative, unsympathetic and binding for people like Geeta. Mohan, the blinded worker in a tea stall can only go back to a home without a future and without hope. Home is the world of traditionally arranged marriages as that of Lalitha, married to an older man whose photograph she sees two days before her wedding. Such a vacuum, however, becomes significant in the phantasmal vision of the writer for whom geographical spaces seem to be of little consequence, concerned as she is with the marginal experience of the other, wherever they may come from. In this sense, her Raven is himself the most alienated, for even without physical migration, he finds that rootedness, security, identity and certainty elude him in a life in which he has grappled with the possibilities of his native Indianness and its continuous denial by his mother. It is an identity he urgently needs to embrace before being able to acknowledge the reality and meaning of being himself.

It is in the context of the "Young American" that the role of Tilo and her emerging search for identity coalesces into the central narrative of the novel. Tilo has always been the rebel, the dreamer and the sceptic. It is with much reluctance that the Old Mother gives her a name and a mission, knowing that her fall would be merely a matter of time. She is a young girl in an old woman's body, daring to dream of forbidden pleasures and temptation. And yet, it is this rebellion, the ability to sympathize with the suffering and the persecuted, at times too intimately, that provides her with the platform to contribute and change contemporary American society. Her amorphous personality in a way makes it possible for her to merge into the immigrants' lives, often attempting to cure the ills of the migrant community. It is not for nothing that she sarcastically calls herself "I, Tilo, architect of the Indian dream" (28) for it is a dream which often goes awry. The Old Mother's island had taught Tilo duty and obedience. The suffering of the entire world is unfolded before her before setting out to her destined location to use her power to help, but never to be helped herself. The warning of Sampati's fire which may rage on the disobedient, the selfish and the indulgent is stressed upon by the Old Mother, her eyes resting on Tilo alone. And yet, Tilo's restlessness, her almost haughty confidence and her quickness to learn and change marks her as damned very early on. Even as she chooses the name "Tilotamma" herself as meaning "the essence of til, lifegiver, restorer of health and hope" (42) the greater social role she envisages for herself is established along with the half-hearted conviction, that, for all her temptations, she would never fall.

Tilo, however, does fall very early on in the novel in her desperate attempt to help others and ultimately, herself. Twice she goes outside her shop to help Geeta and Haroun only to find that she could easily succumb to the temptations of a small supermarket as her basic human instinct had only been suppressed all along and had never really disappeared. She however finds her own powers to cure, to treat and help diminishing as she gets more self-engrossed, more concerned with her own life, more personally involved with the lives of some of her clients and finally, more aware of her own emerging sexuality. In its inverse growth, from aged spinster to a beautiful woman, Tilo's journey is itself one of self-discovery, but one which entails sacrifice, surrender and duty. Caught between the various impulses of her individual self, Tilo reacts variously, at times involved, others distant. What attracts her into the lives of the divided and the marginal is their numerous strifes, their struggles with society within and without, their grappling with their fates, desperately seeking a way of living with dignity, knowledge and pride. It is a quest with which she begins to identify intimately as her own, a quest for identity within the confines of a new land or a new body. It is with the rich American businessman, her 'Raven,' that the possibilities of a new life unfold and Tilo finds herself incapable of resisting the current of passion, indulgence and release. The Native American's story of his childhood and his attempt to grapple with the consequences of a past which had been firmly denied to him by his mother gives Tilo yet another case to cure but this time, it is with an involvement she can neither control nor stop in spite of the constant reprimand of the spices which threaten to variously take away their power from her and even to annihilate the world through her wrong use of their powers. Tilo's growing realisation that her role as mistress of spices would enlarge to being the mistress of something more than the magical spices commits her to a re-definition of the self. It is an exploration in which she discovers that the only form of the true self would be not to deny it but to indulge in it to be able to emerge beyond the boundaries of everyday life. Tilo may, at the end of the novel, no longer be privy to the hidden powers of the spices, but her conquest for herself and the acceptance of her reality, her social responsibility and her physical limitations makes her the ultimate expatriate. Her journey from being Nayan Tara, the 'star seer' (8) to Tilottama who "was banished to earth to live as a mortal for seven lives" (43) to Maya "Illusion, spell, enchantment, the power that keeps this imperfect world going day after day," (317) is not without strife and conflict but it is a journey which confronts and challenges the lives of the expatriate in their many manifestations.

Yet, it is the myriad characters with whom Tilo comes in contact that stays in the imagination of the reader long after the earthquake in San Francisco that shatters many lives but recreates Tilo's. The characters in *The Mistress of Spices* are almost always more real and their predicament more immediate and more sensitively portrayed than the narrator's own quest for identity and meaning, one which predictably brings her back to the already accepted role of being socially and physically responsible rather than deny the reality of human experience, to the almost trite realisation that Tilo, now Maya's destiny and her paradise lies, not in the distant hills of nothingness but "in the soot in the rubble in the crisped-away flesh. In the guns and needles, the white drug-dust, the young men and women lying down to dreams of wealth and power." (315) This is a lesson the rebellious Tilo had learned and a trait she had displayed from the moment she had opened her shop. In this emerging relationship, it is the Raven who learns to leave the dream-like world of the mountains to embrace a more socially responsible, immediate one.

Divakaruni's novel, in many ways, voices the varying experiences of the diasporic writer. Distance, she says, often provides an angle in which to view reality: "moving away from a home culture often allows a kind of disjunctive perspective that is very important—a slight sense of being an outsider, being out of place."[2] In this celebration of homelessness and the creation of new homes, she voices a prevalent attitude among diasporic writing, one which exults in the sense of rootlessness and uses it as a literary stratagem to explore the possibilities of living in two worlds. If indeed the "Differences of gender, 'race,' class, religion and language . . . make diaspora spaces dynamic and shifting, open to repeated construction and reconstruction"[3] the merging of identities becomes an essential part of the process of creation. What is created, however, may be further negotiable as the finality of meanings and spaces are constantly challenged and questioned. Diasporic identity, the shift of Tilotamma to being the bougainvillea girl and beyond points to the way expatriation can confront the realities of everyday existence while retaining its capacity to confront, to dream and to hope.

NOTES

1. Chitra Banerjee Divakaruni, *The Mistress of Spices*, London (Doubleday, 1997) p. 33.
2. Interview with Katie Bolick in "Atlantic online" 5/26/2000 <http:/ www.theatlantic,com/unbound/factfict/f/9804.htm>>
3. John McLeod, *Beginning Postcolonialism*, Manchester, Manchester University Press, 2000, p. 207.

The Enigma of Female Bonding in Chitra Banerjee Divakaruni's *Queen of Dreams*

LATA CHATURVEDI
B.H.U., Varanasi

Chitra Banerjee Divakaruni writes: "Women in particular respond to my work because I am writing about them, women in love, in difficulties, women in relationships. I want people to relate to my characters, to feel their joy and pain, because it will be harder to [be] prejudiced when they meet them in real life."[1] She has emerged as a representative voice on the postcolonial literary scene. Her major contribution lies in capturing the continuity of the lives of women, the South Asian immigrants to the U.S. In the world of Divakaruni, the understanding of men and women are firmly separated and the men often play peripheral roles, only sometimes impinging on the horizon of the women's lives. In *Queen of Dreams,* the novelist not only foregrounds the immigrant experience but wonderfully unleashes the conscious and unconscious bonds between mother and daughter. This paper is an attempt to examine how the story of an emotionally distant mother and a daughter transcends cultural boundaries.

The repository of knowledge that is handed down from the dream-teller, Mrs. Gupta to Rakhi, is highly significant and female solidarity seems the only way of survival. This gets further explored with Rakhi and her daughter Jona. However, the father as a distant figure is also considered, and after her mother's death, Rakhi develops a genuine relationship with her father, who will tell her stories of India that her mother would not.

As in *The Mistress of Spices*, Chitra Banerjee has grappled with women's experiences through female language and the intuitive aspects of female intelligence. Tilo, the protagonist forges an ideality for herself by exacting the Indian women's traditions, by looking at their subcultures, in dialogue and in imagery and at unacknowledged realms of experiential realities.

While depicting the common experiences of the Indian diasporic community, *Queen of Dreams* synthesizes an Indian American experience with magic realism. The major problems faced by the immigrants are those of their search for identity and a sense of emotional fulfillment. And this of course is not confined to small corners of the world. This is a dilemma that most of the sensitive readers can have empathy for.

The narrative explores the connection between wakefulness and subconscious. Rakhi, a first generation American of Indian descent, is the daughter of a dream-teller. Spiked with elements of mystery, suspense and the supernatural, the narrative offers an engaging story.

Like most of Divakaruni's earlier works, *The Mistress of Spices* and *Sister of My Heart*, she here concentrates on the immigrant experience, a central motif in the mosaic of American society. Her objective is to deconstruct myths and stereotypes. She hopes to dissolve through her writing boundaries between people of different backgrounds, communities, ages and worlds.

The Indian experience in America and the conflict between the traditions of the novelist's homeland and the culture of her adopted country is the focus of much of her fictional and poetic works. And this has precisely made her an emerging literary celebrity of the present times. As she proclaims: "As immigrants we have this enormous raw material, which is often very painful and puts us in a position of conflict, which is very good for a writer" and further elaborates, "We draw from a dual culture, with two sets of worldviews and paradigms juxtaposing each other."

But she is highly hopeful for the second generation diasporans because she thinks the duality will diminish for them. Divakaruni assures, "our second generation has the family support which gives them a solid and secure base, so they can go out and take risks."[2]

In *Queen of Dreams* she delves deep into the acculturation and the unconscious and in this process she brilliantly underscores three generations of Indian-Americans in the US. Right since her first book *Arranged Marriage*, she has been articulating the problematic of the clash and antagonism between cultures. Here she keeps oscillating between two worlds, the one that moves towards dreams and the subconscious, the subterranean realities of life and the other toward socio-political scene of the country.

As a female *bildungsroman*, the novel unveils before us a pleasant and unconventional tale of self-exploration. Rakhi, a divorced mother and young artist struggling for her survival in Berkeley, Calif has always been vaguely aware of her own mother's usual gift, the ability to interpret dreams. Mrs. Gupta, her mother, once told her:

> I don't sleep with you or your father because my work is to dream. I can't do it if someone is in bed with me. My work is to dream . . . I dream the dreams of other people, she said, "So I can help them live their lives."[3] (7)

She appears as a mysterious figure before the members of her family. She always evades the question of her past life in India and this causes perplexing despair in her daughter. As one of the reviewers aptly observes:

> The novel is also divided between India and the US, although set entirely in America. To Rakhi, as no doubt to many US born Indians, India represents the mystical and the longed for quite literally land of dreams, and one that she is on a quest to understand, through the cryptic medium of her mother's dream journal. As she and her family try to come to terms with their lives and origins, their peace of mind is totally shattered by events in the world around them. India becomes little more than a myth in the shocked aftermath of the terrorist attacks on the world they know and love, and yet it is also the key to their past and present lives.[5]

Caught between the two-pronged burden of her own painful secret, running the starbucks-esque supercafe and confronting Sonny, her ex-husband, for her daughter Jona's affections, she refuses to discuss the causes behind her divorce. While living in a world of alarming transition, Rakhi longs for enigmatic bond which can bring her closer to her mother and perhaps eventually to her daughter.

In Chapter 6 of the book entitled "Rakhi," she confesses: "Let me not misrepresent facts. My mother wasn't the one who wanted to teach me to interpret dreams. I was crazy for it myself. . . . I hungered for all things Indian because my mother never spoke of the country she'd grown up in—just as she never spoke of her past." (39) Rakhi's real solace comes in the discovery, after her mother's death, of her dream journals, which begin to unlock the long sealed up fragments of her secretive past.

She heralds the new confidence of an Indian woman in foregrounding her mother's ability to interpret dreams as an image for hope. She transforms the female gift of dream-interpreting into a powerful symbol of solidarity, that can be seen as a healing device extending success and solace to people dreams. Mrs. Gupta's intuitive power was in fact, a creative legacy to her daughter Rakhi. Chitra Banerjee suggests new approaches to cultural history by showing the exclusive value of women's experiences. She examines what it means to be a woman in a multicultural American society. The struggle of Indian women in the US to reclaim their identity and self-worth is depicted increasingly through the struggle of Rakhi. Chitra Banerjee is unusually successful in proclaiming that this struggle should be broadly based on the female qualities of love and self-awareness.

By representing the experiences of Indian women in the US, she has taken account of the need to interpret to her community predicament the alienating Americans. The novel brilliantly claims out the question of cultural identity, family and redemption. It is satisfying as well as consolatory.

In this novel, Chitra Banerjee has presented exhilaratingly useful reappraisals of the south Asian immigrant women. Like the protagonists in Black Women novelists, in Alice Walker and Toni Morrison, Rakhi acknowledges how deeply she owes to her mother. It is the dream of her mother which gives her love of language, the ability to affirm self after the humiliation that she undergoes after her divorce. As an engaging tale of acculturation and the unconscious, the text tries to encompass the lives three generations of Indian Americans living in the United States. Rakhi, the female protagonist, loses her mother in a mysterious car accident, and her mother's death propels her to decipher Mrs. Gupta's dream journals in hopes of unlocking the long-kept secrets of her strange double life. The sinister rival figure of a shadowy man in white who appears at crucial moments in the dream journals punctuate the story that mystically churns out an imagined saga of love, forgiveness and new beginnings. Remarkably enough, the nerve-shattering horror of September 11 provides her another opportunity for resolving longstanding issue of alienation. As this terrible event disrupts Rakhi's search for identity, and a vicious attack on her friends and family puts their very concepts of citizenship at stake and they get threatened. As a novelist, Divakaruni defies easy categorization. She displays a passion for forging a free flowing narrative that can captivate readers across the globe. No attempt for synthetic characterization has been made. Current issues have been brought to the ambit of his other novels such as *The Mistress of Spices* and *Sister of My Heart*. The text comes alive before us as a rich and sumptuous narrative delight where mystery and fantasy, realistic and cosmic get harmonized in a composite whole. This is a riveting and politico-sociologically searing novel by a woman writer of Indian diaspora. The story juxtaposes Mrs. Gupta's luminous world of dreams with the everyday concerns of her daughter's life.

The title of the novel takes us to the image of India sealed up in the mind of Rakhi, along with many US-born Indians. 'Queen of dreams' conjures up the image of India as a mystical and longed-for land of dreams. This also reminds us of the cryptic medium of Mrs. Gupta's dream journal and she herself as an Interpreter of the dream journal. Mr. Gupta reveals to his daughter: "Your mother was a meticulous person. You did not find those journals by accident. She left them for you. May be they are her way of telling you what was on her mind." (183) He comes to realize: "Some of the time . . . is like reading a novel written by a stranger—I don't recognize any one, especially myself and the parts about the caves, and her—uh, skill—why, it's like one of those old tales I heard when growing up." Then she has those entries about clients coming to her for help. "I can't believe that all of that went on right in my house," she sighs. "But they must have happened. At least in her mind." (184)

Right from her early childhood, Rakhi was drawn towards her mother. Mrs. Gupta wonders in one of her late *Dream Journals*: "Do all girls go through such a phase of mother worship? Having had no mother myself, I did not know" (255). In the penultimate chapter of the book, Rakhi's mother comes to evaluate her role in her daughter's life when she illumines, "I was not a good mother to Rakhi. I loved her, but not fully. To love someone fully is to give up selfhood, and I could not risk that. She knew this. Perhaps that is why she constantly longed to understand who I am, to become who I am. I did not have the power to give her the latter, even if I wished such a fate on her. If I gave her the former, it would have destroyed me. . . . And so I attempt these journals. . . . Thoughts rush through me and disappear, memories. I can express only a fraction of what I feel." (328-29).

The narrative brilliantly underscores the possibility of salvaging relationships, if one chooses to forgive and move on—as indeed Rakhi does with Mr. Gupta, her father and Sonny, her ex-husband. And Divakaruni has been successful in achieving this through digging deep into the subterranean layers of the enigmatic female bonding. She has truly concentrated on her creative impulse that she has expressed in such unequivocal terms:

> What has impelled my writing so far . . . is the desire to put women in the centre of stories, to have their voices be the voices of interpretation, their eyes that we see through. There just hasn't been enough of that in the world, if you look back at literary history.[6]

Here, Rakhi, like his other female predecessors in *The Mistress of Spices, Sister of My Heart* and *The Vine of Desire*, acclimatises to her new land and immensely expanding opportunities. And it is in this context that the enigma of female bonding and ties to tradition / homeland are pulled out and unravelled.

NOTES

1 Elizabeth Softky, "Cross Cultural Understanding Spiced with the Indian Diaspora," *Black Issues in Higher Education*, 18 Sept. 1997: 26.

2 http://www.time. com/time/daily/special/india/chitra.html.

3 Chitra Banerjee Divakaruni, *Queen of Dreams* (New York: Anchor Books, 2004).

4. Olga Kenyon, *Writing Women* (London: Pluto Press, 1991).

5. Serena Trowbridge, Review of Chitra Banerjee Divakaruni's *Queen of Dreams*, Column 8, 26.04.2004. Agony Column Review/*Archive* trashotron.com/agony/reviews/divakaruni-queen of dreams. html

6. http://www.theatlantic.com/doc/prem/2004/00/int 2004-10-04.

Bapsi Sidhwa's *Water*: The Voice of the Marginalised

BEENA AGARWAL
D.S. College, Aligarh

Postcolonial literary discourse is a comprehensive mode of speculation related with socio-political, socio-economic and socio-psychological dimensions of human suffering resulting out of the passion to monopolize power resources with a view to sway the fate of those who were destined to lead the life of marginalised. In spite of psycho-biological similarities, the politics of discrimination dumped a large section of society in the slumber of ignorance and injustice. Elitists with their authority became the unacknowledged legislators to weave the fabric of social conventions and personal relationship. In the postcolonial literary texts, the 'silence of the week' became the 'central voice.' The novel *Water* (2006) by Bapsi Sidhwa, based on the controversial film by Deepa Mehta, can be appreciated as a voice of the weak. Here, Sidhwa "historicizes the images, lends greater poignancy to faces and provides speech where the film must leave the women speechless."[1] The present paper is an investigation of female suffering, silence of the women against the domination of patriarchy and ruthless criticism of nefarious norms of the conventions of Brahmanism that were responsible for the humiliation and exploitation of women. The first section of the paper reviews identical grounds treaded by feminism and postcolonialism, while as the second section decodes the postcolonial vision integrated in the texture of the novel *Water*.

I

In the postcolonial discourse, anti-colonial nationalism deflects attention away from internal orthodoxies and injustice, "the nation can become a panacea for not dealing with economic disparities, social injustice and the capture of the newly independent state by national elite"[2] but it also includes attention to "the abused rights of all oppressed classes."[3] It also looks at ideas that "minimize orthodoxy and authoritarian or patriarchal thought that takes a severe view of the coercive nature of identity politics." Chandra Talpade Mohanty in her celebrated article. "Under Western Eyes, Feminist Scholarship and Colonial Discourse" defends the cause of Third World woman and uses the term 'Colonialism' to imply any relation of structural domination which relies upon self-serving suppression.[4] Feminists invoke the narrative of 'double colonisation,' principally to contrast the political immaturity of third world woman with the progressive ethos of Western feminism. The average third world woman is represented as ignorant, poor, uneducated, silent and unaware of her own "sexualities" and "freedom." Spivak, eminent postcolonial feminist critic, urges the academic feminist to 'speak' to the subaltern women and to speak of their real life experience. She protests:

> Between patriarchy and imperialism, subject constitution and object formation, the figure of woman disappears, not into a pristine nothingness but a violent shuttling which is the displaced figuration of the 'Third World Woman' caught between tradition and modernisation.[5]

Hence, thinkers focus on plight of existence of women under the burden of conventions and traditions. American author Katherine Mayo in her book *Mother India* embarks on a furious invective against the unhappy condition of Indian women. She investigates the brutishness of Indian men, the horrors of child marriage, widowhood, illiteracy and unsanitary habits of Indian women.[6] Macaulay formulates the colonial relationship in terms of 'natural' ascendancy of men over women. Nandy writes:

> Colonialism, too, was congruent with the existing western sexual stereotype and the philosophy of life which they represented. It produced a cultured consensus in which political and socio-economic dominance symbolised the dominance of men and masculinity over women and feminity.[7]

In the postcolonial literary texts, the efforts were made to record "the direct experience of women"[8] to get an insight into the reality of "being a woman in Indian village."[9] The idea of the real experiences of womanhood implies the objective representation of female experiences untainted by unhealthy cultural practices. It was to challenge the idealised and traditional images of women. It was to fill the gulf between "direct experiences" and their textual representation. In revealing the real experiences, there is a greater authenticity upon the claims based on ontological superiority of females, 'women as women' are seen to have a 'special drive for liberation.' The need was felt for the representation of women as a subject, speaking of her own 'identity,' 'suffering' and urge for 'freedom.' Mody and Mhatre in "Sexual Class in India" asserts that the public voice of Indian women has long been stifled by male-dominated society and see that her present silence is connected to 'self image' which is surely distorted and repressed and there is a need to shake off this imposed reticence. He admits, "The voice and consciousness comes from outside, when women are encouraged to voice their oppressors and to struggle to improve their condition."[10] The traditions are responsible for the misery of women but the efforts are made for their sublimation, they can yield the responses required for the 'universal' goal of feminism. Kishwar observes:

> Our cultural traditions have tremendous potential within them to combat reactionary and anti-women ideas, if we can identify their points of strength and use them creatively. The rejections of the harmful are then made much easier than attempts to overthrow traditions totally and attacks them arrogantly from outside as most of us westernised modernists tend to do.[11]

The reassessment of traditions to represent the voice of marginalised and to enlighten their consciousness for self-dignity has been the whole endeavour of postcolonial socio-cultural ideology.

II

The novel *Water* offers a riveting examination of the lives of widows in colonial India, but ultimately "it is a haunting and lyrical story of love, faith and redemption." (Cover Page) It is located at a village on Bihar-Bengal border in mid-thirties, mourning the suffering of a child widow, Chuyia, an innocent girl of six. Being a child, she prefers "playing with her clay dolls, skipping along a path in her bare feet and collecting the berries in her skirt for her mother to pickle and felt an overwhelming surge of tenderness and longing" (5). After the proposal of marriage from Hira Lal, a man of fifty, Chuyia gets married without even having a realisation of the sanctity of the concept of marriage. For her father, Somnath, the only consolation was, "they don't want a dowry; they will pay for the wedding" (7). He is guided by the traditional orthodoxies of womanhood that dictates that woman is happy only in the protection of her husband. Her dreams and self-dignity is subordinated to the dreams determined by her husband, "a woman is recognised as a person only when she is one with her husband" (8). In Indian cultural ethos, the woman is not expected to have a voice of her own beyond the periphery of marriage, "outside of marriage the wife has no recognised existence in our tradition. A woman's role in life is to get married and have sons." (9) Husband is given the authority of a ruler to control the destiny of woman. Religious conventions further dragged the women in corner, "Her husband was right and his words bore the cumulative wisdom of Gods and ancients" (9). Chuyia's mother in spite of her unwillingness was not capable to express her choice. In contrast to her excitement, unfolded dreams of life, she was pushed behind the bars of marriage. Bapsi Sidhwa shares her anguish, "she has no idea of the troubles that lie ahead of her" (18). In spite of her erratic behaviour and resistance, amid the rituals of marriage recommended by Hindu Dharma, she was decked in bridal make up when she looked like a "diminutive doll" (21). The analogy of doll obviously suggests the idea that she is beautiful to play with but she can't speak. As a property, she was handed over from father to husband, "just as the giver can no longer lay claim to an object that has once been donated" (21). Bapsi Sidhwa with an exceptionally penetrating insight presents the position of Indian woman through the horrors of widowhood of chuyia after the death of her husband. After long illness, Hira Lal's death was evident. Chuyia was invited to her in-law's house. Her mother tormented her on the anticipation of the horrors of her existence, it would be a death of her personal life, social life and even of her own feminity. Her observation on the fate of a widow in the traditional Brahamin family universalizes the misery of feminine suffering;

> In Brahamin culture, once widowed, a woman was deprived by her useful function in society that of reproducing and fulfilling her duties to her husband. She ceased to exist as a person; she was no longer either daughter or daughter-in-law . . . a woman's sexuality and fertility, which was so valuable to her husband in his life-time, was converted upon his death into a potential danger to the morality of the community. (24)

The distinction of Sidhwa's narrative art consists in projection of extremely emotional situations corresponding with the undeserved suffering in the hands of unidentified oppressors. Chuyia too is victim of 'double colonisation': firstly she appears as a victim of patriarchy and secondly she suffers the ordeals of conservative Brahamin cult. For her the whole drama of death and funeral was no better than playing with pulp. After the death of her husband, she was brought to the ghats of Banaras. For her funeral fire was a plaything, "Baba, look at the fire" (30). The poignancy in the novel is superb. Her father said, "you are widow now" but the concept of widowhood was beyond her comprehension. The image of mother-in-law of chuyia in the novel *Water* is projected as the manifestation of imperial authority. Her actions, like jerking of mangalsutra off her neck, smashing the red glass bangles from her wrist, are the signs of oppressive measure to subdue the humanity of the child. She treats chuyia as if she were an "inanimate object." Before she could have registered her protest, the women gathered around "pulled down her skirt and pulled her blouse up" because she was not permitted to wear coloured dresses, "chuyia stood naked as the day she was born, staring at the vibrant little red and blue heap her clothes made" (35). Chuyia, in spite of being the focal point of the whole affair, observes the rituals as silent spectator. Finally, the last but the worst ritual of shaving of hair was carried of in the belief, "If the widow did not shave her head, every drop of water that fell upon the hair polluted the husband's soul" (45). It was an oppression, humiliation and horror. Chuyia, with this frightening apparition starts screaming, "Baba, don't leave me here." But there is no voice even to respond to her call.

The novel *Water* tears the veil of hypocrisy of the Ashrams of widow, where instead of social security and dignity, they are forced to face all sorts of humiliation, torture and prostitution of their virginity. Most of the widows in Ashrams were with their shaved heads and long stern faces look like men deprived of their beauty and social status. Madhumati, a widow with abundance of "slacked flesh," was the ruler of dilapidated ashram. The imperial authority is manifested through her. She shouts, abuses and commands to maintain her absolute authority. Chuyia almost becomes crazy in this horrible atmosphere, "I don't want to be a stupid widow" and in her extreme resentment, she dug her sharp teeth in Madhumati's thick ankle. In contrast of her, Shakuntala Devi, another widow of the same Ashram, with her sympathy and dynamic image consoles chuyia. It was an Ashram situated near the temple. Here widows are given a cup of rice and a fistful of lentils for every eight-hour session of singing and dancing. Inside the ashram, in spite of persistent humiliation, she was not permitted to speak of herself. Bapsi Sidhwa states, "She didn't reply" but the fact is that she "couldn't" reply. Sidhwa exposes the horrors of the life of widows but simultaneously sustains that in the passion of domination, the absolute negation of humanity is not possible. In the life of chuyia, the appearance of Kalyani, another young widow with radical temperament, comes as a ray of hope. In her company, she was swamped by the same feelings of happiness and tenderness. It brings a new zest of life for the innocent chuyia. Another considerate widow in the ashram was 'Bua' who tried to console her by narrating the stories of excitement and adventure. Bapsi Sidhwa promotes that social conventions can suppress human voices but it cannot abolish the innate urges and individuality. The discipline of Ashram deprives unfortunate widows of their rights, self-dignity and even the basic biological urges peculiar to their sex. Kalyani does not follow the code of shaving the hair. Ever since her association with Narayan, she revives her dreams and her quest to seek the company of male companion. Swayed by Gandhian ideology, Narayan develops a mission to liberate the widows of India from their plight. Through the relationship of Kalyani and Narayan, Sidhwa insists that human relationship is the only possible panacea to encourage the marginalised to express their resistance against oppression and injustice.

In the fabric of the novel *Water*, Sidhwa contemptuously criticizes the corrupt religious practices that are a hurdle to the growth of civil society. The conventions of patriarchy are framed in the garb of religious practices. Kalyani in spite of being a widow denied shaving her hair but she was dammed as a polluted woman, "eating with Kalyani would pollute our food" (80). The concept of absolute detachment is only hypocrisy. Shakuntala absolutely denies the illusion of self-liberation and she candidly admits, "If self-liberation means detachment from worldly desires, then, no, I'm no closer to it" (95). Bapsi Sidhwa, for a greater authenticity, tries to capture the inner world of widows through the experiences of Chuyia, Shakuntala, Kalyani and Snehlata. They were reduced to state of beggars, having lost their initial sense of shame and humiliation, sitting on the stairs of temple with the bowl of alms in their hands. Sidhwa emphasizes such religious practices that encourage the politics of 'otherness.' Kalyani possesses the same sensibility, responds to the touch of Narayan but is not bold enough to speak against it. She identifies her suppression of desires with the suffering of innocent chuyia. On one occasion, Chuyia in her innocence reveals, "I'll eat a hundred puris at Kalyani's wedding" (141). This revelation comes as a bolt from the blue to Madhumati. It was a challenge to her authority, her autonomy, her nefarious design to exploit innocent widows like Chuyia and Kalyani. She summons Kalyani and shouts, "We'll be cured. We must live in purity to die in purity." She grabbed her hair to hack-off her head. Her beauty was dismantled and her dreams were gone to shambles. She was forced to shear her hair to live in perpetual mourning and to give up hot foods to cool her sexual energy. However, the experiences of 'sexual energy' are innate and its suppression leads to perversion. If man has a right to express his sexual desires, woman too equally possess the right to assert her desires.

> The psychoanalytic idea that women are moved by strong sexual desires in the same way that men are, had led to the overestimation of sex as significant variable in the lives of women. There has also been a lack of recognition of the cyclic nature of desire and of the strength of maternity—nurturance as a powerful female need.[12]

Chuyia witnesses the whole event but she is speechless to express what she feels. There is one episode in the novel where she grabs Mittu, the parrot, and with a swift twist wrings his neck. It is a projection of her unconscious desire to emancipate herself and crush those who are responsible for her plight. Silence and suffering of Kalyani convert into subterranean fury. With recollected force, she revolts against the authority of Madhumati and announces her *Jehad* against the traditions of the Ashram. She continues her diffident walk toward he ashram exit. All her passion and fear subsides in the company of Narayan.

Bapsi Sidhwa is convinced that man has persistently to work with the desperate ironies of life because the network of social relationship is too hard to cut. Had every Kalyani been able to take rescue in the company of Narayan, there would have been no suffering. The marginalised are the sufferers and the new voices like that of Narayan's, can't bring them in "centre" so easily. The imperialism represented in patriarchy controls the fate of marginalised at several levels. Widowhood is no sin, the real horrors consist in the hypocrisy of ruling class who mutes the voice of the weak to veil their own intentions. Narayan in all excitement and enthusiasm brings Kalyani to her home and reveals the name of his father, Seth Dwarkanath. With this revelation, the blood chills in her veins and turns her body numb. She does not reveal the reason and only says, "ask your father" (174). Narayan is mystified and concludes, "something was seriously amiss between father and son." The radicalism of Bapsi Sidhwa consists in the fact that she not only represents the suffering of marginalised but also unmasks the face of the oppressors. To identify the oppressors and to identify the causes of oppression represent the true cult of humanism and emancipation. In the novel *Water*, oppressors are the custodians of religious orthodoxy and the masters of economic resources like Madhumati and Seth Dwarkanath. Without least shame for the sexual exploitation of Kalyani, he tries to convince, "she is not a goddess, don't marry her, keep her as your mistress." (173). For his impious and shameful acts, she seeks a defence in the name of holy scriptures, "Narayan, perhaps you are not aware of this. Our holy texts say Brahmins can sleep with whomsoever they want, and the women they sleep with are blessed." (174). In the background of this conversation, Narayan's mother perceives the reflection of her own humiliation. She had to tolerate "tawdry infidelities" because she "had no option." The non-resistant vision against male sexuality is a part of the 'real experience' of womanhood in society. For these uncertain liaisons, woman has to bear shame and ignominy. Kalyani maintains silence against childhood injustice, maintains silence against humiliation in Ashram and maintains silence against the treachery of Seth Dwarkanath because there is one standard for males and other for females. It is said:

> When it comes to sex, there is one standard for women and another for men. People consider a woman more sinful than man, if both indulge in pre-marital or extra-marital sex relations. There are double standards governed by the order of patriarchy.[13]

Kalyani realises that "she had no choice" but to embrace death to avoid the betrayal of faith to Narayan and to escape the horrors of Ashram. The text of the novel from socio-political spectrum shifts to the realm of socio-philosophical justification. The death of Kalyani's extends the impression of nervousness and a temporary failure to restore due justice to them. It is not a loss but an investment to stir the strength in Chuyia and Shakuntala to challenge the authority of Madhumati. When Chuyia is employed to complete the nefarious designs of Madhumati, Shakuntala can not tolerate it and shouts to rescue her who has been dragged. It is only in the last scene that Sidhwa seeks the solution in Gandhian ideology i.e. the realisation and response to the call of humanity. In the presence of Gandhi on the ghats of Banaras, Shakuntala feels a terrible aura of warmth and kindness and an "indefinable magneticism and power." In the followers of Gandhi, she finds new awakening, new ideas and the new way of viewing the things. She dreams that they can take her far away from Rawalpur and the ashram and give her a new start in her life. She desperately runs after the train, looks at Narayan and finally hands over Chuyia to him, to save her from the horrors of Ashram and widowhood.

The discussion enables us to draw the conclusion that the fate of these oppressed and silent sufferers can be improved with new ideas and new vision towards the traditions of life. Socio-religious and socio-cultural practices are to be revaluated and reassessed in the light of new ideas, the unconventional way of thinking coupled with humanism and dynamism. It has come close to Lyotard's conviction, "it is both possible and necessary to break with tradition and institute absolutely new ways of living and thinking."[14]

NOTES

1. Bapsi Sidhwa, *Water* (New Delhi: Penguin, 2006). Cover page.
2. Edward Said, *Culture and Imperialism* (London: Chatto and Windus, 1993), 262.
3. *Ibid*, p. 264.
4. C. Talpade Mohanty, "Under Western Eyes: Feminist Scholarship and Colonial Discourse," rep. *Colonial Discourse and Post Colonial Theory: A Reader*, ed. Patrick Williams, Laura Chrisman (New York: Columbia University Press, 1994), p. 192.

5. G. Spivak, "Can the Subaltern Speak," rep. *Marxist Interpretations of Culture*, ed. Carywelson and Lawrence Grossberg (Basingstone: Macmillan Education, 1985), p. 306.
6. K. Mayo, 1986. *Mother India* (Delhi, Anmol).
7. A. Nandy, *The Intimate Enemy: Loss and Recovery of Self under Colonialism* (Delhi: Oxford University Press), 1983, p. 4
8. Helen Roberts, "Doing Feminist Research" (London, 1981), p. 98.
9. Elener Leacock, "Women Development and Anthropological Facts and Fiction," *The Politics of Anthropology*, ed. G. Huizer (The Hague, 1979) p. 132.
10. S. Mody and S. Mahtre, "Sexual Class in India," *BCAS*, Vol. 7, no. 1, 1975.
11. M. Kishwar and R. Vanita, ed., *In Search of Answers: Indian Women's Voices from Munshi* (London, 1984), p. 47.
12. Judith Barwick, *Psychology of Women: A Study of Bio-Cultural Conflicts* (New York: Harper and Row, 1971), p. 59.
13. Promilla Kapur, *Love, Marriage, Sex and Indian Woman* (New Delhi: Orient Paperbacks, 1976), p. 193.
14. Jean-Francois Lyotard, *The Post-Modern Explained to Children: Correspondence 1982-1985,* ed. Julian Penfants and Morgan Thomas (Sydney: Power Publications), 1992, p. 90.

Bapsi Sidhwa's *Water*: A Haunting and Lyrical Story of Love, Faith and Redemption

MEENAKSHI CHOUBEY
Govt. Girls College, Betul

Bapsi Sidhwa is Pakistan's leading diasporic writer. Her novels reflect her personal experience of the Indian subcontinent's Partition, abuse against women, immigration to the US, and membership in the Parsi/Zoroastrian community. Born on August 11, 1938 in Karachi and migrating shortly thereafter to Lahore, Bapsi Sidhwa witnessed the bloody Partition of the Indian Subcontinent as a young child in 1947.

Her novel *Water* is the basis of the film by Deepa Mehta. In this deeply moving story, Bapsi Sidhwa narrates the pathetic state of the widows in the widow's ashram in Benares. The most difficult thing to do is to live in peace and harmony with people. It is, perhaps, easier to live with birds and animals. Why is living with people a problem? Living with the widows in the widow's ashram is not an easy task for Chuyia, a child-bride who is abandoned at a widow's ashram in Benares after her fifty-year-old husband Hira Lal dies. The novel begins with the innocent Chuyia playing with her clay dolls. Chuyia is the daughter of Somnath and Bhagyalakshmi. Chuyia's mother expresses her concern about Hira Lal, her would be son-in-law: "I've heard Hira Lal is a grandfather."[1]

Somnath is satisfied that they don't want a dowry and will pay for the wedding. Bhagya is concerned about Hira Lal's age as she says: "By the time her womanhood blooms, he'll be old and spent." (8) But her husband has the last word and she thinks that he is right. The thought which haunts Bhagya is: "Then why did she not lavish on her the affection and attention she lavished on her sons? Feel the same surge of love and pride for her daughter? Was it because her heart knew that a daughter was only a guest and never belonged to the house into which she was born?" (10)

Chuyia is the most winsome of her characters in the novel. She grows up along with her brothers Prasad and Mohan in a traditional Brahmin family. Her brothers go to school while she helps her mother at house.

The marriage ceremony takes place at a temple, where only Brahmins are allowed to enter. Chuyia looks like a doll, sitting in front of Hira Lal. He applies the red sindoor to the parting in Chuyia's hair and to her forehead. He offers her a new sari with which to cover her head, and with this act the couple is considered officially married.

Chuyia's carefree life does not change after her marriage. She continues to play with her brothers and other village children and wanders off into the forest at will. Two years pass away very soon and Chuyia has almost no memory of her wedding. Somnath brings the news that Hira Lal is ill. After five days he tells Bhagya: "Hira Lal must be dying. Chuyia's mother-in-law wishes for her son to die on the banks of the Ganga so he can liberate his soul and attain moksha. Hira Lal's wife must be at his side. It is the moral thing to do." (23)

The bullock cart arrives at the bank of the Ganga. A boatman is waiting for them. The men lift Hira Lal and place him in a boat. Hira Lal's fever-racked heart finally gives out and the boat slowly approaches the steps to the ghats. Somnath doesn't know how to break the news. Searching for proper words, he asks his daughter, 'Bitiya, do you remember getting married?' 'No' she replies. Somnath declares, "Your husband is dead. You are a widow now." "For how long, Baba?" Chuyia asks her father. Somnath looks away, unable to face the innocent child.

Chuyia's mother-in-law takes the mangalsutra off Chuyia's neck and the beads scatter on the ground. The bangles are also smashed leaving Chuyia speechless. The barber cuts her hair and she is given white homespun cloth to wear. Chuyia is told by his father about her new residence. "This is your home now, bitia."

"Where is Ma?" she asks. Somnath does not have an answer. "Somnath stood helpless, resigned to his fate and the fate of his daughter. Hira Lal's mother pulled the black panels together and firmly shut the door of the ashram on his daughter's fearful cries and on her life." (39)

Inside the ashram, she looks at the strange surroundings. She meets there Kunti, Madhumati, Bua, Shakuntala and Kalyani. Some days later Chuyia learns that she is living in a singing ashram-temple.

In Kalyani's room Chuyia meets a small mongrel puppy, whose name is Kaalu Narayan, a young upper class Gandhian idealist stares at Kalyani when he first meets her. "He stood transfixed, completely enchanted—as if she were the first woman created by God." (63) His handsome face makes Kalyani speechless. She wants to conceal her feelings, but is unable to do so. She speaks to Narayan through Chuyia. An ugly face of the ashram comes forward when the readers come to know that Gulabi, the eunuch regularly takes Kalyani to the clients, mostly to the Seths in the area. Chuyia becomes the secret emissary carrying little notes from Narayan and conveying Kalyani's verbal answers to them. One day Narayan tells his mother that he has found a girl for him and there is no need to search a bride for him. But his mother is shocked when she learns that her would be daughter-in-law is a widow. She stares at him in horror and says: "Hai Bhagwan! . . . How will we show our face to the world?" (138)

She thinks that Gandhi has turned him into a lunatic! Madhumati comes to know of Kalyani's plan to get married to Narayan. One day Shakuntala asks a priest, Sadananda: "Panditji, is it written that widows should be treated badly?" (157) Sadananda says that there is a law recently passed which favours widow remarriage. He also makes it clear that we ignore the laws that don't suit us. The passionate love for Kalyani makes Narayan ask her: "Will you marry me?" (164) When Narayan shows her his house, she asks:

> "What is your father's name?"

"Dwarkanath—Seth Dwarkanath." (171)

Kalyani asks the boatman to turn the boat around. Narayan, not knowing the reason asks her: "Are you feeling sick?" Kalyani simply says, "Ask your father?" Narayan's father tells his son: "So, you've found out she's not a goddess. Don't marry her—Keep her as your mistress." (173) Kalyani decides to end her life as she knows that she has no other choice. She calmly walks into the river. Ma Ganga has claimed her daughter.

Madhumati thinks of a new plan to finance the ashram. She sends Chuyia with Gulabi to Seth Bhupidernath on the pretext of sending her home. Shakuntala comes to know the fate of Chuyia and she decides to help her. She goes to the platform and hears the speech given by Gandhi. She decides to hand over Chuyia to any of Gandhi's followers, who can take care of her. The follower will give her a new start in life. She runs with the train requesting everybody: "Brother, please take her. Please take this child with you." (197) At last Narayan takes Chuyia with him.

The novel explicitly depicts and discusses the problems of child marriage and the woe of the widows. The novel reflects the attitude of the male-dominated society towards widows. A widow is to observe fasts. She has to give up eating 'hot' foods in order to cool her sexual energy. She has to avoid auspicious occasions because she is considered inauspicious. (146) She has to remain celibate and loyal to her husband's memory. The novel presents biased attitude of the society towards the widows. The novel also highlights the state of the widows and the struggle for their survival. It also depicts rituals, values and practices of the colonial India.

The concept of womanhood in India is as divergent as the country itself. Bapsi Sidhwa's characters represent a wide spectrum. Traditional patriarchal Indian society creates several problems for the women. She is supposed to be pativrata, the paragon of all virtues. Yet the same society accepts different laws for marital disloyalty of a husband. The novel *Water* is not the story of Chuyia only, who becomes a catalyst for the change in the lives of the widows, but it is the story of all the widows in colonial India. The novel is to be remembered for the portrayal of some of the immortal characters like Narayan, Gulabi (who never walks but sashays), Kalyani and Chuyia.

Woman is the pillar of the society supporting, strengthening and enduring everyone around her. She is the guardian of culture and the advocate of tolerance and acceptance. Throughout the novel, the women are depicted as tolerating every injustice inflicted on them. Misfortunes engulf Kalyani but Chuiya is lucky enough to be accepted by Narayan at the last moment. *Water* questions the sorry state of the widows of those days. Their own existence is at stake. The tender and loving approach of the novelist makes the novel unforgettable.

The Times calls Bapsi Sidhwa a powerful and dramatic novelist. Her novel *Water* is a tribute to the victims and survivors of those days. The enduring appeal of the novel is due to her balanced treatment of depiction of some of the sensitive issues as well as delicate scenes in the lives of the characters. The positive attitude of Bapsi Sidhwa is commendable. The bitterness of the past is narrated by every widow in the novel. The disillusionment and the dishonesty make the widows speechless and passive. They are the victims of poverty and social taboos. Traditional Indian society's hypocrisy is shown to the outside world by Bapsi Sidhwa. Kalyani, a prostitute who entertains the Seths in order to raise some funds to run the ashram, is a fine example of such a hypocrisy. Bapsi Sidhwa is successful in the depiction of double standards of the society. She shapes and moulds the lives of the characters in the novel superbly. The expressions used in the novel, resourcefulness in characterization are the major strengths of the novel.

NOTES

1. Bapsi Sidhwa, *Water* (New Delhi: Viking, 2006), p. 7.

Feminist Perspective in Arundhati Roy's *The God of Small Things*

C. BHARATHI
KSR College of Engineering, Tiruchengode

> Feminism is a theory which involves women emancipating themselves on their own terms from inequalities and discrimination based on gender. The canon of this political philosophy addresses patriarchal orthodoxies within a male-dominated society. It seeks to bring an end to women's subordination and violence against women by empowering women and giving them control over their own bodies. (Allen 509)

The term 'feminism' was first used by the French dramatist Alexander Dumas in 1872 in his pamphlet '*L'Hommefemme*, to designate the emerging movement for women's rights. According to the *Oxford English Dictionary*, the term 'Feminism' was first used in the latter part of the nineteenth century, and it means having the qualities of females. The meaning of the term has been gradually transformed and it means a theory of political, economic and social qualities of the sexes. In general, feminism is an ideology of women's liberation, since intrinsic in all its approaches based on a woman who recognized herself, and is recognized by others as a feminist.

Feminism is meant "both the awareness of women's position in society as one of disadvantage or inequality compared with that of men and also a desire to remove those disadvantages" (Pathak 19).

Feminism is by no means a monolithic term. If one seeks a common strand in a number of varieties, it is the critique of the patriarchal modes of thinking which subordinate women to men in familial, religious, legal and artistic domains. This patriarchal ideology teaches women to internalize the concepts in the process of their socialization. It brings into focus the concepts of gender which are man-made.

Feminism means a sense of personal courage. The feminist consciousness is the consciousness of victimization. As a philosophy of life, it seeks to discover and change the more subtle and deep-seated causes of women's oppression. It is a concept of raising of the consciousness of an entire culture. Present-day feminism is a historically specific movement, rooted in French tenement wedded in deep critical style and equality. So feminism must be viewed as a rapidly developing major critical ideology or system of ideas in its own right.

The present-day feminist thought seeks to destroy masculinist hierarchy, but not sexual dualism. It is necessarily as a rebalancing factor between men and women within a given society. It is viewed as a humanistic philosophy. It still remains a political change to male authority and hierarchy in the most profound sense. But today the theorists describing its ultimate vision, prefer the word 'transformational' to the term 'revolutionary'.

Feminism as a mode of existence in which woman is free of the dependence syndrome. When women are free from the dependence syndrome and lead a normal life, the idea of feminism materializes.

It is no surprise that more number of Indian English novelists concentrate on feminist issues as the atrocities against women continue to increase. Nayantara Sahgal, Shobha De, Suniti Namjoshi, Ashapurna Devi, Mahasweta Devi, Kundalika Kapadia and Arundhati Roy are some of the present-day feminist writers. They have written of Indian women, their conflicts and predicaments against the male-chauvinist society. They have given the image and role towards the society of Indian women. The changing contexts have placed these women writers in an unenviable position. Their chief contribution consists in their exploring the moral and psychic dilemmas of the women protagonists and their achieving a new harmony of relationship with themselves and their surroundings.

The preset study deals about the three generations of women in Arundhati Roy's *The God of Small Things*. It is basically a saga novel that depicts the life of Mammachi and Baby Kochamma, Ammu and Rahel in Syrian Christian family in Ayemenem. The problems of patriarchal domination and female subalternity and the clash between the two are rooted in the specific geocultural reality of Ayemenem. Of the male characters, Pappachi and Chacko represent phallocratic hegemony.

Pappachi is the father of Ammu, the one blessed directly by the patriarch of Antioch, is a typical member of an upper middle class Christian family. The novelist comments sarcastically on the carefully maintained imperialist postures of the family. Roy presents Pappachi as an anglicized, tyrannizing and wife-beating man. He is suspicious of the emerging woman finding a voice, where anti-patriarchal impulses intersect. He cannot relish the idea of sending a girl for higher education. Nor can he appreciate his wife's efficient management of the affairs of the family's paradise pickles factory.

Ammu uses scathing and even blasphemous language to deflate the vanity and eurocentric pretensions of an authoritarian father whose extreme interventions had traumatized her childhood. Ammu's conflict with patriarchy often assumes anti-imperialist dimensions. She never loses a chance to condemn the hypocritical and Oxford-educated Chacko. She can only sympathize with her mother, who considers him a prime-ministerial stuff. Roy puts him in a ridiculously absurd situation by making him love and marry an English waitress, who walks out of that marriage soon after.

Ammu, the heroine of the novel, challenges the defiled social order by marrying a man of her choice and then breaking that marriage and getting entangled in a forbidden love. Ammu seeks to unsettle the formidable structures of a socio-cultural order by interrogating the traditional grammar of love.

The protagonist of the novel is Ammu, who is the daughter of Mammachi and mother of Rahel. Ammu became a victim of male-dominated society, when she was not allowed to pursue her studies. She finished her school education the year her father had retired from his job at Delhi and settled at Ayemenem. Ammu's father, called Pappachi in the novel, considered the education of women, an unnecessary expense. So Ammu's education had suddenly come to a stop and she had no other alternative than to come with her father to Ayemenem and wait for marriage:

> Ammu finished her schooling the same year that her father retired from his job in Delhi and moved to Ayemenem. Pappachi insisted that college education was an unnecessary expense for a girl, so Ammu had no choice but to leave Delhi and move with them. (38)

After that, Ammu helped her mother with the household duties. Ammu began to grow desperate, when no suitable marriage proposal came in a reasonable time. Marriage for Pappachi is the male's domination over woman and women are nothing but flowers in the hands of man. At home, Ammu felt like a captive lady, fettered to household chores and dull, mechanical routine. Sudden disruption of education, uncongenial atmosphere at home and lack of a viable alternative through marriage made her desperate:

> All day she dreamed of escaping from Ayemenem and the clutches of her ill-tempered father and bitter, long-suffering mother. She hatched several wretched little plans. Eventually, one worked. Pappachi agreed to let her spend the summer with a distant aunt who lived in Calcutta. (38-39)

Ammu met her future husband in a wedding reception when she paid a visit to one of her relatives in Calcutta. He was an assistant manager of a tea estate in Assam, who happened to be there on the vocation from his job. He proposed to her within five days they had met. Ammu accepted the proposal of a man whom she had known so little in a short time. Ammu was in a hurry to marry him, because she knew that in Ayemenem, people were dead against her wishes and so something was better than nothing.

But soon after the marriage, Ammu discovered that she had actually fallen from the frying pan into the fire. Her husband, whom she loved so much, proved to be an alcoholic. Disappointment became unbearable when her husband was suspended from his job for alcoholism, and sought to bargain by procuring his beautiful wife for his boss, Mr. Hollick, the English manager of the tea estate. Mr. Hollick suggested that he could go on a leave and "Ammu be sent to his bungalow to be 'looked after" (42). Ammu's refusal only aggravated her physical and mental torture. Her husband "grew uncomfortable and then infuriated by her silence. Suddenly he lunged at her, grabbed her hair, punched her and then passed out from the effort" (42). Ammu also hit back as hard as she could, but "when his bouts of violence began to include the children" (42) she could not tolerate the situation any more.

Ammu had no alternative but to break off and come back with her twins (two-egg twins, born from separate but simultaneously fertilized eggs)—Estha and Rahel to the very same place from where she tried to run away.

> Ammu left her husband and returned, unwelcome, to her parents in Ayemenem. To everything that she had fled from only a few years ago. Except that now she had two young children. And no more dreams. (42)

At the personal level, she was now burdened with the liability of two children who were not really loved by anybody, and all her dreams had shattered. At the familial level, she did not receive any sympathy at all. Her father would not believe that "an Englishman, any Englishman, would covet another man's wife," (42) and to Mammachi her children were a nuisance.

In brief, at the age of twenty-four, Ammu's life came to a standstill, nothing to hope for, nothing to happen, only to spend the long uneventful days languidly one after another. Her rebellious spirit only made her more and more miserable as the days went by.

At this stage, when she knew that she was "already damned" she became an "Unmixable mix" combining the infinite tenderness of motherhood and the reckless rage of a suicide bomber. She realized that though she lived in her parental house with her mother and brother, she had no "Locusts Stand I." For example when Chacko becomes the owner of the pickle factory which was established by Mammachi, he registers the venture into a partnership and he informs Ammu that she is the sleeping partner.

> Chacko had it registered as a partnership and informed Mammachi that she was the sleeping partner. . . . Though Ammu did as much work in the factory as Chacko, whenever he was dealing with food inspectors or sanitary engineers, he always referred to it as my factory, my pineapples, my pickles. Legally, as a daughter, she had no claim to the property. . . . 'Thanks to our wonderful male chauvinist society', Ammu said. Chacko said, 'What's yours is mine and what's mine is also mine'. (57)

Thus at twenty-four, Ammu had the painful realization that life had been lived, since she had spoilt her only chance by making the irrevocable mistake of choosing the wrong man. At her home and in her family and the society, she became virtually "untouchable." The mood of the patriarchal society is reflected in the view of Baby Kochamma, who

> subscribed wholeheartedly to the commonly held view that a married daughter had no position in her parents' home. As for a divorced daughter—according to Baby Kochamma, she had no position anywhere at all. And as for a divorced daughter from a love marriage, well, words could not describe Baby Kochamma's outrage. As for a divorced daughter from an inter community love marriage—Baby Kochamma chose to remain quiveringly silent on the subject. (45-46)

It should be noted that Baby Kochamma always resented Ammu because "she saw her quarrelling with a fate that she, Baby Kochamma herself, felt she had graciously accepted. The fate of the wretched Man-less woman" (45). What is interesting from the feminist point of view is that although Baby Kochamma is a woman, she is not in sympathy with another woman—her own kin—when she is in real distress. And Ammu's own mother, her "bitter long-suffering mother," refused to have any sympathy for her miserable daughter.

It was at this time that Velutha, son of Vellya Pappen, returned to Ayemenem after spending years away from home.

Ammu knew him since her childhood. Velutha used to come with his father to their house to deliver the coconuts. The Syrian Christians keep themselves away from Paravans because they consider them an untouchable. But Ammu had loved Velutha as her childhood companion, not so much for his exceptional talents as for his fiery spirit of protest, which she herself wanted to articulate. Arundhati Roy remarks:

> As she grew older, Ammu learned to live with this cold, calculating cruelty. She developed a lofty sense of injustice and the mulish, reckless streak that develops in Someone Small who has been bullied all their lives by Someone Big. She did exactly nothing to avoid quarrels and confrontations. In fact, it could be argued that she sought them out, perhaps even enjoyed them. (181-82)

Years later, Rahel still remembers Ammu's expression of love towards Velutha. Ammu loved Velutha—heart and soul—for his indomitable spirit of protest which she also nursed in her heart but could not articulate. So, she touched the untouchable. Velutha's father was angry with his son and profusely apologized to his master.

But, secretly, the love between Ammu and Velutha went on. During this time Velutha was arrested to be tortured to death on a false charge. As soon as Ammu came to know about it, she rushed to the police station to tell the truth. The treatment that she received at the hands of the Station House Officer shows how pitiable is the condition of women in the society, particularly when a woman is a divorcee. The author drops a hint that the police officer knew that he can freely insult the woman without any fear or compunction.

The officer represents the society's attitude to a woman who has loved outside the rules of "Love Laws." Ammu's brother, Chacko had already threatened her with all the authority of a patriarchy in his own house. "Get out of my house before I break every bone in your body" (255). So, having no "Locusts Stand I" anywhere, she had to leave and die helpless, sick, alone in a hotel in the strange place for a job interview. Ammu's last frantic effort is to make a living in her struggle for survival, mainly for the sake of her children. She died at the age of thirty one, "Not old, not young, but a viable die-able age" (161).

Ammu had been humiliated and cornered by her father, ill-treated and betrayed by her husband. She had been insulted by the police and rendered destitute by her brother. Each of them voiced the patriarchy ideology which commanded that she should have no right anywhere—as daughter, wife, sister and citizen. She was not an individual but just an object, a role necessarily submissive.

However it is not malefolk alone who perpetrate her tragedy. It is worth considering how a woman acts as an agent of this society, to undo another woman. Even women who have been deprived in their life choose to come down with all the unspent force of their frustration on another helpless woman.

Mary Roy, Arundhati Roy's mother, a fellow sufferer in real life like Ammu in the novel, says that Arundhati has written neither about people nor about the 1960s. Rather she is talking about a situation "where a Touchable woman—Syrian Christian, Nair or any other-falls in love with a man of lower caste. . . . I think Arundhati is making a point here. Nobody is bothered about the way Chacko has always had these women coming through the side entrance to satisfy his 'Men's Needs'." (Pandey 157)

Baby Kochamma's actual name is Navomi. She fell in love with a handsome young Irish monk called Father Mulligan, who was in Kerala for a year on deputation from his seminary in Madras. He was supposed to study Hindu Scriptures to denounce them intelligently. Baby Kochamma lived her life backwards. As a young woman she had renounced the material world, as an old one, she seemed to embrace it.

Every Thursday morning before the arrival of Father Mulligan, she forcibly bathed a poor village child just to impress Father Mulligan. When all her desperate efforts failed, she went to Madras, joined Roman Catholic Convent to become a Roman Catholic, against the wishes of her father, so that she could be with Father Mulligan. Being aware of her plans, Baby Kochamma's father went to Madras and withdrew his daughter from the convent. She returned but remained a Roman Catholic. By this time she had gained a 'reputation' as a Roman Catholic and was unlikely to find a husband. Since she refused to marry, she was sent by her father to do a course at a university in America. After two years she returned home with a diploma in Ornamental Gardening. But her love for Father Mulligan did not die.

The decision of Baby Kochamma's father made clear the society's priorities. A girl can be given education only if she cannot be given in marriage. Marriage in the eyes of the Indian society is the summum bonum of a woman's life. Her physical separation from Father Mulligan largely accounts for her growing narcissism and eventual sadism.

Baby Kochamma accepted the reality of living a manless life at Ayemenem. But still she loved the priest and made regular entries 'I love you, I love you' in her diaries. On the other hand, Father Mulligan, instead of denouncing the Hindu Scriptures, is fascinated by their beauty and becomes a Vaishnava. He went to an ashram north of Rishikesh, lived there for two years and died there of viral hepatitis. As long as he lived, he maintained a link with Baby Kochamma by writing to her every Diwali and sending a greeting card every New Year. Baby Kochamma's diary entries continued even after the death of Father Mulligan.

Baby Kochamma's frustration in love and the unspent force of repressed desire are instrumental in making Ammu's life miserable. She also poisoned the minds of Mammachi and Chacko against her. She was also responsible to a large extent for the children's unending suffering. Baby Kochamma is a study in meanness and perversion that may result from unnatural self-repression and the consequent frustration. When the novel opens, Father Mulligan has died four years ago. Father Mulligan's death did not affect the attitude of Baby Kochamma. On the contrary, she felt that she could possess him more now. She felt that "her memory of him was hers. Wholly hers. Savagely, fiercely, hers. Not to be shared with Faith, far less with competing co-nuns, and co-sadhus or whatever it was they called themselves" (298).

Mammachi's case is different—a different tale of woe. Although her husband was a high up in the society, a noted entomologist, he is seventeen years older than Mammachi. He had always been a jealous man. In Vienna, when Mammachi took her first lessons in violin, the lessons were abruptly discontinued by Pappachi when he heard the appreciative comments from the teacher that she was exceptionally talented. A sadist, every night he used to beat her with a brass flower vase.

Mammachi regularly suffered this ignominy with increasing frequency, till one day Chacko, on vacation, strode into the room, caught Pappachi's vase-hand and twisted it around his back. The result of it was always a thin bond between Mammachi and her husband. He never touched her again. He never spoke to her. If he needed something, he called either Kochu Maria or Baby Kochamma as intermediaries. He had other ways of insulting his wife. He never allowed Mammachi to sit in his car. And when some visitors were expected, he would sit on the verandah and publicly sew buttons which were not really missing, only to give an impression to the visitor that his wife neglected him.

In brief, Pappachi rejected Mammachi and insulted her in every possible way. Mammachi accepted the rejection passively and submissively. In other words, she accepted the female role model imposed on her by the society—docile, submissive, ungrudging, unprotesting. It is possible because of the trained sensibility.

> In the Indian society mother feels more for the daughter's agony, but here Mammachi due to her failures, did not feel much for her daughter's agony and it may be perhaps she was secretly jealous of Ammu's courage, happiness and her fulfilment, however brief it was.

Mammachi's attitude to Margaret Kochamma and her feminine jealousy for the woman, whom her son had loved and married, is the natural outcome of a woman in patriarchal society. She hated Margaret Kochamma, though she never met her. Arundhati Roy further tells us:

> Of course Mammachi would have despised Margaret Kochamma even if she had been heir to the throne of England. It wasn't just

> her working-class background Mammachi resented. She hated Margaret Kochamma for being Chacko's wife. She hated her for leaving him. But would have hated her even more had she stayed. (168)

Ammu came to understand that her brother Chacko still loves his wife despite the fact she left him. When she expressed this to Mammachi, she disagreed with that opinion. In fact, her maternal love grew into an obsession since the day Chacko prevented Pappachi from beating Mammachi. She was impervious to her daughter's frustration, yearning and love. She was ready to arrange even a prostitute to fulfil 'men's needs' to her divorcee son. Thus Mammachi exhibits the double standard of the society. Her treatment of Ammu and Velutha reveals the ugliness of narrow orthodoxy. Arundhati Roy's portrayal of Mammachi exposes the higher caste feudal values which she represents. Mammachi evokes no sympathy from us.

The story commences with the return of Rahel to her home in Southern India, Ayemenem, and the reunion with her brother Estha after twenty-three years. Thus the story begins near the end of the story and it is presented by a third person narrator: 'It was raining when Rahel came back to Ayemenem" (1). Rahel has come back leaving her job in America, hearing that Estha is in Ayemenem again. The narrative moves backwards and forwards to the arrival and the aftermath of the death by drowning of Sophie Mol, the English cousin, and ill-fated love between Ammu and the untouchable Velutha. Rahel recollects with pain these bitter memories of her mother's suffering life.

Rahel was one of the twins. She was child of a broken home and daughter of a divorcee mother and presently staying in her ancestral house. She was not fortunate to receive the love and affection from her elders that a child so badly needs. Her emotional needs remained unfulfilled. Of course her mother had all the concern for her, but in a hostile atmosphere she was utterly helpless. When Ammu died at the age of thirty one, Rahel was nearly eleven. As a child she had seen the sufferings of her mother, the insults and ignominies that were inflicted on her all the year round and the tortures she had been subjected to when her affair with Velutha was detected.

Estha and Rahel were also very fond of Velutha. They were deceived into giving false evidence when Velutha was arrested and brutally tortured to death. Rahel, after all these years, still remembers how they were made instrumental by Baby Kochamma in doing wrong to their mother. It is a memory that Rahel could never put out of her mind and in a way, it is this memory that practically ruined her conjugal life. After the death of Ammu, Rahel was more neglected than ever. With the death of her mother, Rahel had lost the last moorings that she had and she began to drift, from school to school, and spent eight years in a college of Architecture in Delhi.

She spent eight years in Delhi, unable to finish the five year undergraduate course. But it was here that she met Larry McCaslin, who happened to be in Delhi collecting material for his doctoral thesis. He met Rahel and found in her 'a jazz tune.' He followed her into a bookshop where neither of them looked at books and Rahel drifted into marriage "like a passenger drifts towards an unoccupied chair in an airport lounge. With a Sitting Down sense. She returned with him to Boston" (18). Initially things went well. Larry held Rahel in his arms, her cheeks against his heart, and saw the dark tumble down of her hair. He held her as though she was a precious gift. But things went wrong when they made love. While making love, he was offended by her eyes that seemed to have belonged to someone else and watching someone, "Looking out of the window at the sea. At a boat in the river" (19). He could not decode what that look meant. He could not understand what was in Rahel's eyes. He was unable to understand "that the emptiness in one twin was only a version of the quietness in the other. That the two things fitted together. Like stacked spoons. Like familiar lovers' bodies" (20).

Rahel realized within the short time of their marriage that something was lacking in their love relationship. They could not understand each other and decided to divorce. After this bitter experience, Rahel worked as a waitress, a night clerk, at different places. At that time, she was informed that Estha was expected to return to Ayemenem. This made Rahel give up her job and leave America.

When Rahel returned to Ayemenem, she was a divorcee like her mother. But luckily, she was not encumbered with a child, with any 'Millstone' round her neck. She developed a casual attitude to life and did not suffer from the various restrictions generally imposed by the society. Instead of feeling any kind of shame or moral weakness for a divorcee, she shocked Comrade Pillai by informing about it:

> "We're divorced." Rahel hoped to shock him into silence. 'Die-vorced?' His voice rose to such a high register that it cracked on the question mark. He even pronounced the word as though it were a form of death. (130)

To a large extent, Rahel is an emancipated woman. In terms of mother-daughter relationship, we notice that Rahel understands her mother much better than Ammu understanding Mammachi. There is enough evidence in the novel that she shares the agony of her mother, realizes the great injustice and cruelty done to her mother. Ammu has always remained a living presence in her memory. Seen from the feminist perspective, the novel records a progress, albeit slow, in feminism, offers some rays of hope and seems to suggest a distinct possibility of redemption.

The contemporary generation of women is represented by Rahel who is a rebel and a non-conformist throughout her life and proves herself. Arundhati Roy makes it abundantly clear that Rahel is not a traditional woman. She is a transgressor. She is guilty of incest as well—a taboo not to be violated even in contemporary society.

The novel presents three generations of women—Baby Kochamma and Mammachi, Ammu, and Rahel, and all are unhappy in their own way. Viewed from the angle of the narrator, *The God of Small Things* is authentically a feminine narrative.

The novel is a sad story of a woman who became a decentred subject in a world still clinging to a single, unified, unrelenting patriarchal authority. Ammu is a woman who loved "not wisely but too well," and was ruthlessly crushed down by the patriarchal love laws that lay down "who should be loved. And how. And how much" (328).

The God of Small Things is a feminist novel in the pity and terror that it evokes for the condition of women in a particular cultural milieu. The enclosure of marriage is analysed from the angle of woman's point of view. The horrors of self-willed, the failed or the successful endeavours of escape are recorded authentically. Female preoccupations with specific roles and images are carefully diluted.

Arundhati Roy's characters have their weakness and have their distinct personalities. The characters' unquenched desires, unfulfilled assurances, broken marriages, shattered faiths, unreasonable hate and planned revenge—all these are the crux of the novel. These complex and complicated problems bring them nothing but frustration, which culminates in perpetual suffering.

The major issue of feminism discussed in this novel is the struggle engaged by women for the establishment of their identity, their economic and sexual freedom. Ammu is a valiant fighter for these causes, though the options open to her in the male-dominated order are not viable at all.

Roy is concerned about matters that prove to be devastating and dehumanising for all. Her anxiety is for the mortals in general. Female preoccupations with specific roles and images are carefully diluted. The institution of marriage as an enclosure for both the sexes is envisioned by Roy in *The God of Small Things*. For women, total equality in marriage may still be a Utopian dream, but for men also, as Roy records, the road is not impediment free. Women can overcome the debilitating effects of marriage, overtly or covertly, to discredit male power or energy. This constant competition breeds the psychology of the victor and the vanquished.

The first generation of women—Mammachi and Baby Kochamma—represent the generation that submits to the norms of patriarchy. The second generation—Ammu—pays a heavy price for non-conformity and defiance. The contemporary generation of women is represented by Rahel, who lives the life of a rebel and a non-conformist.

The God of Small Things pretty well fits into a feminist text foregrounding many invisible barriers. Patriarchy has continued to rise in women's way to gain parity with men. One of the key issues which very often figures in contemporary feminist discourse is the patriarchal powers within the household, the society and the economy. It is so because "in spite of a number of face-saving laws made by the State, practices like dowry-based violence or female foeticide are carried on with impunity within the household" (Pandey 143).

The God of Small Things is the truthful portrayal of the plight of the women in society and their marathon struggle for seeking the sense of 'identity' in a male-dominated conservative framework. The social structure of an Indian woman is full of many ups and downs. Life offers little choice for a forsaken woman like Ammu.

Arundhati Roy identifies herself with Rahel who is also an architect by profession. Ammu and her tragic travails are a fictional adaptation of the various kinds of social ostracism that Arundhati Roy's mother had suffered due to her rebellious outlook. The novel projects the writer's own life through Ammu's character. The autobiographical touches are definitely traced in the setting of the novel, characterization etc. In brief, the novel is full of autobiographical elements.

Works Cited

Ajayan, C. "A Segment of Existence: Arundhati Roy's *The God of Small Things*." *Journal of Literature and Aesthetics*, July-Dec. 1997: 97-99.

Bhatt, Indira, and Indira Nityanandan (1999). *Explorations of Arundhati Roy's The God of Small Things*. New Delhi: Creative.

Dass, Veena Noble (1995). *Feminism and Literature*. New Delhi: Prestige.

Davees, C.J. "(De)sign in *The God of Small Things*." *College English Review* (Nov.-Dec. 1997): 13-19.

Dhawan, R.K (1999). *Arundhati Roy: The Novelist Extraordinary*. New Delhi: Prestige.

Dodiya, Jaydip Singh K. (1999). *Indian Women Writers: Critical Perspectives*. New Delhi: Sarup.

Jha, Surendra Narayan. (2001). "Dreams Re-Dream-ed.: A Study of *The God of Small Things*." *Indian Women Novelists in English*, ed. Amar Nath Prasad. New Delhi.

Kaul, R.K. "*The God of Small Things*." *Indian Book Chronicle* (4 April 1998): 8-9.

Khot, Mohini (2001). "The Feminist Voice in Arundhati Roy's *The God of Small Things*." *Indian Feminisms*, ed. Jasbir Jain and Avadesh Kumar Singh. New Delhi: Creative.

Nair, Rukmini Bhaya. "Twins and Lovers," rev. of *The God of Small Things, Biblio: A Review of Books* (3 May 1997): 4-6.

Nayar, Pramod K. "Ellipsis and the Formation of Subjects: Arundhati Roy's *The God of Small Things*." 6 (1997): 4-5.

Pillai, Gopinatha C. (1999). "Aesthetics of Post-Colonial Feminism: A Reading of *The God of Small Things*." *The Critical Studies of Arundhati Roy's "The God of Small Things*."

Prabhakar, M. (1999). *Feminism and Post-Modernism in Margaret Atwood's Fiction*. New Delhi: Creative.

Prasad, Amar Nath (2001). *Critical Response to Indian Fiction in English*.

Roy, Arundhati (1997) *The God of Small Things*. New Delhi: IndiaInk.

Saini, Bimaljit (2002). "*The God of Small Things*: A Feminist Analysis." *Feminist English Literature*, ed. Manmohan K Bhatnagar. New Delhi: Atlantic.

Shukla, Shobhushan (2000). "The Bigness of the Small and the Smallness of the Big: An Interpretation of *The God of Small Things*." *"The God of Small Things": A Saga of Lost Dreams*, ed. K.V. Surendran. New Delhi: Atlantic.

Sharma, R.S, and Shashi Bala Talwar, ed. (1998). *Arundhati Roy's "The God of Small Things": Critique and Commentary*. New Delhi: Creative.

Singh, B.N. (1999). "Combating Caste and Sexuality in God's Own Country: A Feminist Reading of Arundhati Roy's *The God of Small Things*." *Contemporary Indian Women Writers in English: A Feminist Perspective*, ed. Surya Nath Pandey.

Surendran, K.V. "Arundhati Roy's Innovations in *The God of Small Things*." *Punjab Journal of English Studies*, 14 (1994): 51-61.

Invisible Barriers: A Study of Gender and Caste in Arundhati Roy's *The God of Small Things*

PROTIBHA MUKHERJEE SAHUKAR
Durga Mahavidyalaya, Raipur

Arundhati Roy has received overwhelming acclaim with the publication of *The God of Small Things.* With this, Roy has successfully hoisted India on to the international stage but let us not forget that the novel portrays India not as a prosperous nation with a glorious past but a nation with a gloomy side of progress where man-made boundaries and divisions bring forth brutality of unbelievable nature. Through *The God of Small Things,* Roy gives the people who have been placed at the bottom of the society and forced into silence a platform to reveal the suffering.

The driving force of the novel stems from the anger at the damage done to people and their kin, to the fundamental laws of love and to the honest way of thinking as a result of gender and caste discrimination. One becomes conscious of the viciousness human beings are capable of when the stability of the society they live in is threatened. In one of her interviews, Roy had said: "fiction has always been a means of making sense of the world, to connect the smallest things to the biggest things" but the fact remains that the small things are no match for the big ones and get crushed by them. The 'small things' like love and warmth, yearning and affection get trampled by the 'big things' like blatant gender and caste prejudice, patriarchy and the effort to preserve the status quo at any cost. Roy categorically hits out on old-fashioned traditional assumption and question the authority of societal hierarchy.

The God of Small Things is a story of star-crossed lovers and how far a community goes to safeguard its old traditions and ways of life. The novel unravels a complex maze of sexism and casteism as women and the untouchables are the two sections of Indian society that have suffered most through the ages. It is a biting account of the veiled beliefs of a patriarchal society which controls the hierarchies in the family system, in the gender roles and in the caste system. By interlacing the fate of women and untouchables, Roy demonstrates that just as women are treated as second sex, in the same way untouchables can never cease to be the lesser mortals.

My purpose is to show how these two types of societal and cultural hierarchy work in *The God of Small Things* to strip individuals of their secular, constitutional, emotional, and sexual rights. By weaving the fortunes of an afflicted woman and an ill-fated untouchable, this paper looks at the correlation between sexism and caste and the consequences of such relationship for the pariahs.

From time immemorial, our society has bound its people with limitations on social interaction. With the caste system deeply rooted in India's legacy, men and woman here have always felt the heat of it in the matter of falling in love. Women on the other hand craving for fulfillment in life·cross the barrier of piety motivated by benevolence or passion of the underdog and break the fence of regulated love. As Roy explains in her story, all this really began in the days when the moral police made the love laws, "the Laws that lay down who should be loved and how. And how much" (33).

The politics of gender and caste converge to tell a heart-wrenching story of Ammu and Velutha. Their fate demonstrates that despite the fact that women and untouchables have been granted the right to vote by the Constitution of India, it is not adequate enough to help erase the long-established conservative forces of Indian (Hindu) society.

Ammu is a divorcee. Velutha is an untouchable. They are outcasts who dare to fall in love. "They . . . broke the rules. They . . . crossed into forbidden territory. They . . . tampered with the laws." (33)The two lovers are separated by social order as the two are from completely different social backgrounds. Ammu is a typical upper class woman who as per the society rules should not even dream of socializing with the untouchable Velutha, leave alone having an affair with him. Such behaviour of Ammu brings dishonour to her family and she herself suffers lasting damage to her own reputation. The "bare bodied" Velutha (6), on the other hand, is a man who is at the lowest rung of the social ladder, specifically called a Paravan. But the well-built Velutha creates ripples in lonely Ammu's heart. The two defy the age-old institution of their particular classes and cross into forbidden territory. Such violation on their part necessarily results in very heavy penalty where Ammu loses her social status completely and worst still Velutha is tortured and brutally killed by aides of her family. Subjugation of Ammu presents a clear indication of prevalent exploitation and discrimination against a woman subordinated in terms of authority to a man in a patriarchal society.

It is important to understand the place in which Indian women are positioned within its tradition and belief. It is a harsh reality that women have been ill-treated for ages and India is no exception. From the cradle to her grave, a woman has always been in the clutches of numerous evil acts like discrimination, oppression, violence within the family, at the workplace and in the society. Though the kind of oppression that a woman in India had to undergo in the past (widowhood, child marriage, sati etc.) is to a large extent done away with but by and large she has always remained at the mercy of her male counterparts, beginning with her father in her childhood, to her husband in her youth and to her own son in her old age. As a result, she turned into a mere object rather than a human being. The incongruity lies in the fact that in India where a woman is worshipped as Durga, Lakshmi and Saraswati—the embodiment of *sakti*—the atrocities committed against her are horrendous.

So what is the source of women's oppression? Women's status in India is bound by social, cultural and economic factors that influence all aspects of their lives. Since a woman is vulnerably positioned at the gender hierarchy, she experiences widespread discrimination and hostility. Her social vulnerability and lack of opinionated voice, when combined with her being female, increase her exposure to potentially violent situations simultaneously reducing her ability to escape.

Roy reveals the condition of women in India through the portrayal of the beautiful Ammu. To understand Ammu's position in particular or for that matter the position of women in the society as complex as that of India, it is necessary to do more than label women as oppressed class, caste or a colonized group. It is necessary to take cognizance of their position, the degree and nature of their subordination, as it varies from one class to another, one ethnic group to another, and the type of society in which they live. Let us not forget that in the case of Indian woman even with the new political systems and liberal ideas of class equality, it is difficult to do away with the old decaying power structures.

Ammu's situation goes on to show that women in India hold no power and have no rights even in their own lives. She is not just combating new hostilities of society, in fact she is fighting an age-old war. Ammu's is the struggle of a woman who against all odds goes in pursuit of love risking everything. Society is a vital part of our lives. The various forms of social punishment and restrictions imposed on women help prevent transgressors from getting away with their insubordination, and teach prospective rebels to abide by the rules and norms of the society. Ammu's sexual relationship with Velutha brings in its wake horror, tragedy and savagery resulting in the brutal murder of Velutha and the incessant victimisation of Ammu (along her children). Ammu has the right over her body and her sexual experiences but her dependent position in the house does not sanction her choice of her partner. The expected relationship between a woman and a man are controlled by the prevailing attitudes of people and social standing that act as great barriers for the autonomy of Indian women.

Ammu wants nothing more than happiness for herself and her children but realises that life offers very little choice to a woman who yearns for happiness. Ammu's search for happiness threatens the existing order, and her society takes every probable step to stop that. Since Ammu lives in a very orthodox society, she is made to suffer quite early in her life and continues to suffer throughout. Doomed fate follows her like a shadow right up to the last moment of her life.

Ammu is a classic example of the denial of a woman's place inside her own family and the emotional abuse meted out by the paternal cruelty. Ammu's standing within the house is very fragile for the reason that her marriage brought shame on all the people of Kochamma family. She made the unpardonable mistake of marrying badly and returning to her parents' home where she is not welcome. The fact that Ammu divorced an alcoholic husband who physically abused her and the children does not make any difference. From the patriarchal point of view which is obsessed with ideas of order and perpetuation, good wives tolerate, and in this way grant stability to the family systems. Ammu does not fit into the bill. Even though the Hindu Succession Act of 1956 states that a girl child has equal claim to her father's inheritance as her male sibling, Ammu has no claims whatsoever to the family property nor is privileged enough to enjoy the same attention and affection reserved for her brother. The ruthless attitude of her family clearly shows that there is no place for an impudent daughter inside an old-fashioned household. It is a well-documented fact that the feeling of being loved and cherished is very important for the development of a person's self-esteem and dignity and gender bias inside families leads to irreparable harm. Ammu is humiliated at the hands of her near and dear ones and shown the door. In the end, she is left to herself and dies a lonely death with no one to ease her pain. Her dire situation exposes the double standards of moral values in Indian culture regarding men and women and the expected passive role of a woman in a man-woman relationship. Ammu fails to realize that the inequality shown to her and her subordination essentially consolidates the rigidly hierarchical and unfair social structure.

Ammu and Velutha's choice to enter into such an illicit relationship does show a glimmer of rebellion. Nevertheless it cannot be denied that Ammu's liaison with Velutha is a blatant albeit hopeless violation of the society's rigid rules. Although the two struggle against the current of social norms but they are still unable to escape the inevitable consequences of their actions in a coldly unyielding society.

Perhaps one of the most striking features of the novel is the treatment of Velutha who stands out as the representative of the untouchables considered lowest on the social scale. He is an out-cast belonging to the group of unskilled people who perform the unpleasant duties of cleaning human faeces and sweeping the street of all kinds of filth. With no apparent way to escape the chain of social order, the untouchables are forced to accept their inferior status. Even though Untouchability was abolished by Baba Sahib Ambedkar's zealous perseverance in 1949, nevertheless the inner prejudice remained firm. Mahatma Gandhi and Baba Sahib Ambedker helped the untouchables fight for their rights trying to redeem them of subjugation yet they are not openly welcomed. While they are not legally excluded from the community altogether, they continue to be below the four main divisions of the original caste system.

Roy develops Velutha to the level of a cataclysmic hero. He is a self-made man, a master craftsman having no parallel as a carpenter. He is full of life, hope and aspirations, is a Communist worker and takes party activities rather seriously. Firmly placed by caste at the bottom of society, he is aware of its taboos, and yet readily breaks out of these strictures. However, the caste-oriented rigidity plays havoc with his life.

In the Indian society, romantic relationships have always been expected to stay within a specified sphere. It is no wonder, then, that people have to pay a heavy price when they choose to go against their parents's or society's wishes and fall in love with someone outside the circle. Velutha falls for Ammu throwing all scruples of caste and community to the air. This in fact is the beginning of the end for him. If Ammu finds Velutha's dark skin fascinating and is drawn to the passion she feels for him, then Velutha's longing grows to match Ammu's aching. Even though he knows that there is no future for his love, yet his infatuation prevails. Ammu offers Velutha, what the society and family refused. In a world which is so hostile, the few moments spent with Ammu offer real happiness to Velutha. In doing so, he seals his fate. He pays with his bleeding, bruised body for the raptures of consummated ardour.

When Velutha's father Vellya Paapen discovers the affair, he cannot imagine in his wildest dreams that Ammu who belongs to the orthodox Syrian Christian community, could ever fall in love with his son who is an untouchable. He exhibits a typical indebtedness to the dominant cultural prejudices as it is a social taboo for a Christian to marry a Hindu and, much worse, a Paravan. A man and his culture are intimately interlinked and the greatest tragedy happens when one become blind to the evils of one's own culture and society. Vellya Paapen considers it a crime on the part of his son and unwittingly acts as the guardian of system, joins hand with the victimizers.

Velutha is accused of assault and rape of Ammu and is wrongly implicated in Sophie Mol's death. He is battered to death at the police station. In reality, Velutha is killed for transgressing the caste barrier.

Vulnerably situated at the bottom of India's gender and caste hierarchies, both Ammu and Velutha experience rampant gender and caste discrimination and violence as the outcome of severely imbalanced power equations. They fail to comprehend that their establishing relationships outside the regular social framework will unleash cultural fear, rage and hostility leading them to their doom. Through the depiction of the fate of Ammu and Velutha and the unyielding positioning of women and the unendurable plight of the dispossessed group, Roy categorically pushes for improved societal reform. She successfully manages to highlight her protagonists' struggle against the human penchant for creating hierarchical structures, the repercussion these traditionally controlled ideologies create, and the destiny of those who go against the tenets of these ideologies. Ammu and Velutha's defying spirits make them take risk but unfortunately they lose everything. Ammu takes the risk of loving an untouchable. Velutha risks marching into a world where he is not welcome; a world so hostile that it costs him his life. It is human nature to destroy things that stand in its way because it is the fundamental urge of man to keep things under his control. Roy builds up her critique of gender and caste discrimination and demonstrates how man's objective to create and maintain hierarchical structure along with his resolve to establish authority ultimately obliterates two lovers.

Work Cited

Roy, Arundhati. *The God of Small Things.* New Delhi: India Ink, 1997.

Concept of Feminism in Doris Lessing and Anita Desai's Fiction

ASHOK KUMAR AZAD
L.P.R.L. Sanskrit Collage, Samaul

Feminism in literature refers to a mode that approaches a text with foremost concern for the nature of female experience in it. The fictional experience of characters, the relation, intuitional or imaginative, capacity of an author, the experience implicit in language of structure that interrogates the cultural prescriptions that subordinate and trivialize woman and treat them as inferiors are the primary concerns of female fiction writers. Feminism demands an activity, not passivity, which analyses our sense of the female presence in the world. A feminist fiction is a work where language and imagery are employed to impart a new vision of reality—reality perceived from a woman's authentic mode of seeing, feeling and measuring her existence without subscribing to the male cultural codes.

Toril Moi in her essay "Feminist, Female, Feminine," distinguishes between 'feminism' as a political position, 'female' or 'femaleness' as a matter of biology and 'femininity' as a set of culturally defined characteristics. The 'feminine' is a culturally produced position of marginality in relation to patriarchal society. It is not a fact of nature. Hence the term 'feminine' gives rise to a ground from which to conduct a feminist politics for change.

Feminism has its origin in the history of woman's oppression all over the world. God alone knows what Adam and Eve were like and how they behaved in their mutual relationship. But one thing is clear and it is the age-old superiority of man over woman. In the *Bible* Adam is presented as the master. He names all the beasts and animals. He also names Eve. St. Paul, too, ascribes a secondary position to woman.

The late 19th century is recognised as a period which thrust women at the forefront of political scenario. Beneath the facade of democratic ideals, women were subjected to unfair treatment. In industries they were paid less than men and were denied the right to vote. These issues assumed importance in their collective movement for equal rights in 1906-1914. Finally all over the world, women were granted suffrage by 1928 and after the Second World War the women's movement, which was a marginal movement up to 1950s, came to full swing.

The present article is focused on Doris Lessing and Anita Desai's fiction. English has come a long way both in Britain and in India, as have the women of both India and the West. English having been introduced in India when the British arrived here has grown so much that now we have what one many call Indian English. This study is by no means intended as a comparative analysis or an influence study. Although, I have tried to state the concept of feminism as understood in India and England, made sweeping generalizations, contriving the parallels either between the Western feminist theory or the fiction of these writers of the British and Indian tradition, the study brings out the mutual irradiation of literature and theories.

The present article is an attempt to study feminism in British and Indian English fiction. It also incorporates the study of different cultural and historical backgrounds to trace the presence of the woman question. I have tried to focus my study on two major novelists—Anita Desai and Doris Lessing. In fiction, the women writers appear to be seeking freedom from the male version of women by speaking out, naming, defining and deconstructing themselves. The British portrayal of the inner world of female psyche happens to be amazingly diverse, ambiguous and multivalent. In matters of love, sexuality and maternity, their characters not only reveal bizarre responses, secret logic but also daring self-assertion.

An author is willy-nilly influenced by her social milieu. Conditions being very different in India and England, the novelists selected for this study—Doris Lessing, Anita Desai—view the issues from different levels. In England, an average woman does not have to struggle for bare existence. In India, where abject poverty is not unusual, people have to strive for sheer survival. Under such trying conditions, we cannot expect men or women to be lost in romantic fancies. No heroine of Doris Lessing or Anita Desai has to crush her conscience simply to keep the wolf from the door. Women novelists like Anita Desai portray the lives of women belonging to the educated and affluent sections of the society. With these women, the problem is not economic but psychological. With a happy background as children and being financially well off as married women, they can afford to attend to more refined feelings and emotions. Things which mean less than a trifle to the weather-beaten, thick-skinned common people are of vital importance to them. Like the sensitive heroines of Doris Lessing, Anita Desai's heroines have psychological problems and are, in fact, regarded as abnormal by the people who come in contact with them. These female characters show much affinity to their counterparts in the Western novels.

One of the many causes of concern in Indian society is the institution of joint family which demands a lot of flexibility and adjustability from a woman. If the other members of the family are not sympathetic and broad-minded, the newly married girl has to face a lot of trouble and her experience may embitter her life, as happens in the novels of Anita Desai. Such a condition does not exist in the West, and so, it does not appear in any significant form in the Western novels.

These dissimilarities in our values and approach to life are reflected in the novelists under study. In India sexual freedom for women, for example, has not assumed the enormous proportion it has in the West. As a matter of fact, barring the negligible periphery of the uppermost and lower-most sections of the Indian society, it is looked down upon. In India economic freedom for women is more important than sexual one because it often subjects them to male tyranny. Barring a few writers like Shobha De and Uma Vasudev, Indian women novelists avoid the kind of frank discussion of sexual matters found so frequently in Doris Lessing.

Women's approach to the problem of establishing their identity is again different in the East and the West. In the West, more often than not, women equate identity with independence and equality with men; in India, on the other hand, the guiding principle appears to be cooperation. In spite of conflicts, the Indian woman in the last three decades has learnt to assert herself as an autonomous human being. Her responses to her femaleness have been diverse and differ according to her class and upbringing.

The first factor that influences the identity of a person is heredity. All the novelists attach great importance to parental influence. In Doris Lessing's *The Grass is Singing*, Mary inherited her mother's 'contempt' and 'derision' for her father and an arid feminism. Consequently, she seemed to take no interest in men. The perversion of a normal instinct plays a decisive part in her tragedy. Too late she realizes that she had allowed others to guide her life and in future "she would walk out her road alone."[1] Death grants her no respite and she fails to realize her identity. The personal scenes in *The Memories of a Survivor* are used by the novelist to emphasize the fact that thought patterns are set in childhood and the family plays an important part in this matter. The novels in *Canopus in Argos* series deal with matters that that transcend sublunary trivialities like the effect of heredity.

Doris Lessing analyses the concept of freedom for women and discovers its insubstantiality. Regarding freedom, she says that every human being is unfree from the moment of conception since he is a chance conglomeration of inherited things, his parent's attitudes, the people who chance to influence him. *The Golden Notebook* with its 'free women' sections is a total debunking of the concept of 'freedom'. S. Jameson misses the point when he says that these anxiously independent women are caught in their sexuality like flies in treacle. Experience, in fact, tells them that sexual freedom is a very poor substitute for real freedom and for real freedom they have to depend on a life partner who regards them as human beings. We are told that sex is essentially emotional for a woman. In this novel no marriage is shown as successful or happy and yet women wish to get married. The lovelorn Maryrose finally marries a middle-aged man. When Marion says to Anna she is free, Anna answers who would like to be married but she does not like her mode of living. Ella says to Maitland that every woman wants to get married and sums up the woman's case: "My deep emotions, my real ones, are to do with my relationship with a man."[2] Ella without Paul was "unable to enjoy sitting at a table publicly without a man's protection." This shows the interdependence of man and woman. In an interview given in 1969 at Story Brook, Lessing said: "I'm impatient with people who emphasize sexual revolution. I say we should all go to bed, shut up about sexual liberation and go on with the important matters."[3]

Mercury in *Briefing for a Descent into Hell* by Doris Lessing says that truth will be part of new soon-to-be-developed equipment of humanity. Clearly the focus is on all humanity, not simply males or females. Doris Lessing admits the limitations of women, their dependence on men to live which leads to fulfillment and the inadequacy of mere physical sex. Lessing's *The Children of Violence* series consisting of five novels studies the relations of the individual conscience with the collective. Martha Quest's family has no sympathy with her intellectual aspirations and her goal is the visionary Four Gated City "where white and black and brown lived as equal." As a child she had ecstatic visions: "There was a slow integration during which she, and the little animals, and the moving grasses became one." In this mystic union of herself with the universe lies the core of her identity which she succeeds in establishing only in *The Four Gated City.* In this context it is important to distinguish between the real and the apparent identity of a woman. Martha's youthful rebelliousness and idealism were the facades of her identity; her real identity emerges when she comes in contact with the Coldridge household where her selfless service helps to bring out her real personality.

Doris Lessing regards *The Children of Violence* as a study of the individual conscience in its relations with collective. The first distinctive feature of self-development is the conscious and unavoidable segregation of the single individual from the undifferentiated herd. Martha's mother, the Cohen boys, Donovan, people at the Sports Club, all seek to model her personality and thus curb her autonomy. The Sport Club is symbolic of the action of the collective. Thus Martha discovers that "her own idea of herself was destroyed."[4] Later, she washes her hands off the Sports Club, a step in her liberation from the pressure of the collective. In each volume, Martha has to struggle against some factors in order to preserve her individuality. Later she concludes that no social group with a dogma can effect the balanced healthy development of a person or society. Thus, in *The Four Gated City,* she works for developing the psychic abilities of the race because of her faith that only a change in the individual can usher in a change in the collective. From the beginning, we see Martha doing things reluctantly. She even repudiates the child she has borne. Her actions merely add to her problems and the split in her personality widens with the passage of time and in the Four Gated City, like Anna in *The Golden Notebook*, she has to seek the help of a psychiatrist. As Selma Burkom observes with special reference to *The Golden Notebook*, the problem of integration is of perennial interest to Lessing.

Mental illness may be more apparent than real or it may be the consequence of the unhealthy restrictions on an individual's perceptions. Social pressure forces people to repress their instinctive drives and reactions which constantly seek an outlet and thus create tension in their minds. In *Landlocked* by Doris Lessing, Thomas Stern suggests that the present suffering of humanity may be the augury of a transformation in the human race like the straining of a caterpillar before its metamorphosis into a butterfly. Many of these mentally ill persons may well be the harbingers of our mental evolution. Society however, rejects these harbingers of the evolutionary design. After coming in contact with Lynda, in opposition to the intentions of the society, Martha learns to see things steadily and to see them whole. She comes to realize that these forces are benevolent and she learns to live in harmony with them. Martha's newly acquired wisdom helps her to realize her identity that mystic sense of her union with the universe. It is, thus in the Four Gated City, that Martha realizes her identity, the seed of which had been latent in her personality since childhood, but not burgeoning out.

Doris Lessing has deeply probed the problem of female identity in relation to sexual relationship with men. She shows that nature of female instinct itself propels woman towards union with man, though most of the unions resulting in marriage prove hazardous owing mainly to the situation of being a woman in a male dominated society. In *The Grass is Singing,* though Mary's marriage leads to her tragic death, Doris Lessing presents an interesting aspect of female nature which is reflected in Mary's wish to be dominated by man. Though Dick's "abasement before her was the greatest satisfaction she knew," she needed a man stronger than herself and even tried to force her husband to "take the ascendancy over her." What strikes her most about Moses is his masculinity, his strength that would enable him to dominate her physically.

Lessing's other heroine Martha finds marriage as an encroachment of her identity and freedom. In *A Proper Marriage*, Douglas doubts Martha's fidelity whereas she is not accorded the right to question his numerous love affairs. In *A Ripple from the Storm,* Martha marries Anton Hesse for political reasons. Her friend Maisie, a widow and pregnant by the son of the local magistrate, affords another instance of the instinct controlling and guiding women. She marries Andrew. In the next novel of the series *Landlocked,* Martha and Anton are shown maintaining separate identities before a proper divorce while Maisie, already divorced, brings up her daughter alone. In this novel Martha is shown as having her only meaningful sexual relationship with Thomas Stern. Martha has all sorts of romantic notions about sex and what she most dislikes in the older women's attitude towards sex is their bargaining conventional approach. She is asked to make men respect her not for moral reasons but for the practical reason of doing well for herself. However, she soon discovers from an affair that casual sex cannot satisfy. Neither 'free love' nor marriage seems to satisfy her. Her behaviour before her marriage is simply an extreme form of reaction against her mother and all she stands for. She even admits to entertaining a desire for a strong man she could defer to. She is overtaken by her biological destiny and gives birth to a child: "It was of no interest to anybody, not even herself."[5] Only her relationship with Thomas Stern helps her in the integration of her personality.

The Summer before the Dark is Doris Lessing's best statement on the problem of female integration. She concentrates on a problem which is common perhaps to women all over the world. The novel depicts Kate Brown's efforts to establish her identity to regain her neglected personality. Kate Brown has been performing the roles prescribed for her by her society, never caring for the dictates of her inner self. She takes a job as a translator and builds a maternal identity for herself. Kate Brown, however, receives her warnings in fifteen dreams, in each one of which a seal appears. The seal, many critics hold, is the symbol of her real personality. In her home and in her job, she has to follow the will of others. This has given her a fake personality. She has to stop acting and start living as herself. Even at her next job, she is required to play the role of the mother. Evidently, she cannot establish her identity. This is a lesson to the housewives that they should prefer pleasing themselves to pleasing others if they want to establish their identity. She leaves her sick lover, Jeffrey. The moral is pragmatic—one has to be ruthless for the sake of one's identity. Her dream of a turtle which after laying its eggs, loses its sense of direction and is stranded on land is symbolic of Kate Brown as a mother after fulfilling her biological role. This clearly shows that the family in patriarchy is a hindrance in the path of a woman's realization of her identity. In her last dream, Kate releases the seal into the water. This is symbolic of Kate's new identity. Her personality now includes everything that her inner self wants to be or is.

A close analysis of Lessing's novels enables us to gather that despite her sympathy for women, she is by no means a rabid feminist. It is true that women are placed at a disadvantage both by the exigencies of nature and the machinations of patriarchy. All the same, the realization of their full potentialities is the concern of the women themselves. Goodness or badness is not the ineluctable consequence of belonging to a particular sex.

Feminism being an important movement in the modern world, woman's place, position and especially the question of her identity are the major issues in India also. In India, since ages, a women's role in life was strictly compartmentalized; she was a daughter, a wife or a mother. In all these roles, she had to adhere to certain appointed norms; she had no separate identity as a human being. Things are changing nowadays especially amongst the sections where educations and material prosperity have ushered in a degree of enlightenment. In common with women all over the world, Indian women are also voicing her desire to be emancipated, to get rid of the unjust restrictions imposed on her and the pervasive discrimination against her. She is seeking the right to be regarded as a whole human being, not simply as an adjunct to her male relatives.

In the present context, an important point about the novels of Anita Desai is the weight she attaches to the upbringing of men and women. Generally her protagonists are not brought up in a healthy way being either pampered or else utterly neglected. Mothers, in her novels, do not enjoy the status traditionally extended to them as their natural right, and they almost invariably, fail their children. Their case being worse than their children's they themselves require help from the latter. Under such conditions, women naturally turn to their husbands and families for seeking their identity. In *Cry, the Peacock* by Anita Desai, Maya, the protagonist craves for identity, sympathy and understanding, endeavouring in her own way, to make Gautama, her husband, see her need and to respond to it. Unfortunately, this sensitive impressionable woman is obsessed by a childhood forecast of death in her family four years after her marriage. Had theirs been a true marriage of minds, the love of her husband would have proved a palliative to her inflamed mind. Gautam blames her upbringing for what he regards as morbidity. "Neurotic, he said, 'Neurotic, that what you are. A spoilt body."[6] Maya, with all her susceptibilities fails to see any meaning in the beaten track of routine duties. Seeking a richer, fuller and more meaningful existence, she says an emphatic no to it. This rebellion is called neurosis. It ends in disaster and after the death of Gautama, we learn that she is to be taken to a mental asylum.

Similarly Monisha in *Voices in the City* can't adjust herself to the soulless mechanical life of the city Calcutta, or the household of her husband, Jiban. She is a refined soul, interested in the life of the intellect but elicits derision from the ladies of Jiban's family. Her wardrobe stacked with books simply annoys them as it is something beyond their comprehension. Monisha finds this atmosphere suffocating. Her husband, Jiban, is stolidly personified. She can either surrender or commit suicide. She chooses the latter one. Of course, people could not read her psychology and fulfill her emotional needs. She found no way of expressing her self and preserved her identity by killing herself. In *Fire on the Mountain,* Nanda Kaul lives in Kasauli. To her comes Raka, her grand-daughter, who, young as she is, has experienced the darker side of life, She has seen her father "stumbling home and wept."[7] Her early experience has blighted her soul. It has embittered her nature. She is defiant, destructive, perversely interested in the darker aspects of nature rather than in the brighter and healthier ones. All this is the effect of heredity on one's personality.

Sita in *Where Shall We Go This Summer*? belongs to the same group. Her childhood influence has been of immense significance in moulding her identity. Her childhood has not been the usual smooth running period of average persons. Her mother had vanished, her father was a freedom fighter with something of a glow of a national hero, living in Manori, having acquired the fame of a magician among the simple islanders. He had little time to bestow on his own children, so the daughter lived a solitary life. After her marriage she found that the women of her husband's family were busy with planning and preparing meals, their predilections being in no way different from those of animals. Sita found the atmosphere suffocating as there was no way out for expression of her identity. It is seen that as there was no communication between Sita and her father, so there is little sympathetic understanding between Sita and her children. This is again an apt illustration of heredity influencing people's personality. In *Clear Light of Day* following the usual pattern, the parents are unable to attend to their children, the mother being an invalid and the father busy with his club or his ailing wife. The childhood influence is visible in the life of Tara. Bimla, however, is an exception and takes a challenging decision of remaining unmarried. But Tara, timid by nature,,wants to marry and become a mother.

Anita Desai's novel *Cry, the Peacock,* also presents a picture of married relationship. Maya and Gautama are enveloped by a silence that is stifling, that offers no scope for dialogue. There are only misunderstandings and misinterpretations. Each character lives in his cocoon constructing illusions about the other. The very beginning is the end. Gautama and Maya are incompatible, poles apart in temperament. The relation grows worse and irreconcilable. Marriage appears like a vicious circle that leads to the pathetic derangement of Maya. The grotesque ending of the novel shows how the mating of diverse kinds could bring about tragic doom. Maya, as the name suggests, is Prakriti while Gautama is Purusha/reason. Prakriti/root imprisons, possesses, creates and liberates. Maya, unfortunately, could not realize her true nature. Unharnessed, her overwhelming longings and desire induce trauma partly brought about by her husband's indifference and mostly by herself. Unlike Saru, Jaya or Indu, she is not capable of resolving her problems rationally. The unconscious impulses, fears, fancies and delusions impinge upon her conscience and overwhelm her producing a schizophrenic state of mind. In Anita Desai's *Voices in the City,* Amla sees the bitter outbursts of anger by Nirode against her mother. She feels that, perhaps, her parents' marriage was a sort of economic contract. Her father married her mother neither out of love nor because it was settled but to get some economic support from her parents. It was what Amla calls a financial settlement.

Anita Desai seems to be an exception as she debunks motherhood. In *Cry, the Peacock* the mother is very much involved in social welfare. Hence, she finds little time to attend to the travails of the children. There are crèches which she is running. She follows her husband, a freedom fighter, and hence finds little to provide help to distraught Maya. Nanda Kaul, in *Fire on the Mountain,* fails to provide succour poor Raka. Raka's father is a drunkard. Her mother is frequently going to various nursing homes due to successive nervous breakdowns. Raka is in need of mothering. But who will do it for her? The mother herself needs nurturance. Sita in *Where Shall We Go This Summer?* has no clear idea of her mother. She is informed during childhood that her mother could not stand her father and went to Banaras. Similarly Sita is of no support to her four children. *In Clear Light of Day*, we are deprived of the appearance of mother on the stage. It is only her ghostly appearance that fills the back stage. She is diabetic and whenever she finds time, she enjoys a game of bridge at the club. She is not the least concerned about her children. It is Mira Masi, an old aunt, who becomes the caretaker of Tara, Baba and Bimla.

The powerful, rich, beautiful mother in *Voices in the City,* writes poetic letters to her children. The irony is that she is poetic but soulless to the children. When the mother is in need, none of the children comes to her help. They fail to identify their mother with nurturance and mothering. Nirode terms her as she-cannibal. Her daughter Monisha can not even think of some help from her. She moves alone to meet whatever is her fate. To the wonder of the readers, when Amla goes to her for consolation, she is brushed aside. Nirode is also pushed away: "He fell away and felt himself drained of blood and passion, he realized she did not want him anymore."[8] Later on, she is identified with the idea of destruction, Kali. According to Shantha Krishnaswamy, "it is as the agent of rejection, of destruction that she is brought before us. This is a far cry from the idea of conventional motherhood, where days of glory are numbered and its attraction to women diminished."[9] Of course, Anita Desai seems to be deglamourising motherhood.

It can be said that the theme of motherhood, mothering and nurturance is multifaceted. Some claim motherhood to be an ideal, others says it causes suffering. In Desai's projection of Maya, Monisha, Sita and Raka, motherhood has been subjected to multivalent treatment. Shantha Krishnaswamy's comment that

Desai's portrayal debunks motherhood seems convincing in the light of the subterranean motivations, constituting their circumstance, their early background and their paranoid insecurities.

It is therefore, we can say that in India the salvation of woman lies in proper adjustment with the males. As our leaders have held, men and women are like two wheels of the social chariot. Both should be treated as equal; only then can woman be happy. And a woman's happiness will lead to all over happiness including men, children and the society.

NOTES

1. Doris Lessing, *The Grass is Singing* (London: Michael Joseph, 1950), p. 279.
2. Doris Lessing, *The Golden Notebook* (London: Paladin Grafton Books, 1990).
3. Jonah Ruskin, "Doris Lessing at Stony Brook: An Interview," *New American Review,* 8 (1970), p. 175.
4. Doris Lessing, *Martha Quest* (London: Paladin Grafton Books, 1990), p. 157.
5. Doris Lessing, *A Proper Marriage* (London: Paladin Grafton Books, 1990), p. 127.
6. Anita Desai, *Cry, the Peacock* (New Delhi: Orient Paperbacks, 1986), p. 115.
7. Anita Desai, *Fire on the Mountain* (New Delhi: Allied, 1977), p. 48.
8 Anita Desai, *Voices in the City* (New Delhi: Orient Paperbacks, 1986).
9. Shantha Krishnaswamy, *The Woman in Indian Fiction in English* (New Delhi: Ashish, 1984), p. 260.

Quest for Self: A Study of Anita Desai's *Voices in the City*

R. KALIDASAN
The American College, Madurai

As a feminist writer, Anita Desai is aware of the peculiar predicament of the Indian women. She also knows the awakening in the modern educated Indian women who are engaged in the quest to determine their place in the society. These women strive to establish their identity in the society so that they may be seen as human beings and not as mere objects. In her novels, Anita Desai depicts women as hypersensitive, introspective and vulnerable who feel exposed and utterly isolated. Most of her women suffer as they are endowed with an exceptional sensibility; they also refuse to conform to the orthodox norms of the society. Past fails to comfort them and the present does not offer any consolation. This awareness brings them fresh pain. Though their material needs are fulfilled, they are emotionally deprived. Consequently, they seek new pastures in their quest for identity and meaning in life. Such women are the pivot of Anita Desai's fictional world.

In one of her interviews Anita Desai has observed, "I am interested in characters who are not average but have retreated or been driven into some extremity of despair and so turned against, or made to stand against, the general current. It is easy to flow with the current; it makes no demands, it causes no efforts. But those who cannot follow it, whose heart cries out 'the great No,' who fight the current and struggle against it; they know what the demands are and what it costs to meet them." (Dalmia)

Monisha in *Voices in the City* (1965) is a typical example of Desai's women. This paper aims to bring out Monisha's travails in her search for self. Monisha, her brother Nirode, and her sister Amla become cynical, freakish and desperate because all the three feel abandoned and ignored in life. All of them are well educated, intellectually gifted and highly motivated individuals. Monisha is trapped in a milieu she cannot identify with and thus ensures the psychic ordeal.

Monisha is different and is not one of those Bengali women, "who follow five paces behind their men . . . generations of Bengali women hidden behind the barred windows of half-dark rooms, spending centuries in washing clothes, kneading dough" (120) She is a voracious reader, an intellectual with a liking for Kafka, Hopkins, Dostoyevsky and French and Sanskrit works. She feels oppressed and persecuted as she is deprived of privacy and solitude. Monisha's attempts to open channels of effective communication with her husband and his family do not succeed because they are insensitive and impervious to her finer feelings. She feels like a caged animal in Calcutta, in her in-law's house. Jiban, her husband, knows very little of her misery. He does not know how to comfort her. Absence of love results in husband-wife alienation. He is not kind and considerate towards his wife. Instead of caring for her feelings, he sides with his own people. He does not sympathize with her. There is neither attachment nor a sense of commitment towards his wife. Intermittent rebuffs and setback in the married life leave Monisha completely dazed and confused. In short, Monisha suffers alienation both at the hands of her husband who cannot understand and his domineering die-hard traditional members of the family. She remains afflicted with the overriding sense of ennui, stagnation and sorrow and leads a solitary and marooned life. Her life becomes a tangle of mischances and defeats, reducing her to a near-neurotic.

Monisha is a psychically fragile person with a hyperactive imagination. A sense of emotional insecurity creeps early into Monisha's psyche because of her parent's irresponsible behaviour towards her. She grows up in an atmosphere of parental discord; Monisha develops a silent and morbid temperament. Disastrously, her father chooses a "rotund, minute-minded and limited official," (198) as her life partner. Aunt Lila's warning that Jiban and his family are not suited to Monisha's tastes and inclinations, go unheeded and her father "decides" that Jiban is the right man for Monisha and that Monisha's morbid disposition should be curbed. His act not only demonstrates the tyrannical authority of the father in the traditional male-dominated society but also gives scope to the suspicion if fathers "unconsciously spite their daughters who were unavailable to them?" (198) Monisha's marriage which should have been the beginning of matrimonial bliss and harmony ironically becomes the beginning of her gradual disintegration leading unto death.

A sense of emotional insecurity gets permanently etched on Monisha's consciousness due to the callous and apathetic behaviour of her husband and his family members. She drowns into her private inner shell when she finds her husband uncaring and unresponsive; the emotional hiatus between herself and others renders her an exile in her own home. Monisha is bitterly disheartened to see life's inscrutability and gets gloomy and pessimistic day by day. As a result, Monisha comes to acquire an abnormal personality.

Though Anita Desai's novels, *Cry, the Peacock* and *Voices in the City* delineate husband-wife alienation, Monisha's predicament in *Voices in the City* is quite different from Maya's—she is forced to a servile existence within the rigid confines of a traditional Hindu joint family. Jiban quotes from Mahatma Gandhi and Rabindranath Tagore, the champions of women's liberation, but never practises what he tirelessly preaches! Amla, Monisha's younger sister, wonders, "How it was that Monisha had been married to this boring non-entity, this blind moralist." (198) Maya of *Cry, the Peacock* is emotional while Monisha suffers from an inability to feel. Yet both are unhappy and take to tragic recourses. Maya eventually kills her husband to protect her sensitive world while Monisha kills herself in search of feeling.

The crisis in Monisha's life begins when Jiban is transferred to Calcutta. The couple moves into Jiban's family home to become part of his "many-headed" joint family. Even as she arrives at her husband's home, Monisha begins to experience the repressions that circumscribe the life and the role of women in a traditional value system. The reception arranged to welcome the couple into the family fold forewarns the subordinated role of women in an orthodox family! She is 'pushed' in the small of the back by Jiban to touch the feet of his mother and 'pushed' on the head by her mother-in-law so that she'd bend and seek her blessings! Thus Monisha is crudely initiated into the rigours of a joint family!

Monisha's days are an endless round of mindless work comprising cutting vegetables, serving food and brushing small children's hair. Her life is a testimony to the critical statement that the Indian wife is often a martyr not merely to her husband's needs, but to those of his family as well; her life is a "thankless round of service demanded and unacknowledged" (Nabar 173). She is weighed down by her duties which consist "of serving fresh chapattis to the uncles as they eat, of listening to my mother-in-law as she tells me the remarkably many ways of cooking fish, of being Jiban's wife" (111-12). She is thankful for the physical drudgery in as much as it prevents darker thoughts but the pettiness of her mean existence constantly troubles her. Monisha believes that "to sort the husk from the rice, to wash and iron and to talk and sleep" (121) is not life. "A life dedicated to nothing" is intolerable to her (121).

Through her bedroom window, through its bars, Monisha sees other bars and other walls in her home, which symbolize her restricted existence. Her individuality is steadily smothered as she finds herself powerless to take even the smallest decisions about her own life or her movements. She is "allowed" to receive letters; she is not "allowed" to meet her sister Amla privately. She is "permitted" to accompany her to the taxi. She is "summoned" to massage her mother-in-law's legs. The expressions, "allowed," "permitted" and "summoned" are highly restrictive in nature and bear evidence to her constricted life. Through the life of Monisha, Anita Desai unfolds the saga of a woman's tragic, servile life.

Monisha's plight is considerably worsened by her childlessness. The Hindu social code concurs with the view of certain Western sociologists in upholding motherhood as the most sacred duty of a married woman. A married woman who fails to fulfill this primary duty of begetting a child forfeits the respect and regard of the society in which she lives. Thus Monisha becomes an object of ridicule and utter disrespect in the eyes of her in-laws. Her sufferings aggravate and her heart aches when she listens to the heated discussion of the household women about her blocked ovary tubes and her resultant sterility in an insensitive manner. This gives Monisha the gruesome sensation of her insides being cut and exposed.

Getting steadily alienated from her surroundings and feeling caught in a loveless married life, Monisha longs for privacy, to be away from the oppressive presence of aunts, uncles, cousins, nieces, nephew, all caught in the shackles of tradition. There is no privacy for her even in her room. It is invaded by others. A stream of visitors barge into her bedroom and pester her with uncomfortable questions. Kalyani 'di' of her father-in law's household visits her room and inspects Monisha's wardrobe. When she finds only books instead of sarees in Monisha's wardrobe, she is surprised. Monisha badly needs privacy to read those books. She muses, "I wish they would leave me alone, sometimes, to read"[2] (116). Monisha desires to read Kafka, Hopkins and Dostoyevsky. Her academic bent of mind and her yearning to devote her time to scholarly pursuits are blunted. As Shanta Krishnaswamy aptly observes, "intellectuality in woman is deemed as a direct betrayal of their fundamental feminine nature" (251). Monisha's world, contrary to her expectations, revolves only around the axis of her domestic life. As a result, her psyche is bruised and battered. As she is left alone, Monisha unconsciously reflects on her resistance to subordination by domestication. In the views of Sumita Roy if a woman is left alone, "it is exemption from the oppression of patriarchal societies" (48). In desiring to be left alone, Monisha is in reality raising the problem of freedom.

Because of her silent attitude, Monisha has become an object of envy in her in-law's house. Monisha observes: "I am too silent for them, I know: they all distrust silence." (119) One day, she takes children to the zoo where she feels some kind of freedom.

When she sees many Bengali women walking behind their husbands like animals, Monisha feels morally indignant. These women spend their whole lives within the four walls doing all the household chores. What do they get back for it? It is actually a desperate wait for death. She compares Bengali women to Bleeding Heart Doves, doves that have blood-coloured feathers on their breasts.

She expects her brother Nirode to come and take her out so that she can get some fresh breeze. But he does not come. As she is not a believer, she can't turn to God either and pray for miracles to happen. The only choice is to maintain the same routine, insipid life with fortitude.

Once Monisha is offered a ticket for a Music concert. This is indeed a golden opportunity for Monisha to have complete freedom at least for a short while. However, she is accompanied by an old relation who lives on the roof top of her house. Monisha is taken by surprise, as she has never spoken to that old man. As Monisha and the old man leave the house, Monisha realizes that her in-laws are laughing at her predicament. She feels, "utter humiliation and desolation" (122). "Only a conundrum that I shall brood over forever with passion and pain, never to arrive at a solution? Only a conundrum—is that, then, life?" (124-25)

Monisha knows her survival lies in acceptance of defeat. She wishes it for herself as she wishes it for Nirode that she should accept defeat but she is unable to do so. She is seized by a confused despair. Slowly the answer to her situation becomes obvious to her. Hers is a "choice between death and mean existence, and that surely is not a difficult choice" (122). Having formulated her choice in her mind, Monisha adopts the strategy of withdrawal. She shies away from touch, communication and love. Monisha's alienation manifests itself in her "unnatural silence and unobtrusiveness." Her silence elicits distrust from the family around her.

Totally ignoring her feelings, Jiban urges Monisha to be a little "friendly" with his family. Monisha is expected to be amenable to all the actions of her husband's people. But Monisha chooses "not to take part" in a life that is devoid of opportunities for self-expression and individuality. She says the great "No" to a system that would make a ragged doll of her, she advises her sister Amla to "always go in the opposite direction" (160). What appears to a conformist like Jit Nair as a "terrible destructiveness" in Monisha, is, in fact, a compulsive urge in the latter to defy the existing order of things. Her perception that she is "different from them all," and her revolt against conformity, do not make things easy for her. Sealed away from reality, her life has been a 'waste.' The realization that she has failed to find a more authentic life than the one available to her fills her with self-hate. As Usha Bande pertinently remarks, "the refrain 'I am different from them all' reverberating through *Cry, the Peacock* also echoes throughout Monisha's diary. It spells disaster for both" (60). Monisha suppresses all her emotions in an attempt to preserve her 'self.' Like Maya in *Cry, the Peacock*, she tries to glorify herself by seeing herself as superior to the other women in the household.

Soon Monisha's feeling of superiority is replaced by a deep sense of isolation and alienation. As Jasbir Jain observes, "This self-alienation and withdrawal, this self-destruction is part of a process of minimal self-preservation in a home where roles are confined and well-defined." (111). As she watches the dancers perform, she realizes that she alone is unable to feel any emotion. Birth and Death and all the intervening drama have passed her by and driven by an overwhelming urge to experience desire and emotion like others, Monisha rushes away and burns herself to death.

Monisha's alienation becomes total when Jiban's family, considered mean and petty by her, accuses her of theft. As Nirode has fallen ill and has to be hospitalized, Monisha takes some money from Jiban's purse for hospital expenses. This she does so naturally and as a matter of right. She never even imagines that she will be accused of taking the money without her husband's prior permission. But Jiban's retort, "Why didn't you tell me before you took it?" (162) cuts her to the quick. It almost destroys their tenuous marital status. Her "mental exile" is now complete. Monisha loses weight as her unhappiness eats into her.

The changes in her are more marked internally than in her external appearance. Her 'self-image' sinks as she thinks of herself as a "shrunken, etiolated, wasted thing" (139) whose life appears "traceless, meaningless, uninvolved" and hence a "non-existence." Both Aunt Lila and Amla sense with growing unease, that Monisha is with them only physically but in reality she is slowly but surely sinking. Monisha has withdrawn "from reality into a realm of still colourlessness" (146). Filled with a sense of loneliness and isolation, Monisha gradually withdraws herself into a shell. Her emotional springs are almost dried up due to her sense of dejection and alienation.

Nabar Vrinda views that the ignorance, in which women are traditionally kept, has a stranglehold on their ability to contemplate, revolt, and change or to challenge prejudices (69). They are resigned to a meaningless existence. Monisha's plight is succinctly encapsulated in the above observation. Monisha is a sensitive woman who loves privacy but this is totally denied to her in her husband's house. As a result, she becomes restless and bitter. As Shanta Krishnaswamy says, "her [Monisha's] marriage is the excruciating, destructive and negative of all social institutions that trap and torture her isolated, sensitive psyche." (250). Monisha, the uncompromising individual, is pitted against a cruel, unrelenting, hard-hearted and insensitive social environment.

Many a hapless woman who leads an excruciating married life like Monisha lives like an automaton and finally dies like a puff of earth settling upon the earth. But Monisha prefers the dignified death of a tiger in the zoo, caught as she too is, behind the bars!

Monisha's search for self ends up in failure. All her attempts to make others understand her do not fructify. If there are instances of happiness in Monisha's life, they are only when she nurses her brother Nirode back to life and when she visits the zoo and the music concert. When she dies, Nirode feels that Monisha's splendid death symbolizes the fighting spirit of one who cares deeply for a meaningful existence. To Amla, Monisha's death reveals what lies on the other side of the stark uncompromising margin that separates the conforming world from the painful and the tragic world of non-conformist! Monisha's search for an identity, though silent, is a revolt no doubt and she exerts her will only in the final moments of her life. Her death however helps her brother Nirode and sister Amla to come to terms with life. They realize what they lack—love, affection and lack of communication!

Anita Desai severely indicts the traditional patriarchal society, which is narrow-minded and can see only with the 'blinkers on'! Neither Monisha's husband Jiban nor his family members realize that Monisha is an intelligent and sensitive soul longing for acceptance, recognition and approval. Monisha takes recourse to the extreme step of committing suicide—that too through self-immolation—as all her other measures in her search for self prove to be unsuccessful. Thus Monisha in *Voices in the City* is a typical symbol of an Indian woman who suffers at the hands of all and sundry and is compelled to sink into a world of despair and disillusion!

Works Cited

Bande, Usha. *The Novels of Anita Desai*. New Delhi: Prestige, 1988.

Desai, Anita. *Cry, the Peacock*. New Delhi: Orient Paperbacks, 1980

Desai, Anita. *Voices in the City*. New Delhi: Orient Paperbacks, 1965

Dalmia, Yashodara. "An interview with Anita Desai" *The Times of India*, April 29, 1979. 13.

Jain, Jasbir. *Stairs to the Attic: The Novels of Anita Desai*. Jaipur: Printwell, 1987.

Krishnaswamy, Shanta. *The Woman in Indian Fiction in English*. New Delhi: Ashish, 1984.

Nabar, Vrinda. *Caste as Woman*. New Delhi: Penguin, 1995.

Roy, Sumita. "Paradoxes of Patriarchy: Feminist Motifs," *Indian Women Novelists*, ed. R.K. Dhawan. New Delhi: Prestige, 1991.

Paper presented at the UGC Sponsored Seminar at SFR College for Women, Sivakasi, Tamilnadu on Women Writers: World View on August 28, 2004.

The World of Anita Desai's Short Stories

KETAKI DATTA
A.B.N. Seal College [Govt.], CoochBehar

"Art is not truth. Art is a lie that makes us realize truth," said Picasso. Much later, Eudora Welty too reminded us the same, "Fiction is a lie." But while we go through the novels or short stories of Anita Desai, don't the sayings appear utterly nonsensical or too academic? Anita Desai has carved a niche in the readers' minds much more for her novels than her collections of short stories. Again, she has only two collections to her credit spanning her writing career: *Games at Twilight* (1978) containing eleven stories and *Diamond Dust and Other Stories* (2000) with nine stories i.e. only twenty stories lie divided in the two paper-back volumes. Surprisingly enough, she has written eleven novels while just two volumes of short stories. But why? The reasons are not far to seek. Anita Desai loves to deal with a bunch of human beings on a sprawling backdrop of society—sometimes sliced-up slivers of the ambience serve to be her backdrop. Naturally, Anita Desai feels a little suffocated in the limited confines of a short story. The characters she deals with, too, engage her for quite sometime and she remains ungratified till she can portray the protagonists and other lesser characters to her heart's content which require greater compass and far more minute details. Interesting it is to note that the long-accustomed wont of novel-writing leaves its shadows on the short stories too. While in Ruskin Bond's stories, the story snugly fits into the given confines, Desai's stories stretch a little beyond the etched limits. The story weaves round the characters, incidents (the plot, to be precise) but the readers wait for something more even when the story comes to an end. Perhaps there is something beyond. Anita Desai is somewhat unparalleled there.

The nature-lover, the poet Anita Desai gains supremacy over the story-teller. If "Games at Twilight," the first story of the first volume is taken for analysis, it leaves much to be said; much more to cogitate even. On a hot afternoon, the children go out to play after the "long day of confinement" in school, "to see the sun and feel the air." There is a touch of ruddy happiness in the surroundings. But the story gets a sudden lugubrious turn when Ravi being unnoticed in a hide-and-seek game chances upon a sad truth of existence. Ravi hid himself in a secluded corner till he came out bawling, "Den! Den! Den!" "All this time no one had remembered Ravi. Having disappeared from the scene, he had disappeared from their minds clean." Again, the game started this time accompanied by a sad song,

> The grass is green
> The rose is red
> Remember me
> When I am dead, dead, dead.

Only a few hours' disappearance made them forget him, how could they remember him "even after his death?" The dawning of the ultimate truth on a little boy leaves the readers dumb-founded, rather sad. Anita Desai sounds philosophical in the concluding lines! "The ignominy of being forgotten—how could he face it? He felt his heart go heavy and ache inside him unbearably. He lay down full length on the damp grass, crushing his face into it, no longer crying, silenced by a terrible sense of his insignificance."

Similarly, the stories like "Private Tuition by Mr. Bose," "Studies in the Park," "Surface Textures" highlight slivers of human existence from particular corners. As human life is a summation of moments, the significant moment of a man's life or a woman's life surface in these stories. Anita Desai does so with élan too. In "Private Tuitions by Mr. Bose," Mr. Bose enjoys the 'heavenly' moments when he imparts tuition to the girl who comes with 'poems' to him. When he reads out to her the lines from Jibanananda Das he gets transported to his dreamland. But daily actualities shove a person to irksome boredom. Dreams get shattered with the continuous clash with the reality. But even then Mr. Bose loves his wife, his children, his daily existence in his own family, shouldering sundry responsibilities.

"Studies in the Park" deals with the psyche of the young boy "Suno" who runs away from the din and bustle of his own house to the park where he tries his concentration and succeeds partially. But, an otherworldly or a cryptic vision topsyturvies his within. He seems to chance upon a hereto-unknown truth which inspires him to go for a 'quest.' In the conclusion, Anita Desai seems to support his interminable journey on the path of quest, "Yes it is a search, a kind of perpetual search for me and now that I have accepted it and don't struggle, I find it satisfies me entirely, and I wander about the park as freely as a prince in his palace garden. I look over the benches, I glance behind the bushes, and wonder if I shall even get another glimpse of that strange vision that set me free. I never have but I keep hoping, wishing." The moment of "ultimate realisation" in the park kept Suno tireless in his search for a long time to come. Similarly in "Surface Textures," the psychological aberrations of Harish have been beautifully explored to the core by the short-fiction writer. Harish being drawn by the surface—smoothness or—roughness, began to undergo metamorphosis. His gradual insouciance to the job and family shoved him to utter solitude. But luck had some pleasant surprise in store for him. As his family left him for his growing insensitivity and he was turned out of his flat, he took to a life of a 'nomad.' Kinks cropped up on his hair, his hairs grew matted on his head, prolonged starvation changed the colour of his skin. And one day the children seeing him "stumble about the reeds . . . in order to pull out a water-lily, they took him for a saint for his skin-texture, his bizarre movements. He began to be worshipped as a tight-lipped saint." There is a touch of humour underlying the fictional mode. Anita Desai adeptly portrays the character of Harish who can be taken as an excellent representative of the "existential man" who counts "existence prior to essence," perhaps!!

In "Sale" and "The Accompanist," the mental make-up of a painter and an accompanist (tanpura-player) has been shown simultaneously. The painter in "Sale" who plies his own trade with brushes and colours with élan, hardly can make both ends meet. Even if a party comes to buy paintings for their new house, his hopes do not get any boost. Even after praising his works of art to the skies, they do not buy a single one. Understanding their demand, he promises to paint "a snowy scene." But they do not help him neither with money nor any promises of lucrative prospects! Perhaps, Anita Desai cannot come out of the hazardous memories of portraying Nur of *In Custody*. It haunts her, gives her pain. Even in these couple of stories, we find a shadow of the great poet caught in a faint penumbra. In "The Accompanist," Bhaiyya, the gifted son of an instrument-maker who plays tanpura for Rahim Khan, at last is nudged to comprehend the truth that his talent is being wasted. He can be a good sitarist even. But as he worships Rahim Khan right from the age of fifteen, he can hardly demand anything save playing for the Ustad. But Anita Desai prefers to be a wee-bit suggestive, as per her wont. The conclusion of *Cry, the Peacock* was suggestive, the last lines of "The Accompanist" too are no less. Does he remain gratified with the role of a tanpura-player sitting on the bare-floor, behind Ustad Rahim Khan? Or does he want to proclaim his talents by being an honest and devoted disciple to him? The last lines are suggestive, no doubt: "It made me smile to think anyone could be such a fool. Even I, Bhaiyya, had known when the hour of my destiny had struck. Even a backward, feckless boy from the streets had recognized his god when he met him. I could not have refused. I took up the tanpura and played for my Ustad, and I have played for him since. I could not have wished for a finer destiny. Leaving the park I hailed a tonga and ordered the driver to take me to my Ustad. Never in my life had I spoken so loudly, as surely, as I did then. You should have heard me. I wish my Ustad had heard me. "

In "A Devoted Son," there is an underlying irony running through the story. The conventional norms are mocked at. The over-caring attitude of the 'doctor son,' the son's return from the scheduled period of study abroad, the son's showing of respect to her parents by marrying the girl of their choice and at last, the old father's utmost care by his son—all portray the picture of a dream-family. But to the father the son's solicitous attention is simply an obligation. He is debarred to take any fried things, he is not allowed to consume sweets. The palatable food that he enjoys is denied to him. He thinks the son is actually neglecting him, as he is not allowing him to have the diet of his choice. Actually the son wants from the bottom of his heart that his father must live for long. A paradox too runs parallel to irony. It bears the covert influence of Isaac Bashevis Singer so far as the gripping narration, arresting dialogues and a befitting conclusion are concerned.

The next story "Farewell Party" comes to put the society, especially the higher rung of it, well-exposed to all of us. In this story, Bina and her husband Raman, who are going to Bombay on a transfer, arrange a farewell party at their residence. The ear-stud, ring-sporting, talcum-sprinkled women come to display their sadness on their parting. Bina has a spastic child, Nono, who scrounges maximum time from her daily schedule. In the party, snippets of most conversations appear simply artificial, mindless. After the wives of the so-called bigwigs and company-directors leave, the 'real' party commences, where the 'cultured' wives of the medical men catapult to the helm. Dr. Banerjee's wife sings a soulful Tagore's song and fills the atmosphere with a new meaning. Anita Desai seems to keep a vigilant eye on every nitty-gritty, every detail that remains involved. John Gardner in his *The Art of Fiction* cogently opines, "If we carefully inspect our experience as we read we discover that the importance of physical detail is that it creates for us a kind of dream, a rich and vivid play in mind. We read on, dream on—not passively but actively, worrying about the choices the characters have to make, listening in panic for some sound behind the fictional door, exulting in characters' successes, bemoaning their failures." In great fiction, the dream engages us heart and soul, we not only respond to the imaginary things—sights, sounds, smells—as though they were real, we respond to fictional problems as though they were real, we sympathise, think and judge.

The next story "Pigeons at Daybreak" brings to the open the inter-dependence of husband and wife especially when they are burdened with age and loneliness. One such couple is the Basus—Amul (sixty-one, afflicted with asthma) and Otima (a devoted wife). The wife has to read out the newspaper to the husband even when the blistering heat is about to sicken the gasping husband. Otima has to haul him upstairs with the aid of Bulu. At the break of dawn, the whole existence finds a new meaning when the electricity gets resumed, when the fan drones overhead once again. But, Amul prefers to stay there for sometime when the soft breeze arising from the Jumna blows soothingly. He seems to enjoy it. He declines to come downstairs to his room. He fixes his steadfast gaze on a flock of pigeons who soar high, higher above the morning sky. Anita Desai's pen runs with the perfect poetic élan: "Then with a swirl and flutter of feathers, a flock of pigeons hurtled upwards and spread out against the dome of the sky—opalescent, sun-lit, like small pearls. They caught the light as they rose, turned brighter till they turned at last into crystals, into prisms of light. Then, they disappeared into the soft deep blue of the morning."

Apart from delving into the portrayal of characters and situations, Anita Desai gives a thought to the well-being of the characters as well as moments of relief which add a wider streak to the otherwise simple story and a dash of freedom as well. Reaching the climax and subsequent returning to the normal key—all are smooth and never imposed-from-outside in this story.

The last story of this volume is "Scholar and Gypsy." Perhaps, she had Matthew Arnold's "The Scholar Gipsy" at the back of her mind. The two scholars from abroad, David and Pat visit India on a scholarly pursuit. They both are keen to unravel the beauty of India, precisely the hills of India. The dreamy appeal of Manali really mesmerised the couple, especially Pat." There was a sound of a rushing stream below. A cuckoo called. Above the tips of the immense deodars, the sky was a real turquoise, an evening colour without heat, although still distilled with sunlight. Dog roses bloomed open and white on the hillside. She tried to clasp David's arm with joy: "We might have been reminded of Julia and Winston's thrill while they chanced upon a green corner beside the hills where their romance began to take a final shape in George Orwell's *Nineteen Eighty-Four*. The reference drawn is not at all extraneous as here too David and Pat break with each other, at last.

But, there is a Freudian element in Pat's interest in temples, in dovetailing Hinduism and Buddhism. She blabs, "This isn't like the rest of India, Dave. It's come to me as a relief as an escape from India. You know, down in those horrible cities, I'd gotten to think of India as a horrible temple, bursting, crawling with people—people on their knees, hopeless people—and those horrible idols . . . and then to walk through the forest and come upon this—this little shrine—it's like escaping from all those 'Hindu' horrors—it's like coming into the open and breathing naturally again, without fear . . . you're sitting outside a Hindu shrine, this is a Hindu temple and you are making it out to be a source of Buddhist strength and serenity." This grows into an "obsessional neurosis" with Pat. She frequents the shrine for no reason whatsoever, even David's mild protests could not deter her. She, unawares, came under the irresistible influence of Gnan Dinanath. But, David hated such religious connections Pat kept enjoying on the sly. It sounds a bit outlandish when Anita Desai describes Pat: "Pat set off, striding through the daisy-spattered yard in her newly-acquired hippy rags that whipped against her legs as she marched off, bag and prayer-beads in hand, with never a backward look. "David too left for Delhi the next morning "with a face like a painted baboon's" alone without his wife. Perhaps Pat has a far-fetched similarity with both Martha of Lawrence's "The Mortal Coil" and Janine of Camus's "The Adulterous Woman" as both of them seem dissatisfied with their life-partners though they have to remain together, doggedly-contented. No doubt Anita Desai has portrayed the gypsy-couple brilliantly. An inherent quest for the unknown, a lure of the off-beat existence—these can hardly be lost sight of, though.

The stories in *Diamond Dust* are equally brilliant. In these recent stories, much intricate relations and problems have been dealt with. Post-colonial tensions, nostalgia, tantrums in human relationships, alienation, present-day upheavals in a family-framework and beyond—all have been meticulously attended to by Anita Desai in this volume. The appeal of Isaac Bashevis Singer's short stories, the puerility inherent in Ruskin Bond's stories, the haplessness of the protagonists of Camus's short fictions and a subtle note of tragedy lying embedded in Lawrence's stories—all are present in either overt or covert form in these nine stories of this collection.

In the very first story "Royalty" the arrival of a long-lost friend Raja, the chiaroscuro of emotional swings lend myriads of colours to the human relationships at different levels. Ravi and Sarla again get a chance to roll down the thoroughfare of Eternity back to the days of youth, enjoying the air of "freshness" round them. Perhaps the sojourn to the long-forgotten days of capering and merry-making is a bit too much for Ravi. That's why, it seems, he never hesitates to ask, "Are you all right? Sarla?" She refuses to rejoin, her face taut in a storm of emotions. Despondently he groans, "Oh, aren't we too old?" Raja really arrives by an early-morning train. Though Raja has a whale of time with Ravi and Sarla, he cannot restrain himself from enjoying with Ila Dutta-Roy in Kashmir. A small and faded memory of asking Sarla to join him on a jaunt to Winhaven relives the forgotten days of the past in their mind. Raja goes away while Ravi and Sarla remain together to support and supplement each other's emotional demands. Sarla really gets overjoyed when she hears Raja saying, "Oh Sarla, I would never want to come up here without you, you know." So, the bond of man and wife so far as the Indian norms and notions go is indispensable despite mutual misunderstanding, mistrust and dissatisfaction.

In the next story "Winterscape" a clash of cultural ethos and no-nonsensicality of 'affection' stand out. The two sisters Asha and Anu grew up together. Asha had a misfortune as her husband while going out to shoot partridges for a festive dinner (on Rakesh's birthday) disappeared. Rakesh was Anu's son, who

Asha and her husband reared up showering love and affection. Asha had a frustrated motherhood, hence the decision of looking after Rakesh (Anu's son) as her own son! Later on, Anu too had undergone early widowhood and left for joining Asha and her child. As Rakesh grew up, their dreams too clamoured for perfection. After completing his education in India, Rakesh left for abroad. Marrying Beth, he set up a family there. Hearing that Beth had conceived, Asha and Anu decided to go to the States. They were received with warmth by Rakesh, but Beth's lukewarm attitude spoke otherwise. Rakesh understood everything and was taken aback by the photograph Beth pasted on the refrigerator—the view of the white window and the two widows in white and the whirling snow. Together they stared at the "Winterscape." A hiatus in relationships, a touch of sensitivity, a question of acceptance-rejection, love-and-forgetting—all surface through a soft rejoinder from Beth, "Let it be" some emotions are to be revered, of course! Anita Desai, a master storyteller, is also adept in portraying human relationships in the framework of a society, highlighting the society's demands and an individual's exactitude in fitting himself into its growing necessities. The narration is, no doubt, superb. The dialogues are well-written. A real-life picture, overall.

"Diamond Dust: A Tragedy"—after which this volume is named comes next. It is a sweet story stirring homely instincts, centring round a domestic pet—Diamond. A puppy in the household of Mr. and Mrs. Das grows into a mad dog. One day, Diamond goes missing, as if evaporating from the Das's residence. One morning, Mr. Das chances upon a dog-catchers' van and he runs amuck in frenzy behind it, crying, "Diamond! They will kill my Diamond!" He runs to catch up with the vehicle and suddenly falls with no breath left in him. He breathes his last while the dog casts a hapless look at his master through the bars of the van-window. Man-and-animal bond has been brought to the fore with poetic élan. The story reminds us of D.H. Lawrence's similar narrative, "Rex."

However, three stories of this volume—"Underground," "The Man Who Saw Himself Drown" and "Five Hours to Simla or Faisla"—are quite commonplace, though some readers may claim the second one among the three to carry some shades of Camus's stories from the collection *Exile and the Kingdom*. That however cannot be gainsaid, so far as the dead (otherwise absurd) man's post-death speech goes. In "Underground," the main plot is loosely-knit, so the characters like Jack Higgins or McTaggart can hardly draw the readers' eulogies. Loose-ends are in profusion in this story. It calls for Desai's artistic genius to question.

"Five Hours to Simla or Faisla"—the very name carries a post-colonial tag. A commonplace theme, a very trivial setting, a none-the-appealing point of view mar the points of interest in the story. The pebble shot at the truck shot off the pilot's animosity. All the vehicles come to a standstill on this highway leading to Simla. When darkness falls thick all around, the cops come to disentangle the traffic-jam. Anita Desai is always excellent in describing situations and things. In this story such flashes and strokes are in abundance. For example, "The Ambassador gave a sudden lurch, throwing everyone forwards. The baby whose mouth had been glued to the nipple of the rubber-bottle like a fly to syrup, came unstuck and let out a wail of indignation. Even the mother let out a small involuntary cry. Her daughter, who had been asleep on the backseat, her legs across her mother's lap, crowding the baby and the bottle, now stirred."

Setting of the two stories "The Artist's Life" and "Tepoztlan Tomorrow" like "Underground" is alien locale. Especially, in "The Artist's Life," the teacher-learner relationship comes to the fore through the medium—Art. Polly gets very much influenced by Miss Abigail's way of teaching painting, especially the novel instruction, "Paint your dreams . . . show me what you dreamt last night." Polly looked for an interesting object she wanted to paint, to bring to life. At last, Polly's world of imagination gets a violent jolt when Mabel Dodd's (their tenant) car stands oddly painted with the abominable words PIG by some unknown miscreants. The immediate victims of suspicion were "those kids . . . who came from broken homes or orphanages and some of them with spells in prison." A clash of idealism and realism, a sense of euphoria and anachronism are there in the matrix of this story. "The Artist's Life" is an open window through which Anita Desai takes a deep look into a budding artist Polly's soul. A clash of illusion and reality throws her into the arms of frustration. Her immediate reaction to the nuisance of the miscreants is a scream of faint protest. Anita Desai exquisitely portrays it through words, "Her lips formed the letter 'O' or else 'NO.' She wanted to protest, she was not sure against what but against something that had been presented to her, interposed between her and what she wanted and believed in—something objectionable, inadmissible and imperfection." The feebleness of human frailties comes to the fore. It seems as if a dreamland comes crumbling down noisily.

In another story "Tepoztlan Tomorrow" set in a foreign land, "Mexico City was very far in a sense not geographical, from Tepoztlan." The story opens to get us introduced to Dona Celia, Louis, Nadyn who enjoy homely warmth and togetherness in a house on Avenida Metamoros. Words like 'muy sucio,' 'te de manzanilla' are culture-specific with a certain extent of post-colonial appeal to the readers. The story brings the ambience of today's Tepoztlan seen through the eyes of a modern-day researcher Louis. The curious turn of the amorous tangle between Dona Celia and Pedro, Nadyn's complaining nature, picture of negativism and frustration at Tepoztlan all come vivid in verisimilitude through Desai's easy-flowing narrative. Louis praises Tepoztlan to the skies to Dona Celia, "It's now got a good road and good transport—it's more lovely now." Nostalgia grips Louis when he hears his old school-pal Alejandro singing out bursting forth with indomitable passion before the microphone, "Leave me my streams, leave me my hills—Leave me my Paradise, Tepoztlan." "Who dares to come and steal my Paradise, Tepoztlan?"

The people of today's Tepoztlan are torn between today's frustration and yesterday's nostalgia! Can a word of hope be disseminated among the crowd? Louis is about to bid adieu to Tepoztlan on the eve of Cousin Heriberto's birthday celebrations. Even his parents are coming to participate in the gala festivities.

But he is leaving with a question thrown by Nadyn unanswered, "We are too old for you, not up to date, eh?" He has to go back to his thesis, his classes, the University, after all. The post-colonial silhouette matches the narration quite well.

Last but not least is the story "The Rooftop Dwellers" where the predicament of a single working girl in our Indian social scenario is the cynosure. The setting is Delhi, the protagonist is Moyna, who comes to Delhi with the job of a book-reviewer with the journal "Books" owned by Ajoy Bose, an M.P. from Calcutta. She rents a rooftop tenement (generally named as 'Barsati') in Old Delhi. The horrible and perilous life of a loner with its several disadvantages and gruesomeness has been faithfully drawn by Desai. Her landlord the 'Bhallas' are a peculiar lot. After the big theft in which Moyna has to lose her tape-recorder and quite a few valuables, she feels dejected, as if she is nowhere. Tara, her senior colleague, lends her the necessary moral support. She begins to enjoy her job. But the growing unrest in the tenement, created especially by the Bhallas and their servant really throws her peace off the level. Water-supply was being deliberately cut off quite often, her male colleagues' appearance in her apartment was enough to brand her as a 'slut!'

Naturally she gives in to the oppression and falls ill. Her mother comes all the way from Calcutta to organise the 'Barsati' in order to make it livable. As a natural consequence, Moyna has to return to her parents in Calcutta which she can hardly think. She dreamt of being independent throughout her life! Being jobless, she surely will lose all her interest in life itself, she knows that! But she gets a letter which rejuvenates her lost courage to go on. Her mother has written that her friend-cum-suitor Arun is returning from the States to join them soon. He possesses a degree in Geology and "he is expected to find a suitable job in the field." Moyna pirouettes on her feet as she gets a cause for celebration!! After her long struggle through boredom and uncertainty she at last stands a bright prospect of getting a good partner in her life!! Moyna is now in Seventh Heaven! Anita Desai in a succinct yet simple sentence makes everything clear, "She was free, she was determined, she had made her decision and she

sat up laughing." But she leaves us on the brink of a burning question, "Is marriage the ultimate truth or the 'summum bonum' of existence in an Indian woman's life?" The answer is perhaps "blowing in the wind"!

All the stories bring certain slivers of human existence to life. The characters are as lively as the real-life men and women. Apart from being a brilliant story-teller, Anita Desai is a keen observer of every nuance in each nook and cranny of an ever-changing society, here and abroad. Cultural, a-cultural, political, a-political issues, women here and now, women of the yester-years—all find life and words in the cornucopia of the vast compass of Anita Desai's memorable stories, which in turn can surely stand the test of Time!

Works Cited

Tom Bailey, *A Short Story Writers' Companion* (OUP, New York, 2001).

Albert Camus, *Exile and the Kingdom* (Penguin, England, 1958).

Anita Desai, *Games at Twilight* (Vintage, England, 1998).

Anita Desai, *Diamond Dust and Other Stories* (Vintage, England, 2000).

Sigmund Freud, *Introductory Lectures of Psychoanalysis* (Penguin, England, 1973), Vol. 1.

D.H. Lawrence, *The Mortal Coil and Other Stories* (Penguin, England, 1907).

George Orwell, *Nineteen Eighty-Four* (Penguin, England, 1949).

Communicative Chaos in Anita Desai's *In Custody*

BINOD MISHRA
I.I.T., Roorkee

Human existence in this world faces various onslaughts with changing times and shifting situations. The outside world, which is full of hype and hoopla, affects our inner lives insidiously. Many of us become the unwanted victims and start leading a peripheral existence, taking it as a twist of fate. Living in such a state becomes an ordeal and fans the furnace, the flames burn the bodies and give the souls numerous bruises time cannot heal. The root cause of such catastrophes is the failure of communication, which could bring cohesion and cordiality between individuals distanced by wings of time and pangs of overwhelming desire.

The present paper is an attempt to understand the intricacies emanating from the lack of communication in various characters in Anita Desai's novel, *In Custody*. The paper also endeavours to unravel the miasma of society's expectations from individuals, sandwiched between desires and denials on one hand and reticence and rhapsody on the other. The need to come out of this trap, in the words of Matthew Arnold, is to ensure love for each other. Arnold says in his poem "Dover Beach":

> Ah, love, let us be true
> To one another! for the world, which seems
> To lie before us like a land of dreams,
> So various, so beautiful, so new,
> Hath really neither joy, nor love, nor light,
> Nor certitude, nor peace, nor help for pain;
> And we are here as on a darkling plain

> Swept with confused alarms of struggle and flight,
> Where ignorant armies clash by night.

The realization of such a beautiful thread that can unite can really go a long way in our subsistence.

Anita Desai is an excellent novelist in revealing the intricacies that mar human relationships. Her greatness as a fiction writer emerges in touching the dark unfathomed aspects crippling the existence of people in a fast-changing electronic age. Desai's pen spills not common and day-to-day stories but it portrays the panorama of our lives, the ignorance of which can hamper the once so cordial bond of love. In a world where human beings, queued like ants, want to supersede each other, the so-called small and considered insignificant issue gets so congealed that its outlet becomes anguish. The demon of big things deforms everything and individuals pray for the god of small things, who could reform. Desai ideates such small aspects to awaken human sensitivity gone dud amid the noises of technical gadgets. Desai excels in her novels not because of her neatly woven stories but also because they are like the psychological case studies of a psychiatrist.

Desai is a writer with a purpose. The web of her stories seems complicated at times to the readers but Desai, despite her dexterous use of words, is conscious of her responsibility. She delineates the psyche of her characters no doubt, yet she's wary of the complexities pervading in society. The problem of mankind in a shifting and flexible world, the duties and responsibilities of man to man and the ability to understand the subtle shades of the complex human personality also come under Desai's discipline. Much like Virginia Woolf, Anita Desai marvellously plays with changing time and consciousness. The novel *In Custody* besides telling the story of a young couple Deven and Sarla raises an important issue, namely of the importance of communication in a technologically advanced world. The author is alive to the fact that in a scientific world of today, human relations flourish or famish because of the effectiveness or ineptitude of communication. Anita Desai's superb novel *In Custody*, apart from a commonplace story discusses at large many issues involving man and society. Dealing with the story of Deven, a college lecturer whose infatuation towards the world of imagination, of poetry, of a new world, offers peace and harmony away from the madding world of gains and losses, joys and sorrows. The novel presents a kaleidoscopic picture of the world where love, fondness, friendship and loyalty can change with a gust of wind. In a fast-changing world, even a bond of friendship is based upon selfishness.

The present paper also makes an attempt to show the helplessness that the characters of the novel suffer from. To begin with, Deven, the hero of the novel is an apostle of simplicity and has the depth of boundless sea whose tides are realized by him and no one else. He is a conscious being who realizes his household responsibility yet is incapable of doing anything. His fondness for poetry and his craze for popularity blind him to such an extent where wife and children are the subjects of less importance. But that doesn't mean his neglect of Sarla is not intentional. He feels guilty and is grateful to her parents who satisfy Sarla and Manu's world. Despite his frequent trips to Delhi, he craves for his son and wants to play with him. He oscillates between Mirpore and Delhi, between his college and Nur's Alma Mater of poetry. In his blind search of tracing Nur's poetic sparks, he fails to understand the rhythm that Sarla can offer to his poetry. It's an irony that the great poet, Nur found his inspiration in his two begums and his verses are born of his two mistresses. No doubt, Deven, too, like Nur, has his two mistresses but he prefers poetry to be his first mistress. The portrayal of women in a lighter vein in the novel is based on Desai's real experience of women's condition in Urdu poetry. In one of her interviews, Anita Desai has admitted:

> I could hear them always screaming in the background, banging on the doors, being very hysterical. I asked myself "Why have I made all these women so awful?," and I thought "Well, if that was the house they were made to live they would probably be awful."[1]

Deven is a victim of his ambition. He places his ambition high over other diurnals. He goes an extra mile and of course, is cheated by all. His one time classmate and his only friend, Murad has an overwhelming effect on him. The editor of an Urdu magazine uses Deven for his self-vested interest. He is more business-like than Deven and milches him literally. The purchase of a second-hand tape-recorder and the appointment of a boy for operation are the tricks played by Murad. Behind the mask of friendship, Murad exploits Deven's weakness for Urdu poetry. It's only at the last moment that Deven realizes the ugly face of Murad who denies him an advance for his article. Deven loses more than he could really get. But then the pecuniary loss is not a debatable question as compared to Deven's urge for poetry. The proposal for going abroad and making money as one of his colleagues suggests cuts no ice for him. He suffers all because the poet in him is alive. The bills sent by Nur's begum and the demand for the room rent trouble him. Nur's increasing demands and Deven's sense of gratitude criss-cross. Poverty-stricken yet love-lorn Deven sympathizes with Nur. His words, though in the form of letter, affect Deven with their poetic tinge. Nur's verses have a magical impact on Deven. It's a moment of delight when after much brainstorming and hectic sessions; one of Nur's begums agrees to arrange for the interview. The remuneration for such an arrangement is not a barrier at all.

Deven and Sarla's marital life suffers disharmony because of the lack of communication in it. They are familiar with each other but cordiality seems to corrode out of their union. They live like ghostly, ghastly appearances crawling reluctantly, perhaps having lost the purpose of being united or brought close to each other. Their company frightens each other and a sizzling silence stupefies where both of them want to come out to get an emotional release in the free firmament. The couple seem miles distant from the coercion, which can bring consummation in their lives. The reasons of this untimely breakdown in their coalescence are caused by their inability to make a proper rapport with each other. They fail to understand the fact that impaired communication can create chaos only. Since they communicate less, they find it difficult to face each other. Their brief chats comprise taunts and undesirable queries put under duress. Desai describes the chaos succinctly:

> The door opening on to the courtyard creaked as he released the bolt, making him fear he would wake up the child as well and anger Sarla, but there was silence from both of them and once he was out, he felt relived after all. In place of some emotional release from all that choked him, this simple physical one from the small, stifling room into the open night air would have to do.[2]

Deven's wife, Sarla, a housewife, is conscious of her position in the society. Delineated as a minor character in the novel, Sarla is alive to what's happening around. Choked inside at times and not happy with Deven's dissipating Delhi trips, she sometimes wants to burst but maintains self-restraint. Her confinement to her own world provides a camouflage to her argumentative ability. Despite the arrival of summer, Sarala is opposed to moving out cots in the courtyard since she had nightmares about 'robbers climbing over the wall and attacking them in their sleep.' The nightmare is symbolic of her insecure position in this world. Their dreams of a progressive life have had a premature death and they seem to accept what fate had in store for them. Initially a choice of Deven's family members, Sarla later feels neglect because of her unattractive features resulted by the ravages of time. Deven, too like the members of his family, had not suspected Sarla's aspirations. Sarla's great expectations are thwarted and she resigns to her fate. But both the husband and wife share a secret. Desai sympathizes deeply with the couple:

> Although each understood the secret truth about the other, it did not bring about any closeness of spirit, any comradeship, because they also sensed that two victims ought to avoid each other, not yoke together their joint disappointments. A victim does not look for help from another victim; he looks for a redeemer. (168)

Deven's inability to understand the non-verbal feature of communication often results in his angry outbursts. Tearing his unwashed shirt and turning Manu out of the room because he was crying are signs of his emotional eruption.

A charge commonly labelled on the women characters of Desai is that they are confined to their inner selves. A number of scholars and critics attribute it to the impact of independence which provided education and gave room to a rethinking of various social stigmas. The elimination of these stigmas in later years provided women with a free environment and earmarked more space. But with some good things came some disadvantages too. And that affected not only the women but mankind as a whole. The disappearance of joint family system and the emergence of nuclear family, in a way affected the adults as well as the children. Anita Desai herself realizes the catastrophic impact of this change.

> Only the last two generations can be said to be educated, and only one has experienced the luxury of privacy. Having broken away—often amidst tears, tempers and threats—from the accepted system of daughters not receiving a regular education and from the large noisy, busting joint family, she has now acquired an education and set up her own home. This had its disadvantages—no grandmother to lull the squalling infant to sleep, no sister-in-law to help with the cooking and washing and no one, for the most of the day, to gossip with it does afford woman who craves it, with a degree of silence and privacy in which to work.[3]

We find the lines of communication severed because of the absence of an elderly person (father or mother) who could facilitate the couple to break the silence and encourage the growing kids to bubble and jostle by their bedtime stories.

Deven proves himself a poor communicator throughout the novel. The reasons of his failure can be traced in his vulnerability. His ambition of being popular through his passion for Urdu poetry blindfolds him. He has ambition but he lacks the tact to fulfill his ambition. The lack of practical wisdom and cleverness of purpose have always eluded him. It is his simplicity and meekness that tempt him to be bamboozled even by his friend, Murad. Deven's message gets a wrong channel and the intermediary cause a severe barrier in his way. Neither a glib talker like Murad, nor a charmer like Nur, Deven is exposed to the outside world and becomes a laughing stock. He is unable to effectuate the timing of his message and as a consequence, his entreaty falls on deaf ears. His impatience and excessive avidity to interview Nur are ample proofs of his immaturity as a communicator. Ignoring the sombre mood in Nur's house when Imtiaz Begum's illness takes her to hospital, Deven asks the poet for the interview. His inability to understand the gravity of the situation at times enrages the poet. He not only ignores the role of time and place in communication but also the psycho-physical condition of Nur, the poet. Desai decries and pities in the following lines:

> But he had little gift for speech, for conversation, so little practice in it, and knew only how to stumble awkwardly to the point. Gracelessly. Nur Sahib, you remember I spoke to you of this special issue of Urdu poetry in *Awaaz*? I had hoped that today—since I have come so early—we might be able to discuss it a little. (113)

The lack of proper communication dogs Deven not only at his home front but also at his workplace. Blinded by his passion for Urdu poetry, he ignores his responsibility as a teacher. His dereliction of duty had made him a boring teacher and students looked at him with utter disregard. It is quite ironical that Deven, the poet is unable to command the attention of his students. He's unable to satisfy students' curiosity not because he lacks knowledge but because he lacks the ability to understand them. He feels bored with them and tries to avoid eye contact with them. One can find Deven's reluctance and his nervousness in the following lines, "The expression he saw—of boredom, amusement, insolence and defiance—made him look away quickly and focus his eyes upon the door at the far end of the room, the door that opened on to the passage, freedom and release." (12) One of his senior colleagues of Hindi department, Mr. Trivedi is furious to understand Deven's frequent absence. Deven's request for a week's leave angers him and poor Deven bears Trivedi's ire. Deven is threatened to be demoted and transferred. He controls himself and leaves Trivedi's room without giving any convincing explanation. Deven ignores his position and shows no interest in College Board's meetings. He lacks self-confidence and depends on his colleagues even for petty matters. Worried most of the time because of his job, he remains docile and maintains a low profile.

Technology, a major part of communication today, plays an equal role in creating commotion in Deven's mission of recording Nur's poetry. Advised by his trusted friend and sponsored by Deven's college, the tape-recorder brings with it all sorts of complexities. Murad technically handles the show, lures Deven to buy a second-hand tape recorder and also bear an appendage in the form of Chiku who'll assist in recording Nur's renditions. Desai, through the use of this mechanical device, shows how our inclination to technology results in chaos. Chiku, in his effort to record Nur's verses, records all that's dross and leaves all that is to be recorded. Unable to understand the subtleties of poetry and the ever-changing moods and whims of the poet, Chiku often feigns, forgets and fails. The machine, too at times whirrs, jerks and on some occasions roars. The inexperienced Chiku fails to realize the acoustics and contributes to the chaos. The benediction of proper intonation in the recitation of poetry is lost amid the hue and cry of the outside world, "A pause would follow, not exactly of silence because outside the traffic blared and bleated and in the room the electric fans clicked wildly and a restful of sparrows in the skylight flapped and twittered but certainly of silence from the poet." (155)

Time plays an important part in creating communicative chaos in the novel. It takes long to organize an interview with Nur who in his crapulent mood decides to recite everything without caring about the mood and backgrounds of the audience. The listeners in Nur's poetic soiree comprise street urchins and yokels having nothing to do with poetry. Their presence is because of their temptation for sumptuous food and drink. Nur, too considers himself a know-it-all and times without number responds to Deven's queries crazily. In reply to Deven's curiosity about his youth time poetic leanings the poet bursts:

> Poetry of the period? Do you think a poet can be ground between stones, and bled, in order to produce poetry—for you? You think you can switch on that mincing machine and I will instantly pro-

> duce for you a length of raw, red minced meat that you can carry off to your professors to eat? (156)

Ironically enough, we find the poet reciting his verse soberly sometimes early in the mornings before the agents of Bachchus overpower him. Even Chiku is upset with the odd hours of Nur singing in his full-throated ease with doses of meat and biryani. Chiku, the so-called technician, grumbles quite often of the singing spree twelve hours a day. He often feels drowsy and induced to sleep, forgets to turn the tape in time to record the gems sprouting forth from Nur's lips. This not only adds to the chaos but also makes Deven angry and repentant on having lost the remarkable renditions he and the world of poetry vouched for. The basic purpose of recording Nur's poetry receives a severe jolt when Nur's crowd pullers, all idle men, ask him foolish questions and the poet answers them with aplomb.

Not only Nur and his followers but Deven's students, too consider him vulnerable and want to exploit him as much as possible. The tapes, which contained less of poetry and more of noises, exchange one hand after another in order to be edited and freed from redundancies. This process brings Deven across many multi-dimensional mechanics that are good for nothing. To name a few, Chiku, Pintu and some of Deven's students with their self-vested interests of getting extra marks for fixing tapes make the communicative process more chaotic. Deven feels himself trapped since the tapes give much cry and little wool. His failure to provide something memorable to Urdu lovers tears him beyond repairs. The money procured from his college hangs like a Damocles' sword on him. Nur, the pernickety poet also makes Deven's life prosaic by sending his orgiastic demands. Deven's blind fascination for poetry makes him a plaything in the hands of Murad, Nur, Chiku, Pintu and others. Deven is exploited mentally and monetarily. The poet considers even his cataract operation as Deven's responsibility and wants him to arrange for it. The mediums of Deven's communication with the poet lead him to such a chaotic stage where he smoulders and yet does not shriek having squandered much of what he had. He feels isolated and the exorcists of the charges of misappropriation of funds haunt him. He longs for a backward journey:

> He hoped his former life of non-events, non-happenings, would be resumed, empty and hopeless, safe and endurable. That was the only life he was made for, although life was not perhaps the right term. He needed one that was more grey, more neutral, more shadowy. He sifted through alternatives like torn pieces of grey paper, letting them fall to the floor of his mind with a whisper and bury him in sleep. (183-84)

What sprinkles salt to Deven's injury is Nur's last letter, which is an entreaty for the arrangement of his pilgrimage to Mecca when the last of his pigeons is gone. The poet puts Deven in a panicky situation considering him an all-time serendipity. The failure of communication in the novel is also born of some circumstantial lapses. To call Deven a total failure would be a lop-sided view. He communicates intra personally when he finds himself unsuccessful at inter personal communication. It is the penchant for poetry enables him to ignore the practical needs and necessities of everyday life. Sarla tries her best to mend the walls but feels snubbed realizing her position. She believes in renewing the bond and goes to her parents' house. Sandwiched between Nur and Murad, Deven keeps himself plying from Mirpore to Delhi. Engrossed wholly in his pursuit, he forgets to open Sarla's letter and later feels guilty when she comes back on her own. Deven undergoes an inner journey and feels the emptiness lying in his room. The atmosphere of the house too becomes chaotic when Sarla goes to her parents' house. The novelist sympathizes with the dissatisfaction of the couple in the following lines, "It was not like Sarla to leave behind largesse in any shape. The state of dereliction here was only a reflection of the dereliction of their marriage, perhaps even of themselves." (177) This vacuity gives Deven time to realize his lapses. Nur's dilly-dally and Murad's mish-mash shatter Deven. He feels the pangs of his guilty conscience on having ignored his home and hearth. His communication with his inner self leads him to self-discovery. The readers, too, are touched to the core when Desai says, "There was after all nothing left to do. Oddly enough, the certainty that he could expect no more help from Murad had a calming effect upon him. Perhaps when everyone had cut him off and he was absolutely alone, he would begin to find himself and his own strength." (190)

Deven is benumbed with sensations and feels ill-at-ease. Painfully aware of the damage done to Sarla, he longs to bridge the gaps. Distraction from the outside world because of its falsities, Deven longs for relief in the sweet and sober soothings of Sarla, who appears soigné and sophisticated despite her worn-out clothes. Desai shows her compassion with Deven in the following lines, "He considered touching her, putting an arm around her stooped shoulders and drawing her to him. How else could he tell her he shared all her disappointment and woe?" (94) Despite his longings, he is unable to do so since his position of power over her will be challenged. This shows his frozen evaluation and his resistance to change. He asks for Manu and snaps the tie.

Desai is also keen to say that too much of communication can mislead mankind and create chaos. Starting from Murad and then the pack of letters, reminders, requests and bills blur the basic purpose of communication. Nur's nefarious nuances of extracting much from Deven keep pouring in. His first wife's letters also add to Deven's despair. Finally when Deven decides to come out of the ludic project, Safiya Begum's couth communication comes as a phantasmagoria to tempt Deven. But he feels disillusioned:

> How many more bills, more requests from Nur could he place before them after all? Nur would never stop writing, demanding. The letters would keep pouring in the way the tapes had kept on grinding. He had launched himself, and them, upon a course it now seemed impossible to stop. (197)

Deven wonders if these bills would ever come to an end or he'll have to arrange for Nur's funeral too. The wish with which he had undertaken this dream project leads him nowhere and Deven's miserable condition reminds us of Shakespeare's Macbeth, who, too, is ruined because of his over-ambition. One can find an echo of Macbeth in Deven's character:

> I have no spur
> To prick the sides of my intent, but only
> Vaulting ambition, which o'erlaps itself
> And falls on the other. (I, vii, ll. 25-28)

Surely Deven needed a Lady Macbeth who could expedite his ambition by obviating the milk of human kindness from him in order to catch the nearest way. Macbeth, too, accepts his defeat in the end when he finds the great Birnam woods moving to Dunsinane as predicted by the witches. Deven realizes his lapses at last while explaining everything to Siddiqui. What he tells him is not only a realization but also remorse:

> I worked hard—I prepared for it and I worked—but I was fooled and cheated by everyone—the man who sold me the secondhand equipment, the technician who said he could do the recording but was completely inexperienced, by Murad who said he would pay and did not, by Nur who had never told me he wanted to be paid, and by his wife, wives, all of them. (199)

Thus an overall view of the novel tells us how communication is at stake though there's too much of it. Deven, who initiates the communication, comes across many who communicate and confuse him. Deven's interview with Nur undergoes serious threats because of restrictive environments, which include several distractions. The interview arranged in a busy marketplace, a room with poor acoustics, and a second-hand tape recorder with an inexperienced operator records the sounds and furies only. The audience in the room, all tipsy, cheer the panicky poet and distort the message. The poet unscrupulously seeks personal gains and worsens the aim of the interview. The various agents, too, with their biased notions and self-vested interests add to the commotion. Nur's wives endeavour their best to claim their dues from the poet and their rivalry tears the poet apart. The poet's poor health, too, is behind his garbled voice. He is unable to make a balance between his personal story and poetry. This results in information overload and worries Deven. He tries his best to edit and compile and this process has many transfer stations, which cause distortion to the real message.

Likewise, Deven's communication with Murad suffers breakdown because of their differing background and lack of existence of co-operation despite a common frame of reference. Murad is every inch a professional and Deven a poet to the core. Deven's communication with Sarla suffers because they fail to sustain interest in each other and both of them hesitate to initiate meaningful conversation. Sarla's parental background and her pride over possessions given by them are impediments for Deven. Sarala and Deven also differ in their perceptions. Sarla fears Deven and Deven finds hard to face her because of his inability to fulfill his responsibilities. At times, we also come across Deven's negative emotional behaviour. Deven is of a rigid category and fails to understand Sarala. Deven's students and his colleagues also underrate him. He receives thrashes from his seniors and threats from his students. The atmosphere in his home also stifles him. His only consolation is his son Manu, with whom he feels relaxed and rejuvenated.

There are other symbolic agents in the novel. The neem tree in his courtyard symbolizes sourness. Nur's pigeons also are sources of communication to the poet and he decides to go on a pilgrimage after the death of the last pigeon. As we all knew that for a successful communication, the importance of internal as well as external atmosphere is essential. The novel fails to establish a balance between the two. As a result, an academic endeavour of preserving a culturally rich Urdu poetry's representative voice of Nur Shahjehanbadi for the succeeding generations is defeated. At the close of the novel, the protagonist finds himself worried by the phantoms of future and foresees his son 'consider his father a failure.' The fiction *In Custody*, thus, as a whole, appears to be suffering from a communicative chaos.

NOTES

1. Anita Desai in an Interview to Magda Costa, *Lateral*, March 2001.
2. Anita Desai, *In Custody* (Great Britain: Penguin, 1984), p.130.
3. Anita Desai, "Women Writers," *Quest*, 65 (April-June 1970), 40.

Defiant Daughters:
A Study of Manju Kapur's *Difficult Daughters* and Anita Rau Badami's *The Hero's Walk*

SUMAN BALA
S.B.S. College, University of Delhi

Women are an integral part of civilization. No society or country can ever progress without an active participation of women in its overall development. Although the place of woman in society has differed from culture to culture, yet one fact common to almost all societies is that woman has never been considered the equal of man. In verse 148 of Chapter V of *Manusmriti*, the ancient Hindu lawgiver Manu states that all through her existence, woman must remain dependent on man:

> In childhood must a female be dependent on her father; in youth, on her husband; her lord being dead, on her sons; if she has no sons, on the near kinsmen of her husband; if she be left with no kinsmen, on those of her father; if she has no paternal kinsmen, on the sovereign; a woman must never seek independence.

Right from birth, a woman is thrust with social images, rewards and punishments that are carefully designed to ensure that she does not develop the qualities associated with men. Thus, gender discrimination starts from birth itself. Unmarried girls feel the constraints of parents and of the society to which they belong.

As in life, so in literature. In most of the novels, we find portrayal of a meek, submissive woman who plays a subservient role to father, husband or son. This is the image of woman that is depicted in most of Indian novels, like Kamala in R.K. Narayan's *The Dark Room*, Rukmani in Kamala Markandaya's *Nectar in a Sieve* and Sarita or Saru in Shashi Deshpande's *The Dark Holds No Terrors*. With the spread of education and awakening amongst women, the scenario has changed. Several of the writers have portrayed the 'new' woman who is inclined to take "the road not taken." Such a woman is independent, assertive and even defiant. In this paper, I will look at protagonist in two prize-winning novels, Virmati in Manju Kapur's *Difficult Daughters* and Maya in Indo-Canadian writer Anita Rau Badami's *The Hero's Walk.*

The novel *Difficult Daughters* opens with a cryptic statement: "The one thing I had wanted was not to be like my mother." These words are spoken by the young narrator Ida. Every text contains several entry points. For this novel, the narrator's opening words constitute one and I would explore and analyze in this paper why she did not want to be like her mother, and then relate the answer to the larger issue of patriarchy, which denies women voice, choice and freedom.

Set around the time of partition, *Difficult Daughters* is the story of a woman torn between family duty, the desire for education and illicit love. The protagonist Virmati is the eldest child of the ever-pregnant Kasturi. She looks after ten younger siblings. Virmati has a traditional upbringing and her mother's priority for her daughter is marriage to a nice boy selected by the parents. However, Virmati refuses to settle down to marriage and child-bearing after the high school qualification. She falls in love, instead, with the romantic Oxford-returned professor who lives next door and is already married. Caught in hopeless illicit love, she breaks her engagement with a suitable decent boy Inderjit, attempts suicide and finally seeks refuge in further study. She goes to Lahore to live alone and pursue her studies. Later, she goes to Nahan to work as a principal in a school.

The time Virmati spends in Nahan, the capital of Sirmaur, the small Himalayan state run by an enlightened maharaja, is the happiest and most satisfying period in her life. As headmistress of a girls' school, she is able to regulate her life in a positive way. She is a competent teacher and her performance gets her a deserved respect. In this small place, she has no family to look after, no responsibilities to fulfil. For the first time in her life, she has a house of her own, where she lives independently. To use

Virginia Woolf's phrase, here Virmati has a "room of one's own" which provides her with some degree of psychological and mental stability.

When Virmati eventually returns as the professor's second wife, she has read more books and gained more varied experiences than girls of her time and society were expected to.

Virmati's initial rebellion against her very traditional Arya Samaj family consisting of her parents, her paternal grandfather and Aunt (father's sister) in first postponing her marriage and then refusing to marry the person she was engaged to, constitutes a radical rebellious act, which predicts an individual, who would go on to carve out a niche for herself, and make a personal exemplary feminist statement. Her stoic and heroic suffering for the sake of her love, and marriage to Professor Harish Chandra, who is already married to Ganga and has a child, point towards a 'self' which is tenacious and assertive.

It may be noted here that the two factors which enable the modern woman to assert are education and economic independence. Virmati comes to us as a modern woman, being both educated and having a job before marriage. The very fact that she is able to break the patriarchal mode in the 1940s is in itself a great achievement. In comparison, her daughter Ida, an educated woman, divorced and childless, leads a much freer life than her mother. In fact, she has achieved much more than her mother was able to achieve. As Dora Sales Salvador, the Spanish translator of *Difficult Daughters* says: "In *Difficult Daughters*, we do not listen to Virmati's voice. She could not speak out, being certainly situated at the juncture of two oppressions: colonialism and patriarchy. What we have is her daughter's reconstruction and representation."

The defiant daughter in Badami's novel *Hero's Walk* is Maya, a brilliant, accomplished and headstrong woman. Her father Sripathi Rao is proud of his talented vibrant daughter when she wins a scholarship to study at a Canadian university. Partly to ensure that she returns, an engagement is arranged for her with a young Brahmin named Prakash whose horoscope suitably matches hers, and Sripathi and the young man's father become close friends. They remain so until Maya writes to say that she had met and fallen in love with a fellow student named Alan Baker who is doing his Ph.D. in Vancouver. She asks her father to tell the family of Prakash that Maya had made other plans. She breaks her engagement with her fiancée Prakash to marry Alan. Maya defied tradition, rejecting her proper Brahmin fiancé for a Canadian husband. Like Virmati, Maya spurns an arranged marriage in India and goes on to marry for love.

Maya is happily married to a Canadian and lives in Vancouver but she is banished from Sripathi's life for defying his wishes. Sripathi, who had sacrificed so many passions to family obligations, including the offer of a journalist's job in the capital city of Delhi, refuses to allow Maya to return to India for an Indian wedding. Sripathi feels that "dishonour was what [Maya] had given them in return for the independence they had granted her." In a desperate attempt to convince his daughter to abort what he sees as a social and spiritual suicide mission, Sripathi tells Maya that if she insists on marrying the foreigner, she will never again be welcome in her father's house. "If you persist on doing this foolish thing," he shouts into the phone long distance, "never show your face in this house again. *Never*." Embarrassed and angry, Sripathi cuts off all his ties with her and refuses even to read her letters or hear anything about her. He forbids her very name being uttered in the house.

Estranged from his only daughter, Maya, whom he shunned on her marriage to a Westerner, Sripathi finds his life turned upside down with a single telephone call. His daughter and son-in-law are killed in a car crash in Vancouver, leaving him as the guardian to their only child, the seven-year old daughter, Nandana. The news totally shatters Sripathi Rao and his wife Nirmala. All Sripathi is left with are his regrets and his own guilt at having cut her out of his life. Sripathi is guilt-ridden for having refused to communicate with Maya because she humiliated him by marrying out of her caste and race. Maya's seven-year-old-daughter Nandana whom he had never seen is now his responsibility. The rest of the novel deals with how Sripathi comes to terms with the death of the daughter he had disowned for marrying a man of her choice.

It may be noted here that we never get to know Maya directly. It is through flashbacks that we learn about her defiance. In the novel, we do not hear Maya speak. To an interviewer, Anita Rau Badami said that she had written a chapter in which Maya interacted with her father but she later dropped it. She decided to focus on the family that was alive. In the novel, Maya remains a memory, and by her silence, she becomes more powerful than if she had been alive. She lived a happy life with her foreigner husband for about a decade till she died in a car-accident. As her aunt Putti says, Maya, even though she died young, had lived as full a life as most people who live to old age. By all standards, she was a successful woman.

Thus we see that the era of subjugation is gone and the women have started asserting themselves. They are no longer traditional Sitas or Savitris. The two daughters portrayed in these two novels rebel against their parents and the society and are successful in their struggle against the oppressive mechanism of a closed society.

Works Cited

Anita Rau Badami, *Hero's Walk* (London: Bloomsbury, 2000).
Manju Kapoor, *Difficult Daughters* (New Delhi: Penguin, 1998).

Image of Mother India in Manju Kapoor's *Difficult Daughters*

PUSHP LATA
BITS, Pilani

Modern Indian fiction has given vent to Indian feminine sensibility; their increasing awareness, unyielding determination to combat men's hypocrisy and search for self-fulfillment. It has obtained its sustenance from various socio-political events like Indian freedom movement, independence, right to vote, spread of education, employment opportunities and legal developments for the protection of women's rights etc. Therefore, the depiction of the Indian women has undergone a metastasis. In this period Manju Kapoor, unquestionably in her debut novel entitled *Difficult Daughters* has left an indelible imprint among the modern female writers in English, as she truthfully mirrors the socio-political scenario of the era. Bhgabat Nayak has befittingly remarked that Manju Kapoor seems to give a tribute to country's celebration of fifty years of independence in her novel as her protagonist, Virmati is projected as a cult to impugn the set norms and taboos imposed on women in the male dominated Indian society.[1] This paper aims at tracing this kind of metamorphosis, which Manju Kapoor has successfully presented by drawing a parallel between Virmati's struggle for self-liberation and the freedom movement that was prevalent during that aeon.

Set against the backdrop of the turbulent years of Indian freedom movement and partition of India, Manju Kapoor has unostentatiously intertwined both the political upheaval of 1950s and the changing feminist perspective of modern times in her novel. While depicting the women of three generations with the mind sets they possess and relationships they hold, she has taken into account the increasing complexity of life, different structures of values and solidarity in relation to socio-cultural scenario of the epoch. In order to portray women's journey of liberation clearly, she has made an attempt to juxtapose the position and perception of women of different generations: A woman, dependant on men for her social and sexual identity and economic needs i.e. Virmati's mother named Kasturi; and another woman who is trying to cross the threshold of the patriarchal system and becoming self directing through various trials and tribulations of life through the character of Virmati. She has masterly sketched the mental conflicts, the restlessness, the percipiently accumulated personal screams and simmering revolt in the minds of women characters through Virmati, Swarnalata, Shakuntala and Leela. The novel thus draws a parallel between the state of the country and women by converging on the issues like the awakening of the country for freedom, women education and feminine emancipation.

Manju Kapoor's *Difficult Daughters* is a story of a girl from a wealthy and distinguished family residing in Lahore before Independence who comes and settles in Amritsar after Independence. Virmati's mother, Kasturi is educated too. Though Kasturi and other family members believe in value of education for girls, they also opine that girls must be married off at the completion of necessary education. Girls are not encouraged for higher studies and selecting a career or a life partner for themselves. However, Shakuntala, Virmati's cousin, is an M.Sc. in Chemistry and works at Lahore College. She is strong-willed and career-oriented. She is self-assured and cherishes the idea of being something other than wife. In an intimate conversation, she tells Virmati: "Here we are, fighting for the freedom of the nation, but women are still supposed to marry and nothing else." (14)[2] Shakuntala always inspires Virmati, the protagonist, to think above the vested interest and get involved and fight for social and national cause. She says: "Times are changing, and women are moving out of the house, so why not you?" (16)

Virmati too often marvels at the ways of Shakuntala, her cousin and has all appreciation for her. When Virmati comes to know that Shakuntala reads papers, attends seminars and travels with her friends. Virmati replies, "I want to be like you, Pehnji." This reflects that the seeds for aspiration and emancipation are already lying there in the heart of the protagonist even much before she meets Harish, the professor. We find the novelist speaking the protagonist's mind in the very ensuing paragraph:

> It was useless looking for answers inside the home. One had to look outside. To education, freedom and the bright lights of Lahore colleges. (17)

As the story proceeds, we are apprised of the fact that Virmati, the representative of pre-independent India is not granted the freedom to pursue her studies. As a corollary, the task of shaping her future lies in her own hands. She feels awfully bad when she fails her F.A. and her parents start looking for a match for her but she insists on reappearing in the F.A. exams and starts studying in the college. Harish, the professor neighbour who makes her understand his need for companionship, in reality takes interest in her as a beautiful female being. Manju Kapoor while describing the classroom scene writes:

> Ignoring the half-dozen young men who rose to give her their place, Virmati sat on the floor in front of his desk, looking up at him with large eyes. The professor drank in the symbolism of her posture greedily. (46)

Further, in last line of chapter VIII Manju Kapoor remarks the following where she informs the readers how Virmati finally gets embroiled in professor's wily predilection: "But by then, the professor's desire to possess had extended to her heart and mind." (47)

Harish is, in fact, responsible for this bi-directional pull in her life. Being caught in hopeless illicit love, she refuses her engagement with Inderjit, a decent boy. At the beginning of her love, Virmati feels that "Professor Sahib was not formidable" (40) but later she finds her life in difficulty oscillating between education and marriage. (38) Here Virmati reminds us of Sarita, the protagonist of *The Dark Holds No Terror*, a novel by Shashi Deshpande. Virmati like Sarita dares to challenge the age-old traditions. The only difference is that Sarita goes to marry a man outside of her cast whereas Virmati marries Harish who also does not belong to Punjabi community but she agrees to become a second wife. However, both the marital bonds finally prove to be fruitless. Nevertheless, like Sarita, Virmati sounds bold, outspoken, determined and action-oriented when she lifts cudgels against male chauvinism, yet she realizes the hopelessness of her illicit love soon as she comes to know about the pregnancy of the professor's wife. After she becomes the second wife of Harish, she turns into a block of wood even before the first year of her marriage lapses. In her husband's company, she becomes a penumbra, a cast shadow as she fails to exercise her rights and freedom as an individual. Though the social opprobrium is not expressed openly, yet she apparently becomes isolated, silent and withdrawn. She is unable to discover her own identity in Harish's world. She fails to get a sense of belongingness, which is usually shared by couples. She finds herself dislocated, displaced and disoriented. She suffers both from the loss of identity and alienation at her marital home. Their love does not seem to be profound but a nauseating apology. Consequently Virmati faces intense frustration, bitter disappointment and awful disillusionment. Her mind and her heart are constantly agitated, rippled and tumultuous with thoughts of her freedom and position in the society and family. When Harish takes pride in discussing the political scenario at national and international level, she is worried about her own freedom. In the conversation that takes place on 8 May, Harish tells Virmati:

> Now it's our turn next. Now they will have no excuse. Cripps had given a commitment. At the San Francisco Peace Conference the eyes of the world will be on Britain. There will be pressure put on her to recognize our sovereignty. . . . No, Britain is now finished, Viru, finished. (254-55)

She does not respond to the above statement by Harish but she reminds herself of her dormant dream of emancipation:

> And me, thought Virmati, what about me? The war, or the end of it. . . . Suddenly he is transformed. He becomes visionary. . . . I feel

> so utterly left out, so utterly cold. Will there be any change in my life, I wonder? (255)

She starts pondering over her own position and wishes her voice to echo so that her needs are acknowledged. For this obvious reason she refuses to go back home and tells herself bluntly:

> I will relate to you with dignity or not at all. None of this hiding and whispering and keeping my voice down and struggle over who is going to wash your underwear and who is going to clean your shoes. None of this for me. (155-56)

The marital home and the bed that she seems to have craved for years, she is ready to renounce and look for an opening. She displays a prodigious strength of mind to fulminate her dejection. After she dares to cross the patriarchal threshold, she finds her free spirit curtailed and chopped. Professor's arms do not provide solace to her any longer. She feels his interest in her is merely lustful. He requires her company for inflating his ego. What we observe is that she is 'undergoing a gradual process of self-effacement, her energies are directed towards pleasing him while she herself remains parched.'[3] During her stay at Lahore when gets engaged in trashy love affair and unwed pregnancy, she aspires for wider spectrum and canvas. At the Punjab Women's Student Conference, she starts at 'How large an area of life women wanted to appropriate for themselves.' (132) She finds herself to have been wronged and victimized in a subtle way by selfish Harish. Later, Virmati gets enrolled for master's degree in Philosophy though she hates this subject very much she is rather instructed to opt for this subject, only because Harish considers Philosophy a noble subject. In spite of the fact that she finds this to be dull, abstract and meaningless subject, Virmati considers it as her only means of escape. As readers we are startled at her state of mind that gets reflected in her monologue on 12 Nov. 1944, the INA Day:

> The child shows such courage, while I fret about my petty domestic matters, at a time when the nation is on trial. I too must take a stand. I have tried adjustment and compromise, now I will try non-cooperation. (159)

Mahatma Gandhi's non-cooperation movement, which is stirring millions of Indians to raise their voice for political freedom, also provides an insight to Virmati, the cult of women liberation for focusing on her personal salvation. A corollary to this thinking of hers, the battle of her own independence, which she started in her youth, she takes it up again. The conflict between her desires and reality intensifies and thus ensues an inner struggle in Virmati's heart as she is drawn into a life of chaos and confusion. The inner voyage of Virmati in the novel is greatly influenced by what Virginia Woolf maintains: "Life is not a series of gig lamps arranged symmetrically; life is a luminous halo, semi-transparent envelop surrounding us from the beginning of consciousness to the end."

Thus, Manju Kapoor has dealt with mind and the soul of protagonist, her inner workings and hidden and silent thoughts rather than her appearance. Though this psychoanalysis does not stand to the degree to which Anita Desai does to her characters, yet she succeeds to a great extent in doing so.

This odyssey of her own liberation creates irrevocable lines of partition, pain and suffering around Virmati, as the freedom movement of the country results in India-Pakistan partition, affliction, anguish and agony of millions of homeless lifeless tortured souls of the country. Virmati feels stronger with the certainty of the nascent life within her womb and when it is considered safe, she wants to help in the camps. On the contrary, Harish does not allow her to do so. According to him, she must think of the baby as she already had an abortion and one miscarriage. However, she gives away all the clothing left unused in the house for the unclad inhabitants of the city.

In another incident we, as the readers, can easily envisage the sustenance of her struggle clearly. When Virmati gives birth to a girl, she names her 'Bharti' since she feels God has blessed her with the child at the dawn of freedom of the country. But this is outrightly rejected by Harish and he names the child as 'Ida' which sounds as a Persian name to Virmati. Over this, Harish irritatingly remarks: "Let anybody think what they like, for us it means a new slate, and a blank beginning." (277)

With the advent of freedom for the country, it can be easily comprehended that the man who talks about freedom dogmatically, does not provide liberty to his wife who bore the pangs and suffering of keeping the child in her womb for nine months even for such a trivial matter like keeping the name of the new-born child of her choice. Virmati who has sacrificed so much in her life to marry Harish, is insouciant of her own identity. I believe that it is Virmati who has taken the first step towards the journey of women liberation from the clutches of the egoist male society but her daughter Ida takes this voyage to culmination. She vehemently opposes male-supremacy and wishes to exercise her right to equality. She clearly repudiates the role of being victims at the hands of dominating males of the society. Ida is able to sense clearly that women need to staunchly believe in the strength of their womanhood if they want the world to recognize their existence. When Ida remarks "The one thing I had wanted was not to be like my mother," she probably means just by defying the patriarchal uphold, women cannot achieve their self the way her mother did. She recognizes her mother's weaknesses, but while tracing her life events, she becomes aware of the pugnacity that Virmati undergoes for creating a space for herself. She acknowledges this fact in the concluding paragraph of the novel where she says, "This book weaves a connection between my mother and me, each word a brick in a mansion I made with my head and my heart. Now live in it, Mama, and leave me be." Perhaps Ida has dedicated the work to her mother as it is about her. And she asks her mom to leave her as she needs to take up the journey ahead in a bolder way.

Thus Manju Kapoor has written with immense concern and understanding for her female characters, particularly Virmati. The suppressed and subjugated world of Indian women comes to full light in the character of her protagonist. She dexterously delineates all kinds of visible and invisible pressures that kept Indian women suffocated for long. I feel in a very symbolic manner Manju Kapoor puts the whole story against the backdrop of Indian freedom movement. Like Anita Desai and Shashi Deshpande, Manju Kapoor can be considered a prose rhapsodist of female sentiments, feelings and emotions through human conscientious awareness. She can be termed as one of the most powerful forerunners of women's emancipation movement on Indian soil.

Works Cited

1. Bhagabat Nayak, "Manju Kapoor's *Difficult Daughters*: A Feminist Reading," *Indian Journal of English Studies*, Vol. XXXVIII, 2000-2001, p. 98.
2. Manju Kapoor, *Difficult Daughters* (New Delhi: Penguin, 1998), p.14.
3. Seema Malik, "Crossing Patriarchal Threshold: Glimpses of the Incipient New Women in Manju Kapoor's *Difficult Daughters*," *Indian Women Writers*, ed. R.K. Dhawan (New Delhi: Prestige, 2001), p. 135.

Readability of Manju Kapur's *Difficult Daughters*

MANJU ROY
C.M. College, Darbhanga

Manju Kapur's debut novel, *Difficult Daughters*, was published in 1998 and it has been winning several accolades since then. It was short-listed for the Crossword Book Award in India and also earned the prestigious 1999 Commonwealth Writer's Prize for the Best First Book category in the Eurasia region. *Difficult Daughters* has been hailed as 'an impressive novel' by Meenakshi Mukherjee, 'a part of the new and vital wave of Anglo-Indian fiction' by Shirley Kossick, 'an eye opener in many ways' by Bibi Shah and 'a novel about female desire and entrapment, about compromise and compliance' by Nira Gupta-Casale. Critics also talk about the 'fluidity' of Kapur's style, but surprisingly, no systematic attempt has been made to evaluate the readability of the novel. Nira Gupta-Casale also considers it 'an extremely readable novel.' When an informal survey was done, several teachers working in the area of Indian Writing in English confirmed Gupta-Casale's opinion intuitively. However, no one, it seems, has taken pains to assess the reasons for its high readability. So, it becomes incumbent to assess the reasons for its high lucidity. This paper is a modest attempt to dig deep into the factors responsible for the novel's very high readability.

One of the sources of high readability lies in the use of a lot of Hindi and Punjabi words in the novel. These words have been taken from different areas of experience. In fact, the English used by Manju Kapur is geared towards expressing a distinctly Indian sensibility. Therefore, her English has definitely a local flavour. This variety of Indian English may be frowned upon by puritans but Kamala Das defends it well in 'An Introduction' to *The Old Playhouse and Other Poems* (cited Nihalani 29):

> The language I speak
> Becomes mine, its distortions, its queerness
> All mine, mine alone. It is half English, half
> Indian, funny perhaps, but it is honest,
> It is as human as I am human, don't
> You see? It voices my joys, my longings, my
> Hopes, and it is as useful to me as cawing
> Is to crows or roaring to the lions, it
> Is human speech, the speech of the mind that is
> Here and not there, a mind that sees and hears and
> Is aware

Manju Kapur also voices her joys and hopes by using rich and colourful expressions of colloquial Punjabi and creates the cultural context of her plot. An example of this creation is evident in 'the devotion with which the native Punjabi extols the soul satisfying virtues of butter and lassi' (Gupta-Casale):

> The milk had a thick layer of *malai*, yellow, not white, like nowadays. And when food was cooked, ah, the fragrance of *ghee*!

At this point, words fail them.

> I had grown up on the mythology of pure ghee, milk, butter, and *lassi*, and whenever I came to Amritsar, I noticed the fanatical gleam in the eyes of people as they talked of those legendary items. Perhaps, if I could have shared that passion, the barriers of time and space would have melted like pure ghee in the warmth of my palm. (4)

The source of high readability can also be traced to the novelist's use of code-switching devices. Code switching is normally defined as the use of more than one language in the execution of a speech-act. She uses this device on the level of lexis and phrases, usually noun phrases, to express herself in a better and satisfying way. Her use of this device seems to be governed sometimes by the non-availability of an equivalent word in English and at other times by a mere choice to make the context or narration more realistic. In the sentence, "A woman's shaan is in her home" (13), Kapur's choice of 'shaan' instead of 'pride' lends this expression a homely and realistic touch. Her use of Hindi/Punjabi words represents a vast area of experiences, but it is remarkable that the words are mostly concrete ones as opposed to abstract ones. Here concrete words refer to the objects normally perceived by our sense organs. Below is given a list of these words used by Kapur which not only refers to a wide spectrum of her experiences but also shows that she is trying to make all the details of the novel realistic, thus increasing readability.

- Food: Atta, Malai, Lassi, Puris,Luchis, Kulchas, Tandoori, Morraba, Sherbat, Papad, Dal, Pakora, Chutney, Khas, Dahi, Paneer, Mathri.
- Place: Ghat, Angan, Gully, Kothi, Dharamshala, Zenana, Aangan,
- Profession: Chowkidar, Randi, Dhobi, Munshi, Bania
- Event: Chauth, Uthala, Shaadi
- Relation: Bhai Saheb, Bua, Maji, Chachi, Bade Pitaji, Baoji, Bhai, Beta, Masi, Pitaji, Bhenji.
- Dress: Pyjama, Kurta, Kameez, Dhoti, Dupatta,
- Utensils: Thali, Katori, Karahi, Patila,
- Miscellaneous: Sandhya, Havan, Durries, Sandhya, Furlong, Lauki, Baithak, Kewara

Manju Kapur switches code on various aspects like reduplications, religious invocations, exclamations and compounding.

- Reduplication: Seedha-saadha, Shor-shaar, Bas-bas
- Religious Invocation: Allah-o-Akbar, Har, har Mahadev, Bole so Nihal
- Adjective: Shaan, Gandi, Badmash
- Exclamation: Bap re, Arre, He Bhagwan, Hai re, hai re, Arre wah
- Compound words: Puris and parathas, Zenana angan, Gajjar-mooli, Dhoti kurta jooti

Further, she uses this device in expressing agreement, affirmation and consent. The following extracts illustrate this point:

> 'What a lovely place to be finally laid to rest!'

> 'Hoon,' said Virmati absently who saw nothing so remarkable about the gravestones. (176)
>
> At the doorway she [Kasturi] turned back once to say, 'Indu, . . . use the fresh butter in the doli, the old one is for ghee.'
>
> 'Han,' said Indu. (74)

Kapur extends the use of this code-switching device to phrases also and forms the expressions like,

> 'puris and parathas wrapped in Britannia-bread waxed paper' (2)
> 'aalu ki sabzi in mithai boxes' (2)
> 'They . . . skirted the zenana angan' (180)
> ' . . . and pull her sari palla' (213)

Readability is also caused by the narrative technique used in the text. The major part of the story is narrated by the author herself, who seems to be omnipresent and does not take part in the story. This type of narrator is called 'heterodiegetic' (Genette, 255-56). Only a very small part is narrated by Ida, Virmati's daughter, who is a participant also. A narrator of this type is labelled as 'homodigetic' (*Ibid*). Ida starts narrating the tale with a very cryptic statement: "The one thing I had wanted was not to be like my mother" (1). And from this very point readers get curious 'to explore, and analyse why she did not like to be like her mother and relate the answer to the larger issue of patriarchy' (Bala and Chandra). And the book ends, as it began, with the angry Ida's comment:

> This book weaves a connection between my mother and me, each word a brick in a mansion I made with my head and my heart.
>
> Now live in it, Mama and leave me be. Do not haunt me any more. (259)

In this way, the novel appears to form a complete circle and this circularity gives a direction, continuity and speed to readers. Ida takes over the narration of the tale at different points in the novel, but only for a very brief period and this breaks the monotony in the reading of the novel. Ida starts the story in Chapter 1 wherein she talks about her dead mother just after her funeral at Delhi and then she reaches Amritsar where she starts piecing together her dead mother's past, but as she has been able to provide only a small aspect of her life, we get the remaining big part of the story mainly by the author. Ida takes up the job of a narrator again in chapter 9. She, along with Kailashnath, goes to the college where her father worked for a very long time and her mother's love affair bloomed with Harish. Thereafter, she again starts telling the story in chapter 17 (second part) wherein she meets Swarna Lata Sondhi, the roommate of Virmati during her Lahore days, to explore some more facets of her mother's personality. Later, she again tries to reconstruct the story in chapter 19 (second part). Here, she comes to know how Swarna Lata helps her mother to get rid of the unwanted pregnancy. Further, in chapter 23 (second part) Ida talks to her Masi about her mother's marriage and in chapter 25, she tries to pick up the loose threads of her mother's marital life. And finally, at the end of Epilogue, she becomes autobiographical and bids farewell to her mother's memory.

The reader develops a bond of trust with the author who is the main narrator in the novel. Her omniscience can be felt by her presence as a storyteller in about 250 pages of the novel, which runs into 259 pages. This is also realized by her familiarity with the characters' innermost thoughts and feelings, her knowledge of past and present and her presence in locations where characters meet in total privacy. In addition, what makes this novel compelling reading and distinguishes it from other tales of adulterous love and romantic intrigue is the sympathy and integrity with which the author and Ida reconstruct the past of Virmati (Gupta-Casale).

Mukul Kesavan, a famous novelist, commends *Difficult Daughters* as 'a first rate realistic novel' (Bala and Chandra 106). A close analysis of the novel reveals that realism also promotes a high degree of reliability, and realism, to a large extent, is realized in 'verisimilitude' and 'credibility.' Cassirer (144) defines art as 'a continuous process of concretion.' Leech and Short (156) explain this definition in the following way: 'The sense of being in the presence of actual individual things, events, people, and places, is the common experience we expect to find in literature' and this very aspect of the illusion of reality is called verisimilitude. The novel is full of instances where readers get the impression of being participants or observers themselves. For example, Virmati's traumatic experience of unwanted pregnancy mitigates the gap between a reader and a participant, at least for a short while:

> Quickly she calculated dates. . . . She was certain she was pregnant. With this certainty, the nausea came again, ripping through her throat, salivating her tongue. She thought of all the hours she had spent over her practical files, her teaching charts, . . . What would happen to her BT now? (141)

Verisimilitude is closely connected with another aspect of realism called credibility. Credibility is "likelihood or believability of the fiction as a 'potential reality'" (Leech and Short, 157). Kasturi gets surprised at the fuss that people are making in the house after Virmati fails at her FA examination. She does not give importance to the success in the examination—instead, she strongly believes: "it is the duty of every girl to get married" (13). Her belief lends credibility to the novel because the same belief was a part of Indian consciousness till some years ago.

A lot of colloquial expressions also make the novel lucid. Some examples are quoted below:

> Hai re, beti! (13)
> He is ill, he is sick, he has fainted, hai re, hai re. (78)
> Come here beta. (202)
> Mornings, toast and milk. Lunch dal, rice, chappati, vegetable, dahi, sometimes a sweet dish, for tea, pakora or mathri, for dinner, dal, sabzi, sometimes with paneer, rice, chapatti. (108)

To sum up, we may say that the novel is brilliant because it is 'about female desire and entrapment, about compromise and compliance' (Gupta-Casale). Nonetheless, its brilliance also lies in its high readability which is triggered by Kapur's unique handling of the English language marked by an abundance of Hindi and Punjabi words and by her use of code switching devices and several colloquial expressions. In addition, Kapur's narrative technique and her sincere effort to make the novel realistic also enhance the readability of the text.

Works Cited

Bala, Suman and Subhash Chandra. "Manju Kapur's *Difficult Daughters*: An Absorbing Tale of Fact and Fiction." *50 years of Indian Writing*, ed. R.K. Dhawan. New Delhi: Indian Association for English Studies.

Cassirer, Ernest. 1944. *An Essay on Man*. New Haven, Conn: Yale University Press.

Genette, G. 1972. *Figures III*. Paris: Seuil.

Gupta-Casale, Nira. N.d. Online. http://www.cohums.ohio-state.edu/comp/bulletin/ nira.htm. Accessed 28 November 2000.

Kossick, Shirley. 1998. Review of *Difficult Daughters*. Online. http://www.mg.co.za/mg/books/9809/980907-newfiction.htm Accessed 23 October 2000.

Leech, G. and M. Short. 1987. *Style in Fiction*. London: Longman.

Mukherjee, M. 1998. "What caught the eye," *The Hindu*, 20 December 1998.

Nihalani, N. K. (1985) "English in the Third World: Changing Attitudes." *The Journal of Indian Writing in English*, January 1985, Vol. 13, No. 1.

Shah, Bibi. 1999. "An Eye opener." Online. http://www.shop.barnes andnoble. com/bookSearch. Accessed 7 November 2000.

Circular and Circuitous: Feministic Perspectives in Manju Kapur's *A Married Woman*

SUNITA AGARWAL
University of Rajasthan, Jaipur

Virginia Woolf in *A Room of One's Own* (1928) had said that in order for women to come into their own, two things were needed—space and opportunity, both economic and social. Without going into much details of Woolf's initiative feminist pronouncements, the present paper would like to draw parallels between Woolf's hypothesis and Manju Kapur's endeavours in her second novel, *A Married Woman* (2002). The novel, seemingly simplistic, has a polyvalent sub-text that attests to many propositions being propounded about feminism. The narrative skirts through the second and third wave feminist essentials and dramatically ushers in the post-feminist/ postmodernist, though thwarted, era.

The storyline is simple—a married woman struggles to keep her identity intact while seeking equal opportunities within and without the familial threshold. Given the spatio-temporal parameters within which the theme is constructed—a high, middle class, conservative Indian family today—the struggle is destined to be unavailing and the quest a disaster. But what is symbolic of the change to come is the awakened awareness about domination and marginality.

The narrative moves forward toward a resolution but simultaneously it slides back, the paradise is lost in the very attempt to regain it. In this movement, there seems to be a kind of Oedipal logic. The beginning is conventional, highlighting traditional, middle-class Indian attitudes towards marriage. The way protagonist Astha's mother gradually collects a spoon by spoon, a sheet by sheet and jewellery by jewellery for her daughter's marriage locates the story and defines the ambience in which the plot is to be unfolded. The subtle way in which Kapur creates an aura of dissatisfaction around Astha, we know for sure that a revolution is in its making. The generation of Astha is bound to revolt against their lives being manipulated. She shows the expected recalcitrance and debunks the expectation by falling in and out of love a couple of times. Her desires are sexual, "delicious images of a romantic somewhat shadowy young man holding her in embrace." (1) As opposed to her mother's more spiritual ones of attaining salvation, "You know what the shastras say, if parents die without getting their daughter married, they will be condemned to perpetual rebirth." (1) Although Astha did not believe in "all that stuff," it is ironical that she is condemned to a symbolic rebirth in this life itself but yet she does not find satisfaction or solace with her evolved self.

Both her early affairs end tragically, destabilizing her, although she becomes knowledgeable of male exploitation. The experience leaves her both mentally and physically sick as she drifts through college to university. Now she does not put up an obstacle when a proposal comes from "an MBA, foreign returned son of a bureaucrat. She agrees to the marriage and gradually grows to love this man she has to live with. Hemant, the husband, to begin with, gives her all the love, security and material conveniences that a married woman in Astha's place would have yearned for: "Astha's heart was as full of love as a lake is full of water." (42) She submerges herself in the role of daughter-in-law and wife, experimenting in the kitchen, arranging and reordering her life, neatly fitting into the pattern of another. Her time is spent visiting and shopping in the morning and more particularly with "the memory of night past and the night to come insulating her from any tedium she might otherwise have felt." (43) Wrapped in marital bliss and glorying in the satisfaction that she can give her husband, she spends years sinking into oblivion. But soon the dullness and monotony start tainting her new life. She seeks permission to teach to overcome the restlessness. The job that she had never considered with interest now seemed to be the ideal one, at least to overcome the restless hours.

With this new diversion, the margins of her world stretched further and it was no surprise that she started desiring more. And therefore with the entry of Aijaz Akhtar Khan, her well-led plans soon went awry and the pedestal on which she has ensconced her husband was dismantled. Petty vexations started filling in the hitherto unseen gaps. Astha longed to be pregnant, to be a mother to fulfill these gaps. The birth of Anuradha filled both parents with joy. Hemant turned to be a loving and caring father massaging and bathing the baby every Sunday, rejecting the antiquated ideas of fatherhood in India. But this attitude did not last till the time of the birth of Himanshu, their son. By that time Hemant was changed from being an all-American father into an all-Indian one, little caring for Astha and the family. For Astha herself motherly duties occupied her for sometime, but very soon, boredom and monotony of the routine life entered into her life again and she felt the need for a space for herself, an urge to be identified. Her desire for companionship, to be an equal partner in the enterprise of marriage, life and living was outrightly rejected by the too-practical Hemant saying: "Grow up Az, one can't be courting forever." (66)

Astha's effort to adjust and accommodate herself with all these problems of children, husband, servant and job made her sick. She started having regular headaches but giving up the job was immature because there was a change in Astha after the birth of Himanshu: "Astha who earlier was a woman who only wanted love to a woman who valued independence." (72) Despite these emotional voids in her conjugal life, Astha toed the track of an ideal housewife conforming to the demands of tradition. She did not protest but dutifully obeyed her husband. Her position was like a catalyst whose presence is never noticed yet whose absence makes a difference. Astha as a woman was sick of sacrifice. Her relationship with Hemant had grown to be dissatisfying and stifling. "She did not want to be pushed around in the name of family. She was fed up with the idea of Indian womanhood used to trap and jail." (168) Hemant's attitude was befitting and even considerate in his own world of patriarchal hegemony.

On the Goa trip, the ticket of which was arranged by the money earned by the sale of one of Astha's paintings, Astha's desire to buy a carved silver box was ruthlessly crushed down by Hemant saying, "You must be out of your mind." (165) The tone of refusal hurt her she was an earning woman, why could she not have a say in how some of their money was spent. She never said anything when he chose to squander money on airline tickets, why could she not buy a box she liked? The male dominance was clear. Astha felt "limped, attacked and baffled." (167) How ironical the whole thing was: "But their money spending was decided by him not by her." (161)

Disappointed, she tried to seek comfort in her mother. But the mother-daughter relationship failed to provide any emotional solace to Astha as her mother herself was now living in the aura of influence of a Swamiji trying to solve the riddles of life and getting spiritual enlightenment after the death of her husband. Her mother's decision to sell the plot and shift to Rishikesh was incomprehensible to Astha. The relationship of her mother with the Swamiji evoked many questions in her mind, and even a visit to Rishikesh could not solve the puzzle. But her mother's entrusting all the financial matters and a big part of the money, as her father's legacy to Hemant was shocking to Astha. She felt betrayed. Her mother's plea, "it was the same with your father, I only did the household account" (97), was not convincing enough for Astha and it was useless to ask anything about it from Hemant as "she had a good life but it was good because nothing was questioned." (99)

Astha was also pained to learn of the donation of her father's books to the library. "Material possession is a burden," said her mother. But Astha's desire to preserve some of them as her father's memory remained unfulfilled. Her own mother could not understand her: "It is Hemant's house and he said there was no room. Then who am I? The tenant." (87), asks Astha. The question is a very significant one, about the place of woman in her own home. How ridiculous the whole situation was, the woman, the mother who is the nucleus of the family, cannot call her home her own. Before marriage, it was her father's and after marriage it is her husband's. Astha's mother, a traditional woman always took the side of Hemant. So Astha is bereft of any maternal support that could have acted as a ballast to her tottering confidence.

The ferment of dissatisfaction erupts in many wanted and unwanted reactions. Astha, desirous of equality and trying to preserve her independence, tries to shape her life anew. She is attracted to Aijaz Akhtar because he poses to be the alternative that she is seeking. Devoted to the arts and free and encumbered, Astha finds in him those very attributes that she is looking out for herself. She, therefore, relates to him more completely than to her own family who seem to thwart her identity. It is this new Astha under the patronage of Aijaz who crosses her threshold and goes on an Ekta Yatra, which she could not have dreamt of doing earlier. She even grows up to be politically enlightened through the participation in the Street Theatre Group.

Astha's second rebirth is through Pipeelika, a social worker and the widowed wife of Aijaz Akhtar. Astha's relationship grows disproportionately close to Pipeelika: Astha needs her as a support to her new-found independence and Pipeelika needs her to find her own self. It is an unnatural relationship for Astha, for the world from which she hailed, such associations are considered downright asocial. For Pipeelika, as we gradually come to know, it was a stopgap arrangement. She was using Astha to fill the void that Aijaz has created as well as to have a ready peg to hang herself on. Pipeelika gloated as a patriarch to see the way she could sway Astha, Astha in her turn is still the subaltern, now being oppressed by a woman instead of a man. She acquires an unacceptable sexuality in trying to rise above being merely a body. Although she does often brood about her own sexual relationship and its nature, but her desire for Pipee is so linked to that particular person that she fails to draw any general conclusions. It is a way, perhaps of taking revenge. On a deeper level this relationship also implies a woman's independence from man. It has political implications too. Hite (2000) writes that lesbianism can be political too. Sex with another woman could be better because of the more equal relationship possible. Sex with woman can be a reaction against that and over second-class status with them in society. One of the subjects in the Hite's survey says: "Sex with a man is often the beginning of a political education, sex with a woman means independence from man." There is a kind of reciprocity and similarity between two women and as a psychiatrist has pointed out, only another woman knows a woman.

However, Astha is tossed between two longings, the one to which she is maternally attached and the other which her 'self' longs for. This predicament eventually undermines her morale: "Astha's mind boggled. What about their school, their routine, their friends in the colony, their grandparents, their father, who whatever his faults, did love his kids?" (242) Maybe she was deeply conventional but for her the business of raising children had a set dynamics that were the standard ones. That those dynamics did not include companionship and understanding was regrettable, but she had grown used to it. She saw herself as "a bird pecking at a few leftover crumbs from the feast of life." (242)

This image of herself unnerves Astha and makes her feel that she should not have looked for happiness outside the four walls of home and hearth. But once established, such a relationship becomes more and more demanding. The three weeks away together are unembalming and 'unclamping.' Again a three-week holiday, this time with family to the U.S.A., brings about a change. With each passing day of the second holiday she realizes that she had enjoyed the comparative ease between Hemant and herself. And 'she dreaded what Pipee would say when she sensed this.' After all Astha is dependent in her independence, and this is painful, more painful than her fight against conventional dominance. So the break with Pipee is inevitable. Differences creep in and harmony between the two is broken. Astha realizes that the breaking up of this relationship would be a slow process. A new 'carefulness' grows between the two of them and the final cut comes with Pipee's decision to immigrate.

Very skilfully Manju Kapur has brought the novel to a close by bringing a married woman full circle back home. The intertwining forays are the supposed directions that an unquiet mind can take. All said and done, Indian women are respectful of their marriage and even though alternatives are available, they are neither acceptable nor fulfilling. Manju Kapur seems to attest to the third wave postmodernist concept of 'difference.' Each culture cannot retaliate and change in universally acceptable ways, its history, its politics demand a certain patterning that a similar predicament in a different set up would not. Very subtly, Manju Kapur has narrated the life of 'a' married woman who is both specific in an indefinable manner and generic as far as the culture here specifies. A married woman can take liberties with herself but not with her family and she has to return to the fold though she might have stretched herself thin in the process. The last word of the novel 'globe' is symbolic of both the circular and the circuitous route of independence within the prescribed limits of dependence.

Works Cited

Kapur Manju (2002). *A Married Woman*. Delhi: India Ink.

Shere Hite, *The Hite Report: A Nationwide Study of Female Sexuality*.

Context and Text: Technology of Gender in the Fiction of Shashi Deshpande

RASHMI GAUR
Indian Institute of Technology, Roorkee

The calculated and implicitly suggestive construction of gendered identities has supported the binaries which proliferate and continue the marginalization, also the consequential secondary status of women as a class. Gendered interpretation of literary texts enables us to examine man-woman relationship as an axis of prevalent social inequality. Gender identity is a compulsory facet of our cognition—individual as well as collective. Internalization of gendered identities conditions one's own cognitive and behavioural patterns, while simultaneously creating a comfort zone as far as our reactions to different genders are concerned. The difference between sex and gender is symptomatic of the difference between physical and cognitive planes. The cognitive aspect is primarily linked with the psychoanalytical perception of self and others which shapes our relationship with others. It is further extended to a cultural internalization of how men and women should behave and also what type of behaviour they should expect from others. Cultural internalization of gendered conduct intensifies at places of learning, work and social interaction. In turn it affects the very foundation of imagination, coping up strategies and intellect—shaping up the self-hood of individuals. Differences of cultural milieu are incapable to work against this primary aspect of societal structure and power dynamics. The visible distinctions of liberal policies, educational opportunities, career advancement and economic independence may prove to be, at decisive moments, a gloss over the fundamental inequalities with which gender are perceived and responded to. The impact of gendered behaviour, thus, cannot be straightforwardly measured, as it is a phenomenon which has "bodily, psychological and behavioural features" (Alsop et al 14). The present paper surveys various theories of gender construction and reviews to what extent they are reflected in the thematic motifs and character sketches of the novels of Shashi Deshpande.

II

Shashi Deshpande is a major contemporary Indian woman writer, whose fiction can be read as a manual to understand how the circumspectly constructed gendered identity in Indian society comes into being. Deshpande was born in 1938 in Dharwad (Karnataka, India). Her father was a famous Sanskrit scholar. She is a prolific writer and has published nine novels and seven story collections. In her fictional and expository writing and interviews, she has mapped out and uncovered the boundaries erected around a woman's life from childhood to womanhood in the traditional male-dominated Indian society, even though she has refused to be identified as a feminist. Depicting the middle-class milieu, her novels provide a pointer to the catatonic status of women and concentrate on the struggle of women to overcome the constricting dilemmas of pre-fixed definitions and gendered behavioural norms. Her writing convinces us of the need of social restructuring in the light of gender equality and poignantly reveals how the conventional norms of Indian social system mould women's inner life stifling their individuality and encouraging them to put up with the crudity and insensitivity of the male ethos. Her women characters are decisively conscious of their marginalized position in conventional social configurations, and want to achieve selfhood by transcending them.

Interestingly, Deshpande is also the only contemporary Indian writer who has observed that men too are as much the victims of the gendered norms as women are. Her novels indicate how not only women, but men too, have to abide by the mendaciousness of gender which circumscribes their potential for self-actualization. Her novels delineate that though men are also encouraged to opt for a certain type of behaviour only, most of the time these gendered expectations are in their favour, while women are often victimized. She shows the necessity of sensitizing men too, counselling women to treat them as friends and not necessarily as tormenters. In this aspect, Deshpande also comes close to the post-feminist stand, as far as the portrayal of man-woman relationship is concerned.

III

The numerous theories of gender construction highlight the subtlety of the process. In the earlier discussion, it has become clear that gender is the socially projected component of human sexuality. Perhaps the best way to understand gender is to understand it as a process of social presentation. Gender roles are delineated by behavioural expectations and norms; once individuals know those expectations and norms, the individual can adopt behaviours that project the gender they wish to portray. Certain critics have equated gender with a role in a theatrical play. There are specific behaviours and norms associated with genders just like there are lines and movements associated with each character in a play. Adopting the behaviours and norms of a gender leads to the perception that someone belongs in that gender category. Another aspect which may be commented upon is the fact that gender roles, unlike sex, are mutable, meaning they can change. Gender is not, however, as simple as just choosing a role to play but is also influenced by parents, peers, culture and society.

Biological Difference Theory, coupled with the social role theory is perhaps the earliest attempt to outline this suggestion. Biological determinism is often used to support generalisations about men and women, such as 'men are naturally more able in maths and technology' or 'women are naturally suited to domestic duties.' Biological determinism asserts that certain behaviours are justified and unchangeable because there is a basic inequality between the sexes. These inequalities are said to be both physical and psychological. The alleged psychological differences between the sexes include women's emotional instability, greater tolerance for monotonous details, incapacity for abstract thought, and proneness to submission (Singh 27). This conservative view upholds that anatomy becomes one's destiny, and demarcates certain characteristics as being essentially feminine or masculine. Women are supposed to be submissive, dependent, emotional, receptive, intuitive, timid, passive and sensitive. On the other hand, all the active qualities are traditionally linked with men. They are expected to be dominant, independent, rational, assertive, analytical, brave, active and insensitive. This view also encourages the view that 'boys will be boys,' but 'girls should be girls'—a statement which by substituting 'will' by 'should' introduces artificial performance as a social norm. Philosophers like Schopenhauer, Fichte, Rousseau, Nietzsche and Freud have supported such arguments (Jagger 19). It also emphasizes that men and women should perform their own proper social function as this division is astutely based on the intrinsic physical and psychological capabilities of the sexes. However there is little consideration in this view for the wide variety of behaviours among members of each sex, or how masculinity and femininity relate to each other in different settings. This view of 'natural' difference is difficult to support when notions of appropriate gender behaviour are not static, but differ over time, between ethnic and cultural groups, and even between and within families. Society and culture promote separate learning atmospheres to girls and boys, rewarding gender appropriate behaviour and emphasizing structural constraints on children and ensuring that men and women are in different and unequal positions in the social structure. Such cultural climate generates conscious commitment to a specific image of self within the pre-defined gender scaling. The social preprogramming of the individual's experience into the historically precut grooves, conditions individuals to view reality through gendered lenses (Bem.net).

IV

In the novels of Shashi Deshpande, we find an illustration of materialist as well as discursive theories. Her fiction delineates not only the biological essentialism, but also the social role theory in understanding the gender construction. In all her novels, and also in many stories, we find that the roots of girlhood cast their shadow on womanhood, constricting the free burgeoning of women's personalities. Her first novel, *The Dark Holds no Terrors* (1980), exhibits the cruelty of gender discrimination which is inflicted on the girl child—mothers, who themselves are a conditioned product of society, become a vehicle of perpetuating it. The novel shows how the independence of girls, particularly in middle class Indian society, is curbed by the social diktats. Liberties which are routinely given to a boy are denied to girls. Worse, these denials are taken as facilitators for the daughter's future.

Indian society has a preference for boys which has almost religious sanctions. *Atharva Veda* and *Aitareya Brahamin* say that the birth of a daughter is a source of misery. In *Caste as Woman*, Vrinda Nabar comments on this attitude, "It is clear that the birth of a daughter is a let down in some absolute sense. A woman who bears a son, on the other hand, is exalted as someone who has fulfilled her mission as a female. She herself is conditioned into experiencing a sense of achievement at having done so" (Nabar 162).

Deshpande shows how this gender preference generates humiliation, revulsion and even rebellion among girls. Indu in *Roots and Shadows* and Kalpana in *The Binding Vine* suffer from negligence of parents as they are not boys. The middle class society portrayed by Deshpande often denies self–identity to women, and encourages them to mould themselves to fit into the conventional roles of daughter, wife and mother. In *The Dark Holds No Terrors* we have the wives of Manu's friends, who remain in the background. Saru is a catch prize, being a doctor. But when she starts earning more than her husband, frictions occur. List of mothers or mother figures who goad their daughters to remain servile is rather comprehensive. Shakutai in *The Binding Vine*, Manorama in *A Matter of Time,* Indu's Kakis in *Roots and Shadows*, Mohan's mother in *That Long Silence* and various minor figures of Kakis and aajis in Deshpande's fiction lay stress on the feminine functions. Girls are discouraged from asking questions, from raising doubts about prevalent practices. They are encouraged to possess a sheltering tree; i.e. a man by getting married as early as possible. The traditional society still considers that marriage is the final aim of a girl's life. It is the destiny which is "traditionally offered to women by society" (Simone 148). Intellectual emancipation of girls is always frowned upon. In *The Dark Holds No Terrors*, Saru's mother does not want her to opt for higher studies. In *Roots and Shadows*, Indu states that her education and intelligence were always thrown at her like an accusation, "I had sobbed out my heart to old uncle one day. And he had said, "For a woman, intelligence is always a burden, Indu. We like our women not to think" (33). Deshpande's expressions underscore how women are trained to be feminine. Not only the systems of power and control, but also the practices generating social divisions promote a particular interpretation of culture. It reminds us of Simone de Beauvoir's comment that the true woman is "an artificial product that civilization makes, as formerly eunuchs were made. Her presumed 'instincts' for coquetry, docility are indoctrinated, as is phallic pride in man" (Simone 428).

Deshpande's novels suggest that women are taught to inculcate self-abnegation, passivity and self-effacement in order to suit the needs of men. Her protagonists yearn for overcoming it by studying hard and working (like Saru in *The Dark Holds No Terrors* and Indu in *Roots and Shadows*), yet the thought of its absolute contravention makes them feel guilty of deviating from their womanly duties as ascribed by society, generating an intense internal conflict. As a result, they embark on their married life with certain disadvantages.

In *Roots and Shadows*, the protagonist Indu is an educated and working woman. She is shocked to find that women, who toil under a gruelling routine all through their lives, prefer to mould their daughters into better women, and not better human beings with self-identity. Subtle conditioning moulds behavioural patterns of men and women alike. A woman is accepted to be meek, submissive, tolerant, as Mohan's mother and sister are. Their silence is taken as a token of their strength and intellectual accomplishment is thrown at a woman like an accusation. Deshpande vociferously portrays certain aspects of gender construction in her novels—inferior treatment towards girls, association of sin and ugliness with their growing age, emphasis on their preconceived feminine roles. Social ethos accepts that all women must adopt a particular social role, share similar characteristics. Such conditioning, coupled with certain other practices, generates diffidence among women, and does not allow them to nurture relationships on equal footing after marriage. Subtle practices also perpetuate it—in *That Long Silence* Jaya is renamed Suhasini after marriage, in *Roots and Shadows* Indu finds that the names of women are not mentioned on the family tree, in *Come up and be Dead*, Kshama is not allowed to perform her father's last rites.

The burden of social expectations forces women to remain silent. Silence and compromise are often a key to a happy marriage. In *Roots and Shadows*, Indu feels that an ideal woman should merge her identity into that of her husband. In *That Long Silence*, Jaya stops her serious writing as Mohan didn't like it. *In Small Remedies*, marriage fails as the husband is not able to tolerate his wife's adolescent involvement with some other person. Deshpande shows that in all marriages—conventional as well as unconventional—women try to adjust, tolerate forced sex and try to play the idealized roles of wife. Social conditioning is a double-edged sword. Among women it generates self-effacement and a tendency to unquestioningly accept their secondary status. Among men it consolidates the belief that such servile self-effacement among women is natural. This attitude sequesters the wife and the husband apart, negating any possibility of emotional attachment or psychological understanding.

The continued exaltation of self-effacing norms pressurizes women to accept the master subordinate relationship in marriage. Unacknowledged martyrdom becomes a part of wife's existence and hence the socially created gender creates an obstacle in the success of marriages. Deshpande's women, in order to please their husbands hide their desires and feel guilty for not being sufficiently womanly. However, abject submission generates frustration and anger among women. In her interview with Lakshmi Holmstrom, Deshpande talks about the suppressed anger in women which is very common in Indian society:

> I don't know, whether women have been very successful in concealing their anger, or whether men have simply closed their ears. This theme was very important in *That Long Silence*. The total lack of communication between men and women. For example, Mohan's utter inability to understand his mother's despair. He actually calls it courage. A young critic spoke to me once of the 'tone deafness' that Indian men have cultivated towards women. And that seems to me exactly right. (249)

In Deshpande's novels, we find a thorough illustration of the *Authoritarian Submission Syndrome* which has become a part of the collective consciousness of Indian women. The syndrome refers to a defence mechanism which is exhibited in the desire to be subservient to an exceptionally strong and superior role model to protect oneself in an intimidating condition (Leonard 609). For a woman, the role model is often a man, as the emphasis is on an exaggerated need to submit to some external power or control. The individual attempts to overcome humiliation and suppression by an excessively obedient attitude towards superiors. Other attitudes in this syndrome include extreme conventionalism, hard core cynicism and pre-occupation with power—traits commonly found among those sections of the Indian society which has been depicted by Deshpande in her novels. Voicing such sentiments Deshpande has remarked in her interview to Pallavi, given on 21 August 2001 at her residence in Bangalore, "But sometimes with the family we are not completely ourselves. Like I said, we are continuously restricted by our roles. I am so much the wife and mother here that I may not be able to express myself, my whole self." (252)

Deshpande boldly analyzes the epistemology of gender construction in Indian society, though her denouements suggest that women should not be straitjacketed into roles that wrap their personalities. Her women are conscious of retaining family ties. Her women are entangled in the complexities of their life, and face identity crisis. But their relationship with their husbands and family is valuable to them. Instead of rejecting these ties, they want to redefine them on an equal footing. Deshpande suggests through her fiction that a conducive social environment should be created so that women can develop their potential fully and men also can learn to avoid capricious imperialism.

Works Cited

Alsop, Rachel, Annette Fitzsimons, Kathleen Lennon, *Theorizing Gender*, USA: Blackwell, 2002.

Bem, Sandra, http://www.cnr.edu/home/bmcmanus/socialization. html

Beauvoir, Simone de, *The Second Sex*, ed. & trans. H.M. Parshley, London: Four Square, 1961.

Carmichael, Leonard, ed. *Introduction to Psychology*, New Delhi: Oxford and IBH, 1967.

Deshpande, Shashi, *Roots and Shadows*, New Delhi: Penguin Books, 1983.

Deshpande's interview with Lakshmi Holmstrom, "Shashi Deshpande talks to Lakshmi Holmstrom," *The Fiction of Shashi Deshpande*, ed. R.S. Pathak, New Delhi: Creative, 1997.

Deshpande's interview with Pallavi, "Woman's Journey from Self-Effacement to Self-Actualization," Ph.D. Thesis, "Shashi Deshpande's Feministic Concerns," pp. 231-72.

Jagger, Alison, "Political Philosophies of Women's Liberation," *Feminism and Philosophy,* ed. Elliston Braggin and Totowa English, N.J.: Rowman and Littlefield, 1977.

Nabar, Vrinda, *Caste as Woman,* New Delhi: Penguin, 1995.

Singh, Sushila, *Feminism: Theory, Criticism, Analysis*, Delhi: Pencraft International, 1997.

Male-Female Friendship: A Rejuvenating Factor in the Fractured and Restricting Bond of Marriage in the Novels of Shashi Deshpande

PALLAVI
Roorkee

As a feminist, Deshpande is in touch with the real implications of female roles. She has illustrated in her works that centuries-old man-dominated society does not let modern male ego accept the equality of sexes. Deshpande does not believe in following established theories and principles of feminism given by early feminist writers and critics. She believes that the problems of human life can be solved not by adhering to any particular theory, but by concentrating on nurturing positive relationships. Her stories and novels talk about human relationships against a purely Indian setting.

Deshpande has portrayed the violence and insensitivity of incompatible marriages with a rare insight in her novels. Yet she advocates a healthy participation in life by her women characters. In all her novels she has presented friendship between men and women outside the family framework as a rejuvenating factor. According to Shashi Deshpande, husband-wife relationship is always based on the principle of a master and a subordinate, and hence, it can never be truly friendly. A wife can never be her true-self in the company of her husband as she keeps on adjusting herself to suit the needs of her husband. A male-female friendship outside the bond of marriage turns each of them into a better human being as it provides them opportunity to be their true selves and ameliorate their personalities. All the female protagonists of Deshpande, Saru in *The Dark Holds No Terrors*,

Manju in *If I Die Today*, Indu in *Roots and Shadows*, Urmi in *The Binding Vine*, and Jaya in *That Long Silence*, have a male confidant in their lives. Deshpande has exposed the true nature of husband-wife relationship, which is always unquestionably taken as a cohesive social unit of a family by the society. She has pointed out that the society has never taken cognizance of women as equals to their male counterparts. Her novels exhibit that the emancipation of women is related not simply with rejecting the power of men, it also involves the transformation of existing power structures. The picture of devoted housewives has veiled the true image of stifled and pathetic women who want their family to acknowledge their existence as equivalents to men. Deshpande believes that the true-self of women can burgeon only in those relationships in which they are free from the domineering and dictating role of men. Such kind of relationship is seldom found within traditional marriages in the middle class society, while outside the domain of family life, it is considered to be a sacrifice for women. Deshpande views such relationships sympathetically.

Saru in *The Dark Holds No Terrors* discovers her true potential in her relationship with Boozie. Her relationship with Boozie, her professional mentor, is that of a student and a teacher. The timely help and guidance of Boozie helps Saru in the beginning of her career. To Saru, Boozie is, "the fairy godfather who could, with a wave of his magic wand, make things easier" (92). Manu never questions Saru for her growing intimacy with Boozie. Saru's financial help to the family and his inability to tackle the whole situation turns him into a sadist. Saru's better social position as a doctor destroys their marriage. In her relationship with Boozie, she for the first time experiences the charm of being an equal and discovers her existence as a human being which was denied to her as a daughter and wife. According to Shashi Deshpande, such kind of relationship gives men and women the chance to discover and accumulate their lost selves. She states in the personal interview about married women:

> Sometimes with the family we are not completely ourselves. Like I said we are continuously restricted by our roles. I am so much the wife and mother here that I may not be able to express myself, my whole self. It is very rare with a marriage partner. With a marriage partner if you are able to do that it's a wonderful marriage. There is nothing like that because then there is a freedom of both friendship and the intimacy of marriage, both combined in that. Many times it is not possible. So it seems to me that a husband can not be a friend most of the time. (2001)

Manju in *If I Die Today* faces identity crisis as well as disharmony in her marital life. Deshpande has presented a picturesque and realistic view of women's lives, amidst the chaotic atmosphere of modernity. What remains uppermost in our mind is the suggestivity with which the middle-age crisis of women is portrayed by the novelist. Guruji, who comes to the campus of S.D.M. College and Hospital as a patient of cancer, easily takes admission into the life of other people who reveal their hidden secrets to him. Manju recalls Guruji as "horribly frank and open about things" and "an enfant terrible in company" (8). She points out that he possessed "the gift of breaking all barriers, ignoring all formalities and approaching you directly as a human being. That, I think was what made all of us succumb to him finally" (9). Manju, the protagonist of the novel, wants to live a purposeful life. She discovers that she "was almost a redundancy at home" (14), when she becomes pregnant for second time. Communication gap exists in her relationship with Vijay, her husband. Though he looks after her, yet due to the growing silence between them, Manju concludes, "It was that detached kindness of a stranger" (43). The growing silence acerbates the relationship between them to the extent that even the altercations lose their existence in the marital life. Manju and Vijay restrict their lives to themselves and leave no space even for quarrels and disagreement. Manju resents her motherhood and blames it for chopping off her feathers of freedom. She has to leave her job of a teacher due to the complexity in her pregnancy which she loathes. At this juncture Guru explains to her as a friend, "But look . . . you spoke of sperm and the ovum . . . think of that marvellous timing, that beautiful precision . . . can you call the result an accident? No, Manju, there's always a meaning, a coherence. Only if you look for it, of course. The pity is one realises this too late" (11). Gradually Manju develops a healthy relationship with Guru. She recalls, "How did Guru become a confidant? I don't know. But from the beginning, it was as if I had always known him. I could say things to him I could to no one else. There was the time when I said to him a thing I hadn't admitted to anyone, not to Vijay, not even to myself" (10). This healthy relationship with Guru helps Manju examine her situation and the factors responsible for producing disharmony in her marital life.

Indu, the female protagonist of *Roots and Shadows*, represents modern, educated, middle class working women with independent mindset, capable and willing of making independent decisions. Indu is against the traditional modes of finalizing marriages which are not decided on the basis of compatibility. Since her childhood, she had perceived women performing their duties blindly. They toil throughout the day and their gruelling routine never allows them to recognize their true potential. She is shocked when she finds them moulding their daughters to become better women, and not better human beings with self-identity. She decides not to become their replica and works hard to achieve an independent stand. She marries by her choice and in the early phase of her marital life, Indu discovers an intimate friend in Jayant. Gradually she realizes she has lost her true self. She thinks, "Have I become fluid, with no shape, no form of my own? At that moment a savage truth had stared me in the face . . . without wants, there is no 'I'" (49).

Indu too unconsciously treads the path of the elderly women in her family which she has always resented. In the process of pleasing her husband, she hides her desires and emotions. In Indian society, it is the duty of a wife to love her husband which often proves fatal for her marital life as it destroys the companionship between them. Vrinda Nabar states: "There is another difficulty in the way of modern marriage, which is felt especially by those who are most conscious of the value of love. Love can flourish only as long as it is free and spontaneous; it tends to be killed by the thought that it is a duty. To say that it is your duty to love so-and-so is the surest way to cause you to love him or her" (1968: 95).

Indu also contemplates on her relationship with Naren, her old Uncle's grandson. She finds love, care and appreciation for her in Naren. He is a good listener and a confidant in whom she can confide. She discusses her emotional undulations with him, which were causing catastrophic effect on her psyche. She discloses to Naren the stifling effect of Jayant's demeanour, which looks at women, expressing their passions and emotions, as ugly and shocking. Many times, she was repulsed for her sensual approaches which fill her with shame. She deciphers her plight: "It shocks him to find passion in a woman. It puts him off. When I'm like that, he turns away from me. I've learnt my lesson now. And so I'm passive. And unresponsive. I'm still and dead." (3). The repulsive attitude of Jayant impregnates her mind with the thought that she is an impure woman. She concludes, "So that's all I am, Naren. Not a pure woman. Not a too faithful wife. But an anachronism. A woman who loves her husband too much. Too passionately. And is ashamed of it" (83).

Disturbed by her emotional upheaval, Indu establishes physical relationship with Naren. Her momentary physical gratification with Naren was not an outcome of sincere feelings, attachment or bondage between them. Indu finds that they have no "lingering feelings" (171) for each other and even the physical relationship fails to establish "new bonds" (171) between them. Still she decides not to tell Jayant about the infidelity committed by her. She concludes: "For that was not important. That had nothing to do with the two of us and our life together" (187). She knows that there are no genuine and strong feelings of love in her for Naren which may adversely affect her relationship with Jayant. She decides not to disclose her physical intimacy with Naren to him as he might not be able to understand its true nature. Deshpande believes in healthy human relationships between men and women which must be based on companionship, and not on subordination of women. Women continue to be the sufferers in almost all the situations they face as the social norms and moral codes have been so framed as to be particularly disadvantageous to them.

The novel *That Long Silence* observes that the traditional Indian setup finally blocks all escape routes from conventional social diktats unless women determinedly pursue a purpose in life besides domesticity. Women need to liberate themselves from the constraints of 'womanliness' which will erase the existing discrepancy regarding their marginalisation. Jaya, the female protagonist of the novel, has to endure an incompatible and traumatic marital life. She is one of those lucky girls whose upbringing is free from social conditioning. Jaya's carefree childhood has become a part of her existence, while her husband Mohan has a traditional male psyche with all its oppressive cruelty and insensitivity. Frictions occur soon. Mohan finds self-abnegation as strength in a woman as he has watched his mother suffering mutely and still carrying out her domestic affairs. In order to save her marital life from total collapse, Jaya submits before the hegemony of Mohan. Their relationship lacks companionship and Jaya is reduced to the status of a subordinate. Instead of love, care, affection and understanding, silence dominates their relationship. Jaya contemplates, "Like the chorus of Greek drama, we were distanced from suffering; for us there was just living—one foot in front of another, one foot in front of another, until death came to us in a natural form" (4). Jaya had always wanted to become an established and successful writer. Mohan objects to her stories, as her themes portray their marital life. He wants that instead of writing stories based on marital discord, Jaya should write popular articles on superfluous themes. Jaya accepts it in the hope that it shall impart permanence to her marriage. She becomes scared of penning down the stories that were in her mind because she had been scared, "scared of hurting Mohan, scared of jeopardizing the only career I had, my marriage" (144). Jaya remembers Kamat, her upstairs neighbour, who turns out to be her true friend. In Kamat's company her true-self can blossom. She pours out all her thoughts and desires to him. Silence and subjugation that play a prominent role in her relationship with Mohan are completely absent in her relationship with Kamat. In her interview, Deshpande comments on Jaya's relationship with Kamat:

> Jaya is very much aware that with Mohan she is Mohan's wife but with Kamat she is many things. She is that kid Jaya, a rebellious kid, she is a writer; she is a frustrated person who can not write what she wants to. She can be angry with Kamat. With Mohan she can not be angry because he does not like it.

Jaya reveals that it was Kamat who turns out to be her professional mentor. He acts as a teacher, a guide and never spares her writings that were full of flaws. Jaya's problems are gradually curtailed by her frequent discussions with Kamat. Though a good listener, he always condemns Jaya for her weaknesses. She is amazed to see that a man and a woman can reveal themselves before each other without feeling guilty. He asks her to overcome her inanities if she wants to succeed in her profession. He points out that she must overcome her complexes and stop posing as a deprived woman who has to toil like a slave, as this attitude was preventing her from pouring out her true self. Jaya's relationship with Kamat would have solved her puzzled marital life if he had remained alive. During one of her visits, Jaya finds him lying dead in his flat. Instead of paying her last tribute to him, she runs away out of fear of social criticism for maintaining intimate relationship with a man outside marriage. Deshpande has revealed conservative norms of the society that always permit only those relationships to a woman which follow the socially ascribed rules. A married woman is morally bound to her husband only. Deshpande supports healthy human relationships. She says to Lakshmi Holmstrom in an interview:

> But yes, I did bring in Kamat to serve a purpose: to show Jaya the kind of relationship that she could achieve with a man. She gets a kind of companionship with Kamat that she never gets from her husband. Yet that is marriage and this isn't. But perhaps I do realise that kind of relationship, the kind of companionship that is possible, although it is very rare. Often it is missing, because of the predominance of the sexual motif in India, within marriage. (247)

The Binding Vine meticulously presents the strongly knit bonds of human relationships in Indian society. Urmi, the female protagonist, is the only female character in the novel, who is free from social conditioning. She maintains an independent stand and does not rely on her husband. As an educated and independent woman, she analyses the complexity of a woman's life and concludes that even the bitterness of life does not kill the desire to live—may be Urmi wants to state that hope never dies. Urmi often longs for her husband's presence as he works for the Navy and often stays away from home. Meanwhile, Urmi meets Dr. Bhaskar and gradually they become friendly. Vanaa cautions Urmi for her growing intimacy with Bhaskar. Urmi contemplates:

> But how can Vanaa, secure in the fortress of her marriage to Harish, understand what it is like—marriage with a man who flits into my life a few months in a year and flits out again, leaving nothing of himself behind? Often, after he had gone, I find in myself a frantic grappling for his image, as if he has taken it away as well. (164)

Kishore's frequent absence often leaves Urmi's urge of physical gratification, unsatisfied. However, she never breaks the bond of fidelity even when she comes to know that Bhaskar is in love with her. She concludes, "It's so much easier, so much simpler, to just think of virtue and chastity and being a good wife" (166). In the company of Bhaskar she found herself expressing her true thoughts and desires. Bhaskar's growing inclination towards Urmi resists her to continue this relationship any further.

All the female protagonists of Deshpande try to acclimatize, adjust and compromise in their marital life. While going through the phase of transition and self-analysis, they conclude, "It is not that life is cruel but that in the process of our birth we submit to life's cruelty" (92). Thus in their marital life, they suffer due to their submissiveness, servile nature and also due to male chauvinism. As a novelist, Deshpande not only highlights the rigid doctrinal approach of Indian society towards women but also exposes women's habit of self-effacement which is the result of social conditioning. Her novels are an indictment of the male authority, discrimination, social conditioning and duality of moral standards which have victimized women for centuries. Though her novels are a collage of incompatible marriages, yet she advocates a healthy participation in life by her women characters. The void of friendship which these women find in their lives due to their husband's indifference to their desires and thoughts is filled by their male friends. The friendly relationship of the female protagonists of Deshpande with men is not a matter of choice or desire for them but a compulsion. She claims in the interview with the author that such relationship, "gives you a freedom to be yourself. I don't necessarily feel that it has to be an affair . . . . To me more than anything else it's the cheating aspect of these affairs that troubles me." She supports healthy relationship between men and women which is based on mental coordination. She also advocates inter-relationship of men and women into humanism. Deshpande's feminist vision is holistic and life-affirming and offers a fresh perspective on the problems of Indian women.

Works Cited

Shashi Deshpande, *The Dark Holds No Terrors*. 1980. New Delhi: Penguin, 1990.

_____, *If I Die Today*. New Delhi: Penguin, 1982.

_____, *Roots and Shadows*. New Delhi: Penguin, 1983.

_____, *That Long Silence*. New Delhi: Penguin, 1988.

_____, *The Binding Vine*. New Delhi: Penguin, 1990.

_____, "Shashi Deshpande talks to Lakshmi Holmstrom." Interview with Lakshmi Holmstrom. *The Fiction of Shashi Deshpande*, ed. R.S. Pathak. New Delhi: Creative, 1998, 242-50.

Interview with the author. "The Fiction of Shashi Deshpande: Women's Journey from Self-Effacement to Self-Actualization." Bangalore, 21 Aug, 2001.

Vrinda Nabar, *Caste as Woman*. New Delhi: Penguin, 1995.

Self-Identity in Shashi Deshpande's *Roots and Shadows*

F.A. INAMDAR
Aurangabad

The paper aims at interpreting Shashi Deshpande's first novel *Roots and Shadows* (Hyderabad: Disha, 1992) from the point of view of representing self-identity of the protagonist, Indu. In her, we find modern Indian woman who is trying to search out her own self: "Most of the lights were on" (1). That becomes the metaphorical indication that Indu is going to search out her self and the matter related to it and the image of the cobweb to be ultimately devoured by outmoded Hindu tradition. Significantly, the reader notices through Indu's eyes the cobweb: "The pattern of the cobweb was still incomplete somewhere inside it, there was a spider, painstakingly completing its work" (2).

It is a novel about the discovery of self and discovery of others too. During the morning of Mini's wedding, it is through Indu we come to know the two aspects of the personality of Kaka. While he is seen as a genial host at one hand, on the other, he is found out by Indu, when his mask comes off, when he is by himself, as a bewildered and lost man. Indu's awareness of wedding in general reveals what marriage was for her and what it is for all the Indian women in general. Marriage has nothing romantic about it. She realizes this after looking at the bridegroom of Mini who had "heavy coarse features and crude mannerisms" (3). The drab Indian wedded life is evoked by Indu: "What was marriage after all, but two people brought together after cold-blooded bargaining to meet, mate and reproduce so that the generation might continue?" (4)

Similar concept becomes a rooted obsession in the mind of the elderly people like Kaki for whom, "it was marriage that mattered, not the man" (5). Jayant sees in Indu the picture of Akka because to him she is indomitable. And she has her victims as Akka has one of them in Mini. In Mini, Indu sees her own self and the self of women in general: "The women had no choice, but to submit, to accept, and I had often wondered have they been born without wills, or have their wills atrophied through a lifetime of disuse?" (6) As T.S. Eliot evokes in *Four Quartets*: "old stone to the new building." So Indu has become a new woman, a new pillar, as it were against the old one which has been replaced by her. Jayant observes: "New pillars take the place of the old. You're a pillar now yourself don't you know?" (11) T.S. Eliot has rightly pointed out in *Four Quartets*: "our hope may be hope for the wrong thing, our thought may be thought for the wrong thing." Therefore, we are asked to wait without hope, without love, without faith, this neatly ties up with Indu's quest for self-identity. She desired to be loved and to be happy but she realizes that "such demands now seem to me to be an exercise of futility" (13). For here the moments of happiness are something, given and taken, in a lifetime's death in love. For her there is only an attended moment in and out of time as T.S. Eliot puts in *Four Quartets*. Therefore, Indu feels neither love nor happiness come to us for the askin~ But they can sneak up when we least expect them (13).

Her every confrontation with her husband becomes an occasion for the discovery of herself. Her plans to give up the job and take up writing are not liked by Jayant. These conflicts enable her to see her situation. She realizes that their lives are interdependent and her freedom is possible within the limits of the Hindu joint family system: "All things are connected. Yes, they are which is why no one can be completely free. Freedom has to be relative" (14). Significantly, she remembers her talk with her old uncle which shows her a way out of her predicament: "Why not, Indu? There have to be some rules so that life can have both dignity and grace. We can always find measures of freedom within these rules" (15).

She further recalls her old uncle's words loaded with meaning, "To fulfil one's obligations to discharge one's responsibilities, can one not find freedom within this circle?" (15) The idea of the 'the circle' and the concept of within these rules prefigures the web image which she notices on the morning of Mini's wedding. She, as a fly, is struggling to escape from the impositions laid down by orthodox society. Now the awareness dawns on her that her freedom can be achieved within the limits of rules and regulations imposed by the traditional Hindu society. Her initial failure as a creative writer glares into her face even though she wants to put on the mantle of the unacknowledged legislator of the world. She realizes: "It is not in me, the material of which revolutionaries are made, I no longer have desire to mould people to change them, to reform society. There is only one thing I know I can do—I can write" (15).

Further, her dependence and subordination to the editor and to her husband stares in her face when the story that she writes is not accepted by the editor, not only that, but she is called an idealist by the editor and her self is revealed to her: "I could have fought against anger, abuse, hostility. But I could do nothing against this ridicule. I looked at myself through his eyes and saw myself not as brave, but as foolish and naïve" (17).

Added to this, she mildly accepts her husband's verdict not to give up the job: "I went to Jayant and asked him if I should resign" (17). To that he replies: "That's life! What can one person do against the whole system! No point making a spectacle of yourself with futile gestures. We need money, don't we? Don't forget, we have a long way to go" (17).

Consequently, the trap of the womanhood and the spider's web come with a new import: '"Feeling trapped, seeing, myself endlessly chained to the long dusty road that lay ahead of me" (18). In the meanwhile, Akka's summon gives her an escape root from all this mess of subordination. In Akka's house she meets Naren who is instrumental in creating awareness in Indu's self-identity. He has taken a deep interest in her creative writing, through which he recognizes otherness in her personality as opposed to all other people in the novel: "The kind of writing you've been doing. I've my eye on you, young woman. I've read most of the things you've written" (24). For the first time Indu got excited and exclaimed, "how long was it since some had really talked to me? Talked about things as if he understood and cared? Reaching across the barriers I had built around myself" (24).

Shashi Deshpande rightly expresses Indu's identity when Indu realizes that she is incomplete without Jayant. Modern or otherwise, a woman can't be complete without her husband: "I had felt incomplete, not as a woman, but as a person. And in Jayant, I had found the other part of my whole self" 114-15). Indu puts on a show of self-survival. She plays hide and seek with her freedom and self-identity. This is revealed through her words:

> I had found in myself an immense capacity of deception. I had learnt to reveal to Jayant nothing but what he wanted to see, to say to him nothing but what he wanted to see, to say to him nothing but what he wanted to hear. I hid my responses and emotions as if they were bits of garbage. (38)

Through this, she becomes instrumental in submitting herself to the whims and fancies of her husband. Purposefully, she merges her identity in the identity of her husband: "Have I become fluid, with no shapes, no form of my own. At that moment a savage truth had stared me in the face—without wants there is No I am I On my way to becoming an ideal woman, a woman who loses her identity in her husband." (49)

Marriage to her after all is a trap or a cage where one's individuality and personality are neatly kept outside: "For Indu, marriage may be the comic strip version of marriage, a cage with two trapped animals glaring hatred at each other . . . isn't so wrong after all. And it's not a joke, but a tragedy. But what animal would cage self?" (61) Her concept of marriage as "glaring hatred at each other" is totally negative and derogatory. Through her conversation with Naren, she reveals that she writes like a man only because "I felt hedged, limited by my sex. I resented my womanhood because it closed so many doors to me" (79).

Her fear of femininity in creative writing is genuine. Because of this, fear scores of women have written their creative work under pseudonym. She suppresses her natural sexual urge only to please Jayant's attitude towards her: "And now I know. . . . It shocks him to find passion in a woman. It puts him off. When I'm like that, he turns away from me. I've learnt my lesson now and so I pretend. I am passive. And unresponsive. I'm still and dead" (83).

As a result of that, she thinks her life to be futile and she contemplates on giving him up: "sometimes I wonder if I will leave him one day and live by myself" (68). Indu discovers that she is an outcast neither belonging to Jayant whom she has left nor to the Akka's family that she has come to: "And yet I don't fit into the world I have left behind me, either, where then do I belong?" (102) Indu discovers that every woman is a world unto herself. She judges others from her own egoistic spectacles:

> I knew these women had their own standards for judging people. Nothing about me. . . . My academic distinctions, my career, my success, my money . . . none of these would impress her. To her I was a childless woman. To get married, to bear children, to have sons and then grandchildren, they were still for them the only success a woman could have. I had almost forgotten this breed of women since I had left home now, seeing them like discovering a new world. Each one of them riddled with ignorance, prejudice and superstition, was a world of darkness in herself. And even more amazing was their ignorance of their own darkness. It was almost superb. (116)

During Indu's discussion with Naren about women as reformers, she discovers what she lacks as a woman: "I knew in that instant what it was that my life had lacked, it was the quality of courage. I looked back in derision at myself and saw that courage had come to me only in rare moments of blind anger. But that was not enough; what I needed was steadfastness, and where would I get that" (150).

Indu identifies herself as a coward for continuing with Jayant in her loveless marriage. This trait has its roots in the traditional concept of the role of a woman: "You must accept everything, even defeat, with grace because you are a girl, they have said. It is the only way, they said, for a female to live and survive. And I . . . I had watched them and found it to be true. There had to be, if not the substance, at least the shadow of submission" (158). And her drab married life drags on because of her conviction:

> I had surrendered to him, step by step, I realize now that it was not for love, as I had been telling myself, but because I did not want conflict. The hideous ghost of my own cowardice confronted me as I thought of this. . . . That I had clung tenaciously to Jayant, to my marriage, not for love alone, but because I was afraid of failure. I had to show them that my marriage, that I, was a success, show whom? The world. (159)

Indu wants to escape from this kind of miserable existence but she is afraid of life and Shashi Deshpande is teased out of thought, and hence the readers are left wondering what lies ahead for Indu to set right her unhappy married life.

> I won't be like them. I won't live like them, and I thought . . . I've got away. But to what, Naren? To what have I got away? Is that any better than this? Is there no more to like than this? Are we doomed to living meaningless, futile lives? Is there no escape? I am afraid Naren. . . . I'am afraid. (160)

Finally, Indu as much as Shashi Deshpande, are confused and they fumble for clarity of vision of life: "How can I live without knowing what I want? I must know to live without fear, . . . Fear of being unloved, misjudged, misunderstood, displeasing without fear of failure, such a tall order!" (174)

The final vision that we got along with Indu is one of non-detachment from life and its problems. Indu cuts away all the uneven edges off herself and thinks herself to be free but not detached. Shashi Deshpande tries to escape her fictional burden of creating self-identity of Indu. Therefore, Indu says: "Yes the house has been a trap too, binding me to a past I had to move away from. Now I felt clean, as if I had cut away all the unnecessary, uneven edges off myself. And free. But not detached. I would, I knew, never hanker after detachment any more. . . . Detachment. . . . It was for the dead not the living." (186)

The Concept of Femininity in Shashi Deshpande's *Small Remedies*: A Study

GIRIJA NAMBIAR
Maris Stella College, Vijaywada

Thinkers and theorists have consistently expressed difficulty in defining the feminine. Most feminists use 'feminine' and 'masculine' to represent social constructs and 'female' and 'male' to denote biological aspects of sexual differences. In this usage, 'feminine' represents nurture and 'female' nature.

Feminism views femininity as a creation born out of patterns of sexuality and behaviour imposed by cultural and social norms. Hence Simone de Beauvoir's famous statement that one is not born a woman but becomes one and Julia Kristeva's contention that "woman as such does not exist."[1] A patriarchal dispensation imposes certain social standards of femininity on all biological women to foster the belief that the accommodating postures enjoined are natural. To be bold, assertive, independent and intellectual is to be non-conforming and therefore unfeminine and unnatural. In the traditional, patriarchal view, the terms 'feminine' and 'female' are interchangeable but to the feminist, women are female but they need not necessarily be feminine, in the traditional sense.

In a patriarchal world-view, it is generally assumed that a number of psychological traits are linked to sex. By an elementary classification, human qualities are divided into two classes corresponding to the division between male and female. Independence, rationality, and aggression are deemed to be male attributes while dependency, irrationality and submissiveness are female attributes. There is a stereotype of femininity in society that encompasses all the aspects of life from everyday conduct to education, employment, public life, art and literature. This stereotype of femininity also sets up norms for the girl child which influences her life plan and is instrumental in shaping her character.

All through Western history, man has been represented as reason, woman as unreason. If man is more spiritual, intellectual, morally good, woman is more physical, animal and sensual. Therefore, woman must be controlled and through this control man could hope to control the animal side of his own nature. Freud, the complete patriarch, accused woman of an inability to remove her instinctual demands in the interests of civilisation.

Feminists' counter claim is that when woman is totally excluded from 'civilisation' or the power and the rewards of community life, she will seek inclusion by the only means at her disposal: by the cunning use of her sexual attraction for men and by intrigue. Thus woman is hostile to the demands of civilization when civilization is totally masculine.

If this is the role of society, religion, too, has colluded in the marginalization of women. As Eva Figes argues:

> Religion is not only a way in which the male projects a vision of the world as he would wish it to be and expresses his attitude with regard to himself in relation to others and the universe at large, a voice he uses in order to lay down the moral law. Religion is in itself a male cult, and like initiation ceremonies, is specifically designed to exclude women and give the male a compensatory activity for the female one of childbearing.

The Judaeo-Christian view of women finds a close parallel in the traditional Hindu concept of women. Manu instructs men to make women dependent on them. Women are described as easily corrupted and need to be kept occupied. Their sexual instincts are uncontrollable and they are promiscuous by nature. They are unfit to be given access to the performance of Vedic rituals. Hindu mythology and socio-cultural traditions are replete with images of feudal gender-ownership.

Freud's psycho-analysis bases femininity on a negation, a lack, and attributes a number of psychological traits to a woman's constitutional disposition: modesty, vanity, inclination to envy and jealousy, lack of social conscience or social justice, a weaker moral sense, a limited urge for sublimation, a greater disposition to neurosis, a weaker sex urge and masochistic tendencies. To Alfred Adler, 'femininity' is a symbol for all those traits which in our culture obstruct social success: weakness, timidity, shyness, passivity, submissiveness and a sense of being marginalized.

Literature reflects socio-cultural reality. Women all over the world were always relegated to a secondary position in relation to men. Consequently, such is the image of woman reflected in literature. Western texts by male writers cast women in sexually defined roles as dutiful mothers or submissive wives. Alternately, they were categorized as bad, dominating seductresses or as prim, single women. Feminist critics are severe in their condemnation of the idealized image of woman projected by the so-called classics.

Femininity and its construction form the basis of contemporary Western feminist thought. Certain important shifts of perspective in the feminist approach to gender have resulted in a re-evaluation and valorization of the feminine identity and traditional 'feminine' attributes during the 80s. With the advent of cultural feminist movement, emphasis is placed on the positive value of 'feminine' qualities which include sensitivity, gentleness, the ability to cooperate and to nurture.

While the basic underlying principles of feminism in the West and the East are largely similar in that both aim at bettering the lot of women, the different historical and social contexts necessitate a socio-culture specific approach to women's fiction in India.

Among the novelists from the nineteen eighties onwards, women writers such as Nayantara Sahgal, Anita Desai, Gita Mehta, Shashi Deshpande, Githa Hariharan, Anita Nair, Manju Kapoor and Arundhati Roy have had considerable success in portraying woman as the protagonist in plots centred around issues such as female marginalization, marital discord, sexual suppression, alienation and the search for identity.

Shashi Deshpande's novels primarily explore experiences of oppression of Indian women in the domestic arena. These experiences are rooted, according to Deshpande, in the assumption that a woman is an inferior being who has to carry "the burden of being an unwanted female child . . . having to battle an ingrained, deeply entrenched patriarchal system—all of which give rise to problems specific to their sex."[2] In her portrayal of the Indian middle-class woman's existence in India, her early novels appear to prescribe a balance between traditional values of security and harmony, and the modern aspirations for an independent, individual self. Her women do not move out of their familial framework in their attempt to discover their potential as individuals. Urmi, the protagonist of *The Binding Vine* and the most overtly assertive of Deshpande's early creations, is secretly fearful of insecurity and abandonment by the husband. Sumi in *A Matter of Time* waits for her husband to desert her before she can think and act for herself. They remain bound to the outward norms of femininity prescribed by society. When Sumi is finally set to begin a new life of her own outside the family, she is killed, suggesting the inability of the writer as a woman to give her imagination free play and to break loose of the shackles of cultural and social codes. In her next novel *Small Remedies*, Deshpande appears to have overcome these reservations to some extent. This paper attempts to examine the representation of femininity in this novel in the light of these earlier depictions.

The story revolves around three women, Savitribai, a renowned singer, Leela, a socialist, and Madhu, the narrator. Savitribai is the pampered daughter of a wealthy Brahmin family. She inherits exceptional musical talent from her mother who encourages and teaches her. Married off as a young girl into a rich, joint family, she is enabled to indulge her love for music by the generosity of a music-loving, liberal-minded father-in-law, whom she dares to approach to plead her case in the first instance of the transgression of boundaries that is to mark her life. Dissatisfied with the "mundane domestic life she was leading,"[3] she braves the cruelty of the other women of the household, the habitual cruelty of the conforming towards the deviant, to pursue music. Repudiating her position as the daughter-in-law of an affluent family, she leaves the protection of the family circle to elope with Ghulam Saab, her Muslim tabla player, an act of religious as well as social transgression. Suffering and humiliation do not swerve her from her resolve to gain acceptance as a disciple of the guru of her choice. This takes her to the small town of Neemgaon where she grows from the despised "singer woman" to the admired doyen of Hindustani music.

Savitribai is, at one and the same time, a woman, an artist and a mother. She is a "woman in search of her genius, of her destiny. But the artist was born of the woman," (133) a woman in search of power and recognition, in the pursuit of which she abandons husband, lover and daughter. She chooses to forget:

> Bai's forgetting . . . is deliberate. She has drawn a line through Munni's and Ghulam Saab's names and erased them from her life. This is something she did long back, when she turned to respectability, when she began her journey to success and fame. Perhaps she thought that to attain these things this denial of her lover and daughter was necessary . . . the denial also made it possible for her to live with herself. (154)

This is part of the contradiction of her situation, a condition of which Janet Sayers comments, "Consciousness of the contradictions in which women are placed by virtue of their sex is the psychological source of their resistance to their social subordination."[4] There is the curious fact of her obliteration of her daughter's existence. Why, when she had the courage to walk out on her marriage and family, is she so frightened to reveal this truth? "She gave the child the name Indorekar—the name she adopted as a singer (from her mother's hometown Indore)—not comprising either her maiden name or her married one. Meenakshi Indorekar. Marking her out as her child alone, not the child of her lover." (168) In psychoanalytical terms, it is a renewal of ties with the maternal. As Luce Irigaray, in a penetrating discussion on the subject of a child's identity in the patriarchal order, comments:

> According to this order, when a child is given a proper name, it already replaces the most irreducible mark of birth: the navel. A proper name, even a forename, is always late in terms of this most irreducible trace of identity: the scar left when the cord was cut.[5]

The erasure of her daughter could be seen in terms of a rejection of the traditional concept of the feminine, which enjoins sacrifice and selflessness on the part of a mother. Irigaray cautions women not to submit to a desubjectivized social role—that of the mother, governed by an order subordinated to a division of labour—man produces/woman reproduces, thereby confining women to a mere function. Pointing out that fathers have never been asked to renounce being men or citizens, she asserts that women do not have to renounce being women in order to be mothers.

The second major woman character, Leela, is Savitribai's contemporary and Madhu, the narrator's aunt. She is a simple, poorly educated woman who has spent a lifetime working closely with the factory workers of Mumbai, an association formed through her first marriage to a factory employee. Though a deglamourized figure, belonging to a much lower stratum of society than Savitribai, the two are alike in their non-conformity. Leela is a rebel in a wholly conventional, tradition-bound family. Like Savitribai, she makes a cross-caste alliance in her remarriage to Joe, a prosperous doctor and a caring husband. Theirs is a union forged on understanding, despite differences of religion, language and interests. Leela, however, retains her identity as an individual, evident in her retention and return to her Maruti Chawl home after Joe's death. The pattern is a repeat of her move when her first husband died. She had refused to return to her parental home and had chosen, instead to carve a career for herself by "connecting" with the workers and their problems. In contrast is Sumi's return to her parents and the painful period of introspection before she is able to take the decision to seek a life of her own.

Like Bai, Leela too goes beyond the acceptable boundaries set for women, though less spectacularly. Bai's daughter disowns her and fantasizes about a conventional family and a make-believe father. Leela is childless. She does not pine for a child as the conventional barren woman is expected to. She is, however, the perfect "nurturing" mother to her orphaned niece, Madhu.

Madhu is linked to Bai through her childhood when she was her neighbour and friend to her daughter, Munni. Madhu has been commissioned to write a biography of Bai. The three women's lives are connected by a series of similarities and contrasts. Madhu's journey in life has been in the opposite direction from that of the other two women. Hers was an unconventional, motherless childhood in which the nurturing feminine role was fulfilled by a male servant and the loved father was not really cut out for conventional family life, being too "elegant" and "debonair." Her mother was not even an absence, "a tabula rasa" on which she could write what she wanted. What little she had heard of her hardly summoned up a "mother figure." As a child, she was struck, not by the drab, harried mothers she saw around her, but by the "glamorous" pearl-wearing mother of her friend, Munni. Their families are exceptional in Neemgaon in not conforming to the norms.

Madhu finds the warmth of an extended family, its rituals, festivities and ceremonies through her son, Adit. She also experiences the world of motherhood. In this new world, there are only the two of them, others being mere shadows. Even her husband Som occupies a space only on the periphery. All her happiness, all her moments of joy centre round him. As he grows, her world enlarges to include all who matter to him. She fears for him. She is overridden with anxiety lest he be left motherless, like her. Madhu is constructed in the conventional mould of the mother, the good mother of psychology:

> It's my baby's dependence that changes me; my place in the universe is marked out now. After the uncertainty, the indefiniteness of everything, . . . here is something . . . steadfast. It is I who am providing the certainty, the central pole of a whirling universe for this small human being, and at the same time, it is he who is keeping me there, making me into this stable figure. . . . His dependence fills me with delight, my power over him awes me. . . . Mother love is one of the great wonders of this world. (183-84)

She revels in the experience of motherhood. The pain, as his dependency decreases with the years, is unbearable until she recognizes it as "putramoha" and accepts her "delusion about motherhood—a small centre, a vast exclusion—I thought this was love." (144)

Sudhir Kakar, writing in the context of the Indian woman's attitude to motherhood states, "In the case of a Hindu woman, maternal feelings of tenderness and nurturance occur in combination with a profound gratitude and the readiness for a poignantly high emotional investment in the child."[6] Madhu's pain at her son's death is, therefore, expected. The pain, is, however, intensified by the feelings of guilt at having had a role in creating a situation that drove him from home.

Madhu had not expected Som's hostile reaction to her revelation, so many years after their marriage, that she had not been the "chaste, virginal bride" of his expectations. She had had a single sexual experience at the age of fifteen with her father's friend, in a peculiarly vulnerable state of mind. In her self-image she remains a "chaste" woman. She has no active memory of her teenage experience until certain unexpected events coincide to stir her memory and reveal the true identity and the ultimate of her lover. What is significant is Deshpande's projection of the incident. There is no attempt to depict the experience as an act of violence perpetrated upon an unwilling teenager. Instead, Madhu recollects that she had felt pleasure. She is made to feel no guilt. She expects understanding and acceptance from her husband. She is devastated by his violent reaction. The oppressive atmosphere which stems from this drives Adit from home to meet death in a bombed bus.

Deshpande raises the issue of female sexuality in *A Matter of Time*, too. The protagonist Sumi decides to write a play on Surpanakha, a feminine image shunned by tradition. In this choice, Deshpande presents her as the radical Other, that can offer hope against the patriarchal repression of women, much as feminist myth critics have done by projecting the most destructive women in Western mythology in terms of their power of resistance. But by killing Sumi before she writes the play, Deshpande stops short of this radicalism. Madhu's attitude in *Small Remedies* registers a much stronger assertion of female sexuality.

Shashi Deshpande does not see herself as a feminist though she admits that Simone de Beauvoir's *The Second Sex* was "like a flash of light."[7] Yet her treatment of concepts such as motherhood, female sexuality and social conformity, particularly in her more recent works, are in conflict with the traditional attributes of femininity. There is an insistent questioning of gender norms in her portrayal of women who break barriers and suffer in their desire for the "unfeminine" right to freedom.

NOTES

1. Julia Kristeva, *About Chinese Women* (London: Boyars, 1977), p. 16.
2. Shashi Deshpande, 'Demythifying Womanhood," Talk with Veena Mathews, *The Times of India*, 25 Sept. 1995.
3. Shashi Deshpande, *Small Remedies* (New Delhi: Viking, 2000}.
4. Janet Sayers, *Sexual Contradictions* (London & New York: Tavistock, 1986), p. 86.
5. Luce Irigaray, "The Bodily Encounter with the Mother," *Modern Criticism and Theory*, ed. David Lodge (Delhi: Pearson, 2003), p. 418.
6. Sudhir Kakar, *The Inner World* (New Delhi: Oxford University Press, 1978), p. 79.
7. Shashi Deshpande in an interview with Chandra Holm, *Indian Review of Books*, May-June 2000, p. 8.

Retrospection in Shashi Deshpande's *That Long Silence*

KAVYA B.
Mysore

Peering into the silent
with closed eyes
marching for that unseen
unheard, unconceived—before—thing
a living light appears
etching across my screen of darkness
so blazingly bright
my whole expose of consciousness is alerted

Paul Fericano, E.California

Shashi Deshpande is a distinguished and potential woman writer. She is careful to distinguish the 'natural' from the bourgeois in her early novels. A great stress is laid on natural favouring bourgeois i.e. to say both naturality and bourgeois class move hand in hand. The moods of her novels are primarily melancholic and self-conscious; its mosaic is mission towards individuality and self-awareness. Characters don't cling to their roots but undergo a transition to accept their shadow. Shashi Deshpande never tries to sympathize or idolize women but portrays them in a very 'natural' way. She is concerned with the integrity of the individuals who kill their individuality for the sake of others. It is all about those who let themselves loose for the sake of their family and in the course of time they come up and grow up.

Shashi Desphande has always voiced against the various forms of exploitation, humiliation and discrimination of women. She has used silence as a metaphor in painting the patriarchal Indian society. Silence is a patriarchal weapon given to women. Without any choice and courage, women have been clinging to it, unaware of the fact that silence would kill her one day silently. Shashi Deshpande's stories begin after marriage since marriage is the institution which affects women most in many cultures, the married lives of many heroines involve constant struggle to find freedom from their shackled lives.

Jaya, Indu, Saru are educated women who are aware of gender equality, egalitarianism, and yet lack courage to fight for their rights. Through the processes of thought, they change themselves and lead a meaningful life. The protagonists in the first group of novels, Jaya of *That Long Silence*, Indu of *Roots and Shadows* and Saru of *The Dark Holds No Terrors* after a moment of crisis isolate themselves, go to temporary exile and achieve Individuality by self-realization. Jaya is one of those heroines who are relieved from her monotonous work as they have shifted to their old Dadar flat in Bombay and even children go out for holiday. She is exiled with her husband Mohan to their old apartment as allegations of business malpractice are levelled against him and are to be investigated. While the future seemed to be in dire peril, Jaya takes retrospective account of her marriage and introspective analysis of her life. Through retrospection she recalls her days of suppression that demanded her sacrifice in writing and Kamat.

The calmness in Dadar flat triggers Jaya to look back at the events that have already taken place. She herself indulged in morbid retrospection. From seventeen long years of her life, Jaya allowed her family to possess her body and soul. She didn't think anything apart from that, thus she was a dedicated bourgeois woman. All had their lives but she gave up hers, she could neither express nor achieve anything. What a bourgeois woman gains from marriage in the words of Simone De Beauvoir is "a gilded mediocrity lacking ambition and passion, aimless days indefinitely repeated, life that slips away gently towards death without questioning its purpose." (1)

Jaya wanted to fit herself to the ideological mould of a traditional housewife though her innate sensitivity revolts against it.

Her married life was based on the foundation of compromise and commitment, not on love and mutual understanding. From the day one, she tried to do what exactly she was expected to do by her husband and of course by the society. She made herself a puppet in the hands of her husband and society. After marriage, Jaya is named 'Suhasini': "A soft, smiling, motherly placid woman. A woman who lovingly nurtured her family. A woman who coped with every solution to safeguard her family and whose sole intention in her life is to be good and serve her family by all means."

George Dmysdale in *The Elements of Social Science or Physical, Sexual and Natural Religion* (1854) says, "Marriage is one of the chief instruments in the degradation of women. It perpetuates the inveterate error that is the province of the female sex to depend upon man for support and attend merely to household cases and the rearing of children." Jaya was submissive and passive. She felt ashamed because she could not admire the classical music of Paluskar and Faiyaz Khan like her father. Her grandmother continuously reproved her inquisitive nature: "for everything questions, question for everything, a retort what husband can be comfortable with that?" When Jaya was betrothed, Vanitamami advised her that "a husband is like a sheltering tree" (137) and that "the happiness of your husband and home depends entirely on you" (138).

There are a set of rules and regulations for the woman—how she has to behave as a wife—but not for man as a husband. "A wife, obedient to her husband, renowned, light-footed, eloquent in speech, sympathetic to the patients, attains to happiness when she lives peacefully with her husband, and nicely cooks the food, highly efficacious, and grown through rain, conducive to our physical growth, brought daily in use, and relished by our ancestors." (2)

Balzac wrote in "Physiology of Marriage": "Pay no attention to a woman's murmurs, her cries, her pains. Nature has made her for our use and for bearing everything, children, sorrows, blows and pains inflicted by man. Do not accuse yourself of hardness. In all the codes of so-called civilized nations, man has written laws that require woman's destiny under this bloody epigraph "Woe to the weak." (3)

Jaya likes to see advertisements that precede a movie show, for they give her "the illusion of happiness." Since Mohan dismissed them as worthless, they start late and miss the advertisements. She never dared to confess it to him as she feared, "What if he too said, 'what poor taste you have, Jaya!'"

Over the years she learns to suppress her wishes and shapes herself "so resolutely to his despairs" that in the end she is left with no identity of her own, "just emptiness and silence." (144) Man can revolt against anything but he can't accept that from a woman. Even Holy Bible supports this. "A Woman should learn in quietness and full submission." (1 Timothy 2:11, NIV)

John Stuart Mill's major achievement though was to spell out with greater clarity than any previous writer the psychological pressures, which kept women in their traditional place; he spotted the indoctrination of sex moles. 'All women' he writes, 'are brought up from the very earliest years in the belief that their ideal of character is very opposite to that of men; not self-will and government by self control, but submission, and yielding to the control of others. All the moralities tell them that it is the duty of women, and all the current sentimentalities that it is their nature, to live for others; to make complete abnegation of themselves and to have no life but in their affection.'

John Stuart Mill in his book *The Subjection of Women* (1869) says that women have always hitherto been kept, as far as regards spontaneous development, in so unnatural a state, that their nature cannot but have been greatly distorted and disguised; and no one can safely pronounce that if women's nature was left to choose its direction as freely as men's and if no artificial bent were attempted to be given to it except that required by the conditions of human society, and given to both sexes alike, there would be any material difference, or perhaps any difference at all in the character and capacities which would have unfolded themselves. The fear to conform to the stereotyped model of ideal woman i.e., 'Suhasini' makes her restless and she is afraid to acknowledge her desires. In the process of becoming 'Suhasini,' she sacrifices her individuality. His desires and approval seemed to be the goal of her life. She was ready to change herself according to his choice. She cuts her hair, wears dark glasses. Ultimately Jaya gets so completely drawn in to the family fold that from fiercely independent woman she is transformed into the "stereotype of a woman: nervous, incompetent, needing male help and support." (76) She desperately clings to her husband as if her life depends on it. At times she is beset with the fear that something may happen to Mohan. Sita in the *Ramayana* asks him, "What would be the meaning of my existence? I could as well be dead. It will be a living death for me without you. I am alive only when I am with you."

> The thought of living without him had twisted my insides, his death had seemed to me the final catastrophe. The very idea of his dying had made me feel so bereft that tears had flowed effortlessly down my cheeks. If he had been a little late coming home, I had been sure he was dead. By the time he returned, I had, in my imagination shaped my life to a desolate widowhood. (96-97)

Her words clearly state that her value is found through him rather than through herself. Faithfully she followed all the edicts laid down by the women's magazines. She says, "They had been my Bible, and I had pored over the wisdom contained in them. Don't let yourself go. How to keep your husband in love with you. Keep romance alive in a marriage. The quality of charm in a woman." Jaya who clutches to the male chauvinistic ideas follows Vanitamami's words: "Remember Jaya, a husband is like a sheltering tree. Keep the tree alive and flourishing even if you have to water it with deceit and lies." (32) Looking up to him as a 'sheltering tree,' she had fallen into a false sense of security. Since husband is the protector, a woman should never complain or protest. Before her wedding Vanitamami's piece of advice is: "If your husband has a mistress or two, ignore it, take up a hobby instead—cats, may be or your sister's children."

Vanitamami's husband has several shoddy love affairs but she remains loyal to him. Mohan's mother does not protest, though her husband piles up humiliations upon her. Mohan's sister too suffers without complaining and the ovarian tumour kills her slowly. Jaya reports, "She sank in to a coma and died a week later, her silence intact." (39) These are the women who use their silence as a symbol of submission. Jaya after a visit to her in-law's house feels, "They had been a revelation to me, the women in his family. So definite about their roles, so well trained in their duties. I had never seen so clear, so precise a pattern before." (83) Jaya after witnessing them wants to conform to their pattern. Simon De Beauvoir points out: "Marriage is 'Woman's One Career,' that she is Angel in the home and that she would be spoilt if she left it." Jaya controlled her anger here after she realized that according to Mohan anger made woman 'unwomanly.' Being 'terrified' of his disapproval, she gradually developed womanly qualities. She began to be praised for these newly acquired qualities. Jaya says, "And when I had been praised for anything, I'd been so ridiculously pleased, I almost wag my tail, like a dog that's been patted by its master."

Nayana is ready to accept co-wife to remain in her husband's shelter. She tells her hubby, "Just you dare, let me see your coverage, take yourself another woman if you want, roll in the gutters, I can't prevent you, but just try to throw me out of this house."

Ever since her marriage Jaya was happy to follow in the footsteps of the mythological role model of Sita. She tries to compare herself with Gandhari: "If Gandhari, who bandaged her eyes to become blind like her husband could be called an ideal wife, I was an ideal wife too. I bandaged my eyes tightly I don't want to know anything. It was enough for me that we moved to Bombay; that we could send Rahul and Rati to good schools, that I could have the things we needed—decent clothes, a fridge, a gas connection, travelling I class." (61-62)

Jaya too sacrificed her creative writing for her insensitive husband. In the early years of her marriage, she was on the threshold of acquiring some merit. One of her short stories bags the first prize and is published in a magazine, which is about "a couple, a man who cannot reach out to his wife except through her body." Mohan thinks that the story portrays their own personal life, and he is very apprehensive of the idea that people may assume that he is the kind of person portrayed in the story. His words were enough to shut the door of her creative writing. She thinks, "Looking at his stricken face, I had been concerned. I had done him wrong. And I stopped writing after that." (144)

Even though she knew Mohan was wrong in his thinking she never dared to reason it out. Instead she turned towards popular writing and wrote for a Woman's Magazine under the pseudo name of Seeta (In Indian mythology, Seeta stands for total self-surrender. Sita and Savitri were strong and individualistic women but their energies were directed not towards self-liberation but towards the welfare of their husbands).

Mohan's actions before and during the sex are so typical that Jaya can predict them. Each time he asks her the same question—did he hurt her? Then he falls asleep turning his back to Jaya. The communication between them ends with the business of intercourse. Even in her sexual life, Jaya is passive, submissive and yielding. While Mohan is callous, aggressive and self-centred. Ruskin remarks in his lecture "Queen's Gardens": "She must be enduringly, incorruptibly good; instinctively, infallibly wise—wise, not for self-development, but for self-renunciation: Wise, no that she may set herself above her husband, but that she may never fail from his side." (60) Jaya was shut within the "Cage of feminity" (Resomaric Tong 9) and was not permitted to think beyond her family. Her helplessness is worse than the deadly boredom of her life. In the desert of her loneliness, Kamat appears as an oasis.

Kamat, who is devoid of any ego, gives that status to Jaya. As Mohan aspired for, there was just physical link with him but she was intellectually linked to Kamat "a middle aged, bulky man" with graying hair. He was "structured to loneliness" (57) and gave warmth and company to Jaya. Jaya was indeed thirsty for that sort of love, affection and courage after her father's death and quite obviously got attracted to him. He had patience to analyze her stories, which got rejected from many publishers and gave ideas for the betterment of it. He teaches her how she could make them more forceful and hitting. (147) "I am warning you—beware of this 'Women are the victims' theory of yours. It will drag you down into a soft, squishy dog of self-pity. Take yourself seriously woman. Don't sulk behind a false name." (145) Kamat encouraged her like her father: "Spew out your anger in your writing, woman spew it out." (147) It becomes so difficult for Jaya that she says: "It became difficult for me to distinguish between him and Appa for a second. Jaya's comfort level with him is traced in her words: "It had been a revelation to me that two people, a man and woman, could talk this way. With this man I had not been a woman. I had been just myself Jaya. There had been an ease in our relationship I had never known in any other." (153)

Marriage is not an ultimate for the heroines of Shashi Deshpande. In fact, after marriage, they learn the truths of life. Boredom in marriage plunges them to isolation and extra-marital affairs. Kamat's concern towards her gave full scope to express the hidden feelings of her heart. She talks to him about everything, including her parents and his "full-blooded smile" encourages her to go on.

Kamat had made her feel that the spontaneous physical intimacy is natural and sets her free of guilty feeling. Occasional sex, with overwhelming urge, becomes a minor aspect of their relationship. His sudden death shocks her and she is heartbroken. But she turned her back to him, as she was keen to protect her marriage. "That night while having dinner I had thought someone I know is dead. I saw him dead. And I had been detached from that woman who had seen him remote from that experience." (157) This behaviour of Jaya highlights the plight of the so-called educated women still bound firmly by the shackles of tradition and convention. Her creative writing and her close association with Kamat are two glaring examples of Jaya's inability to seek her own identity.

Deshpande's heroines are traditional in nature and reason logically. Her characters are not from rustic or aristocratic society. The heroines of Deshpande are aware of the strength given to woman in a traditional marriage and they refuse to come out of that frame. But at the same time they are unhappy and confused about their roles and the expectations placed upon them by a patriarchal society.

NOTES

1. Simone de Beauvoir, *The Second Sex*, trans. and ed. H.M Parshley (1953; rpt. Harmondsworth: Penguin, 1983), p. 447.
2. From *Yajur Veda*, Chapter XXXIII, Verse 59, trans. Devi Chand.
3. Qtd. Simone de Beauvoir, p. 255.

Introspection in Shashi Deshpande's *That Long Silence*

KAVYA B.
Mysore

Shashi Deshpande's novels are exploration of the truths in relationship of married women. In exploring the depths of human mind, she seems to come across many dark and unexpected corners. *That Long Silence* is one of her classic novels. Jaya who evolved as a silent endurer is subjected to revolution in her attitude. The long pregnancy (17 yrs) of Jaya's silence is delivered to an awareness of identifying herself at the end.

That Long Silence is the story of woman, who led her life being invisible and an outsider in the family. Later she ventures on the journey of self-realization and is haunted by the question "who am I"? Jaya explores a New Woman within herself.

Jaya in her Introspection tries to come to grips with a series of truth about her in the silence of Dadar flat and begins to erase the long silence begun in her childhood. She tries to define her identity and selfhood. Jaya who is set free from her routines is puzzled and frightened in Dadar flat. There is gradual change in her thoughts and she is at the edge of a split personality.

> Looking through these diaries, I realized, was like going backwards. As I burrowed through the facts, what I found was the woman who had once lived here Mohan's wife, Rahul and Rati's mother. Not myself. But what was that 'myself'? (69)

Indira Kulshreshtha says: "Generally, a woman's identity is defined in terms of her relationship with man as daughter, a wife and a mother; it means virtually a woman doesn't have any identity of her own." (1) Jaya admits that she did not disclose her true feelings in the pages of the diaries: "Its essential core had been left out. The agonized cries, 'I can't cope, I can't manage, I can't go on—had been neatly smothered.'" This is the first encounter with her real self.

Jaya's father was a source of inspiration; his encouraging words were motivation in her life and she followed his words. She was full of queries, had no affection towards her mother. Her father pampered her, it is he who named her Jaya and often repeated: "Jaya for victory." It is after his death that Jaya's life gets shattered. Somehow she manages to complete her graduation and gets married to Mohan immediately as per the desire of her uncle. Jaya, who was dancing to the tune of her father, later on started dancing to the tune of her husband. She willingly got acquainted to the role of a typical housewife. To please her husband, she transforms her appearance to suit his idea of a modern woman. But she was shocked by Mohan's definition of love. "First there's love, then there's sex that was how I had always imagined it to be. But after living with Mohan, I had realized that it could so easily be the other way round." (95)

Her married life was an unhappy one, with Mohan it is mostly "a silent, wordless love making" (85). She was romantic and Mohan's physical encounters failed to arouse any emotional link between them. "I could stay apart from him without a twinge." She says, "I could sleep with him too without desire" (97). Jaya puts her relationship with Mohan in these terms: "Ours has been a delicately balanced relationship so much so that we have even snipped off bits of ourselves to keep the scales on an even keel" (7).

Jaya who blindly got suppressed like a dumb animal, given a chance to think about herself, says, "To know what you want . . . I have been denied that. Even now I do not know what I want." (25) Jaya had an illusion of happiness. She accepts that she should let that illusion go. "I had to admit the truth to myself that I had often found family life unendurable. Worse than anything else had been the boredom of the unchanging pattern, the unending monotony." (4)

Jaya on her way of introspection is aware of the essentials of the critical analysis and self detachment and says, "Self revelation is a cruel process. The real picture, the real 'You' never emerges. Looking for it is as bewildering as trying to know how you really look ten different mirrors shows you ten different faces."

Jaya always expected a change she had sighed for a catastrophe, a disaster that could pull her out of dull routine. Jaya expresses her exile: "The truth was that we had both lost the props of our lives. My own career as a wife was in jeopardy. The woman who had shopped, and cleaned, organized and cared for her home and her family with such passion . . . where had she gone? We seemed to be left with nothing but our bodies, and after we had dealt with them we faced blankness. The nothingness of what had seemed a busy and full life was frightening." (24)

Both Jaya and Mohan face the crisis in their lives and they react to the crisis in a different manner. Mohan becomes restless and unsettled, away from his routine work. He is caught in the web of insecurity and is thoroughly confused. Even Jaya's sense of security is shattered with Mohan facing an enquiry. She had looked up to her husband as a 'sheltering tree.' Her self-analysis revealed her own flaws and she gradually prepared herself for facing the truth.

Jaya received a rude shock from Mohan, which shook her very existence. He accused Jaya that his malpractice was for her and her children's comfort. His blurt forced her to face the hard reality that she wronged herself by remaining silent about Mohan's activities. He said, "It was for you and the children that I did this. I wanted you to have a good life; I wanted the children to have all those things I never had." (9) Mohan's ego was hurt by Jaya's silence and it provoked him to blame her for his mistakes. It is apparent here that the portrayal of the image of the *serpent* as a mirror of Eve was common in earlier *iconography* as a result of the identification of women as the source of human *original sin*.

Sudhir Kakar says: "Super ego, the moral agency is weakly differentiated and insufficiently idealized in Indians. But in the West, an individual's behaviour is constantly regulated by the proscriptions of the Super ego, in a Hindu it is communal conscience comprises family and jati norms, it is a social man individual format. For an Indian, there are many external 'watchmen' to patrol his activities, relationships especially in all social hierarchies. It is this importance of relationships that rule the life of an average Indian, rather than the importance of healthy social values."

Jaya's crisis leads her to self-analysis. In the solitude of the Dadar flat where she was free from her daily routine, she found that "the ghost most fearful to confront is the ghost of one's own self." Jaya feels she was neither good wife nor good mother; she was not able to balance her life. She was disappointed from all sides of her life; she was unsuccessful even as a writer.

She rejects 'Suhasini' in her equating Suhasini to the sparrow in the story of the crow and the sparrow. She says, "I have a feeling that even if little boys can forget this story, little girls never will. They will store this story in their subconscious, their unconscious or whatever and eventually they will become that damnably, insufferably priggish sparrow looking after their homes, their babies . . . and to hell with the rest of the world. Stay at home, look after your babies, keep out the rest of the world and you're safe. The poor idiotic woman Suhasini believed in this. I know better now. I know that safety is always unattainable. You're never safe" (17). This realization of Jaya is the milestone for self-recognition.

When Mohan bursts out, Jaya is not able to utter any word. She tries to analyze her silence: "The job I wanted to take, the baby I wanted to adopt, the anti-price movement I wanted to take part in. But even as I listed these to myself, it came to me that perhaps it had nothing to do with Mohan, the fact that I had done these things, that I had left them alone. Perhaps I had not really cared enough about these things myself. Instead I said and my choice sounded sullen even to me, 'I have done everything you wanted me to.' And now, I thought, I must add: 'I have sacrificed my life for you and the children.' But real bitterness clawed its way through this self-mockery and I was conscious of having been chained to his dream." (120)

When Mohan left her alone in Dadar flat without any trace of returning, Jaya tried to realize what she had done. (122) "I have failed him. He expected something from me, from his wife and I have failed him. All these years I thought I was Mohan's wife, now he tells me I was never that, not really." (185) The theme of madness is linked with the theme of self-identity. Kusum goes mad because of pressure from her in-laws for not having a 'son.' In her troubled state of mind, Jaya identifies with Kusum and says, "Thank God, Kusum, you're nuts I had thought complacently; because you are nuts, I know I'm not I know I'm sane." (126)

Jaya confesses her creative self, now she feels disgusted by her false writing. "She [Seeta] had been the means through which I had shut the door, firmly on all those other women who had involved my being, screaming for attention; women I had known I could not write about because they might—it was just possible—resemble Mohan's mother or aunt or my mother or aunt." (140) Now she realizes all this happened because of her own idea of becoming an ideal woman. "Mohan had not forced me to do that kind of writing. I'd gone into it myself. With my eyes wide open." (148)

Detached from her family, Jaya was able to question her inner self and get answers. She experiences mental pain and confusion. Her sense of confusion and turmoil meet her, with brutal force. In Adele King's Words: "In a self-referential parody Deshpande makes Jaya a writer of woman's magazine fiction. In Jaya's stories they lived happily ever after although she knows the falsity of the view of life. Also the mixture of surrealism and fantasy in some of the experiences the writer undergoes is an important aspect of the making and unmaking of fictions in *That Long Silence.*"

Jaya's self-analysis reveals her the real fact that she lacked courage and right of making choice. "The truth is that it was Mohan who had clear idea of what he wanted; the kind of life he wanted to lead, the kind of home he would live in, and I went along with him. But I cannot blame Mohan, for even if he had asked me what do you want?—I would have found it hard to give him a reply." (9)

When she is in this deep thinking, Maitreyee comes to her mind who so definitely rejected her philosopher husband Yajnavalkya's offer of half his property. She asked him: "Will this property give me immortality. 'No,' he said and she immediately rejected the property. To know what you want I have been denied that" (25). Jaya feels if Mohan is a sinner, then she too has to accept herself as one.

At last Jaya realizes that she has to make a choice of her own to assert her individuality. Maitreyee made a choice of her own. Shri Krishna told Arjuna that he himself would have to make his choice. Yatheechasi tatha Kuru—'Do as you desire.'

Jaya's final choice is to erase the silence. "If I have to plug that 'hole in the heart.' I will have to speak, to listen; I will have to erase the silence between us. While studying Sanskrit drama, I'd learnt with a sense of outrage that its rigid rules did not permit women characters to speak Sanskrit. They had to use Prakrit, a language that had sounded to my ears like a baby's lisp. The anger I had felt then comes back to me when I realize what I have been doing all these years. I have been speaking Prakrit myself." (192-93)

Jaya at the end realizes that she is the one who can help her in despair. She struggles alone with the trauma and emerges victorious. Finally she comes to terms with herself and her position. She realizes, "The panic has gone. I am Mohan's wife. I had thought, and cut off the bits of me that had refused to be Mohan's wife. Now I know that kind of fragmentation is not possible." (196)

Jaya, Jeeja, Mukta, Vanitamami, Vimala and her mother's story depicts the plight of Indian women. It shows how the prescribed norms of society are encoded persuasively in the female consciousness and her failure to surmount orthodoxy. Mirra Kumarvsy states that the source of inconsistency lay with society itself and not with the individual women analysed in her study. According to her, the remedy for the solution is not in individual therapy but rather in social reconstruction. The fault is with the actively cruel social environment, not with her. (2)

Nature does not force woman to assume a position inferior to man. Modern woman in India is able to select her career rather than marriage as her career. Jaya is very much keen in satisfying the matrimonial responsibility assigned to her and Mohan predictably displays the Indian male's Ego. Writing in the 1950s Simone de Beauvoir writes, "Marriage incites man to a capricious imperialism." (3) Man wants to dominate woman, it is universal and our traditional marriage provides ample opportunities for this. Husband wants his wife to be patient, always suffering, ever faithful, ever-pure wife. If she fails in any of these then as a husband he forces violence on her to tame her like an animal. Evelyn Cunningham rightly says: "Women are the only oppressed group in our society that lives in intimate association with their oppressors." (4)

Jaya always looked at Mohan and herself as two bullocks yoked together but now she rejects that image and says, "I have always thought—there is only one life, no chance of reprieve, no second chances. But in this life itself there are so many cross roads, so many choices." (192)

Jaya is ready to face the reality and with her changed attitude she is optimistic in her views and says, "we don't change overnight. It's possible that we may not change even over long periods of time. But we can always hope. Without that, life would be impossible. And if this is anything I know now it is this: Life has always to be made possible." Clare Boothe Luce rightly says, "Because I am a woman, I must make unusual efforts to succeed. If I fail, no one will say, 'She doesn't have what it takes.' They will say, 'Women don't have what it takes.'" (5)

At the end it is very clear that the protagonist is ready to compromise with her life. It seems that the heroines of Deshpande are aware of the strength given to woman in a traditional marriage and they refuse to come out of that frame. But at the same time, they are unhappy and confused about their roles and the expectations placed upon them by a patriarchal society. Since ages, Indian men have taken the responsibility of Indian women in terms of social security, economic security, protection of women from criminals by sacrificing their own self, whereas the Indian women have only taken the role of "abala nari." But in the 21st century, Indian women are no more "abala nari" or "forced to wear only Sari," they are as equal to men in every respect including refusal to wear Sari. (6)

Jaya is reminded of lemmings, which rush down to the sea and drown themselves. For women, marriage is a sea of suffering where they drown themselves in pain. According to Deshpande, there is no escape from being caught in the web of relations. In an interview, she said to Vanamala Vishwanatha: "It's necessary for a woman to live within relationships. But if the rules are rigidly laid that as a wife or mother you do this and no further, then one becomes unhappy. This is what I have tried to convey in my writing. What I don't agree with is the idealizations of motherhood, the false and sentimental notes that accompany it." Jaya is hopeful after many years of bitter conflict and with glimpses of hope Jaya has positive signs in her life. Jaya who is a typical Indian woman rejects to come out of the dogmas of married life but what is more important is that now she is ready to face the challenges living with her demanding husband. She readily accepts her flaws and comes out of her depression. Deshpande's protagonists gain triumph not only as a woman but also as human beings. Jaya realizes her power as Roseanne Barr says, "The thing women have yet to learn is nobody gives you power. You just take it." (7)

As Shashi Deshpande herself calls her creations as "thinking characters," they undergo self-examination or introspective analysis of their life. She portrays how a woman is sandwiched between rigid traditional norms set by the society and modernity.

NOTES

1. Indira Kulshreshtha, "*That Long Silence*," *Women in the Novels of Shashi Deshpande, A Study*.

2. Mirra Kumarvsy, "Cultural Contradictions and Sex Roles," *The American Journal of Sociology*, 52 (November 1956), pp.184-89.
3. Qtd. Simone de Beauvoir, *The Second Sex*, trans H.M. Parshley (London: Four Square Books, 1961), p. 6.
4. www.quotegarden.com/feminism.html
5. www.quotegarden.com/feminism.html
6. Save Indian Family's meeting with "Youth for Equality," on 24/02/2007 on the role of women in the promotion of gender equality.
7. (www.quotegarden.com/feminism.html)

The Fiction of Shashi Deshpande: Woman's Journey from Self-Effacement to Self-Actualization
An Interview

PALLAVI
Roorkee

Pall: Your themes and ideas revolve round the dilemma and conflicts of Indian women who are mostly middle class, urban, educated and working. Still you have denied to be branded as a feminist writer. Why?

SD: The fact that a writer writes about women does not necessarily make her a feminist. I am not denying my feminist principles; I have been a feminist and continue to be a feminist, but when I say I am not a feminist writer, I mean that I do not use my novels as a tool to propagate feminism. Any artistic work becomes flawed if you try to use it as propaganda. What you do in a novel is to show life through a certain perspective. Now my perspective is bound to be a feminist perspective. I will be giving you a kind of vision, a point of view which you may not get from somebody else who does not have feminist principles. At the same time I do not say that feminism is good, or that this is feminism. I am pursuing the complexities of human beings. However, much of a feminist one may be, one is really a human being and all those complexities are in us. This is what I mean by saying that I am not a feminist writer.

Pall: But it can be branded as a feministic writing?

SD: It cannot be. I would be quite offended, because then you limit my writing. Once you say I am a feminist writer, you are putting some sort of a boundary, an edge around my writing which means that there is nothing else. I deny it very strongly. My writings are not limited in that way. It is about human beings and it is ultimately universal. You know human beings are the same everywhere. Like I said, feminism has given me a certain perspective, a vision which to some extent is bound to come into my novels. Now who would notice that in a family tree the names of women are not there at all. One takes it for granted. But, you know, for me it is important. Now that is the feminist way of thinking. It gives you a vision of how life should be, but it does not mean that life is like that. Life, as I have presented it, is all muddled and all of us have certain different ways of thinking and with so many complexities. So, when you write a novel all these things come into it. It's not one clear line of feminism. No novel can be a good novel if you do it that way.

Pall: Feminism talks of providing women with education and economic independence in order to liberate them from the conventional, oppressive mores of the society. Do you think these two are really related with each other because most of your female protagonists, despite having economic independence, find themselves entangled in the web of female world and also get exploited within marriage, as you have displayed in your novel *The Dark Holds No Terrors*? Do you treat economic independence as a precondition of emancipation, as most of your protagonists are economically independent?

SD: Certainly. I consider economics as a very strong motivating force in human life. Ultimately everything boils down to money—that's the bottom-line. But at the same time, it is not enough for women to be educated and economically independent. You understand that society consists of all kinds of people, so even if I liberate myself it is not enough because the world also has to be liberated to allow me freedom to live within it. That is where the problem lies. All my novels are concerned with liberating oneself.

It doesn't go beyond that, because that is where I stop, that a person ultimately liberates herself from most constricting factors. Economic independence and education are two parts of it which are very important of course. But there should also be a desire to go beyond what you see and reach the truth. Conventions have given us a certain vision of things, but we have to go beyond to the stark truth, like Jaya in *That Long Silence*, she goes beyond these relationships, husband and wife, mother and daughter, brother and sister and goes to the truth of these relationships. You are free only when you've seen the truths. Education and economic independence are the tools. They can help you, they may not, you may be both educated and economically independent and you may still be bound and wrapped by conventions and brainwashed by the centuries of conditioning. There may be this desire to stifle yourself because you have to live with other people. I have to live with my husband, I have to live with my parents, I have to live with my family. So you keep on cutting bits of yourself to fit into what they expect of you. To me it is more important to liberate yourself but even after that you are still living in a society where everybody is not thinking the way you are. It does not necessarily mean that you are going to be free, but then you are able to at least take the first step, which is for me always the most important step.

Pall: So it is the first step towards emancipation?

SD: First step, absolutely.

Pall: Your concept of feminism suits to the Indian environment and social milieu. Your novels propagate the emancipation of women both intellectually and physically while remaining within the family frame and relationships. Thus it is often said that you are not a hard core feminist. How will you differentiate your concept of feminism from other contemporary writers like Shobha De and Anita Desai? Anita Desai has produced neurotic women characters in her novels and Shobha De's women lose their morality in search of self-identity. Marriage to them is a convenience rather than an emotional and psychological attachment as it is in your novels. Do you consider their writings influenced by the western feministic ideology?

SD: I would not rather comment on other people's writing. I mean, there is Shobha De whom I have not read at all. Anita Desai I have read but I would rather not comment because I think it would be very presumptuous of me to speak of other people and what they intend. I am not a student like you who would study their writings. I just read like a casual reader. I can only speak of my writing. Again I repeat that my kind of feminism is what I am writing about and it does not mean either living within the family or living outside the family or living away from it and certainly it does not mean hating men. It means better human relationships and I think this is what has been denied to women so far because you have to live as a subordinate, you have to live as a subject, you have to live as a slave, you have to live as a tool—as a tool to bear children. And none of these are conducive towards good human relationships—not even with other women, because, you know, slaves are not always united by their slavery; on the contrary there is a lot of bad feeling among slaves. So for me better human relationship is what feminism is all about, which definitely includes relationship with men. You can only have better relationship with an equal. For this reason men should also be feminists, because they also have to understand that feminism will give them a better quality of relationship with a woman. A man may imagine that it is nice to have a woman whom he can order about, but he is bound to lose out on companionship. So my idea of feminism is a better quality of all human relationships. To me, the family is important because there is nothing else to replace it. Marriage itself—I am not hundred percent convinced that it is the best arrangement. As a social arrangement, I have my doubts about it. But the family is a very good kind of an institution, because human beings do want to live among other human beings. We cannot survive alone. I think the family is the best we have at the moment. I don't want to give it up. So for me it is very important that any kind of 'ism' which we evolve should not break up a family. I don't agree with this idea that joint family or what you see in these stupid T.V. serials is the best—I mean, everyone staying together. I think these are forced arrangements where things don't work. I would call a family a loosely knit group of people who have many links and ties and are supportive of one another. I think feminism to me is something where women are not all the time suppressing themselves and making themselves less than what they are because they are so afraid of men being antagonised by their competent selves. We are afraid to show our real capabilities because men feel threatened by women. So I think feminism involves men also. I realize that it is very important to include men in feminism. I think that the greatest failure of feminism is that it has not been able to involve men. It has alienated men. They have made men feel that this is a movement which is going to threaten them which is not correct. It is a movement which means better human relationships.

Pall: I think without the support of men it is not possible for women to go beyond the cultural mores.

SD: Men need the support of women and women need the support of men. And we need each other very badly because in this world we are all living together. I would not say that women should be active and men should be supporting. No, I think they are both in it together, equally together only then it will work. So that is my kind of feminism. I do not know which kind of feminism Anita Desai's or Shobha De's is. My feminism certainly does not mean promiscuity. This is not out of any puritan or moral thinking. There are people who are much happier having many relationships. I don't call that feminism. There are some women who want to stick to one man even if he kicks them or beats them. But if a woman has a choice and she prefers to stay with one man—that's her individual choice.

Don't call that an 'ism'. So I differ from people who feel that feminism means loose morals, hating men or giving up the family. No it's not at all that way to me.

Pall: Betty Friedan's *Feminine Mystique* insists on treating women as "human." Simone de Beauvoir's *Second Sex* has elaborately and graphically exhibited various stages of a woman's life and the limitations associated with it. These feministic concerns are visible in your works also. You have mentioned in an interview to Vanamala Viswanatha that the writings of Germaine Greer, Simone de Beauvoir etc. "stimulated" you. Have these writers helped you in moulding your feministic thoughts?

SD: Well the funny thing is, like I told Vanamala that time, that I didn't read these books early. I read these writers much late. I had not even heard of the word feminism until a neighbour of mine in Bombay gave me Simone De Beauvoir's book and then somebody else gave me Betty Friedan and then somebody gave me Germaine Greer. By that time my own ideas had become obvious to me. I had some gaps which I filled up from my own personal life and what I saw around me. Some kind of dissatisfaction with how things were and dissatisfaction with the role which I was supposed to play as a woman. For me it was that which really mattered. It was only later that I got the language for my feelings from reading these books, but the ideas were within me. Of all the books, Simone De Beauvoir's book influenced me the most. I don't think that these books influenced my novels because my novels don't come out of books, nor do they come out of theories. They come out of people. But these books did influence me as a person. They coloured my ideas. My ideas about feminism were clear to me, except that I did not even know the word feminism. It took me sometime to realize that there was a movement like that. I was troubled by these ideas, but the climate was totally different in late 60s. I got married in 1964. In late 1960s and very early 70s feminism still had not entered India. I think it would be 1975—the International Year of Women—that for the first time a lot of things were out in the open; so until then these things were not so much talked about, not so much mentioned. Even in magazines like *Femina* you always find stories of girls falling in love, romantic stories. I could never write like that. I could never write romantic stories. It seemed to me so false because I could see the reality behind these things and there is always this disparity. That was the time when feminism was not really much spoken about and certainly in India it was very muted. It was not loud. For me I had to get it through my own life and I felt a confirmation of my ideas through these books. So it was like a confirmation of my own feelings. Though of course the way Simone De Beauvoir put it was mind blowing. To me that book really was something; it opened a whole world to me. I mean, I am very grateful to her. I may not agree with all that she is saying, but she has very meticulously, carefully analysed what being a women is. And so many of us can identify with what she is saying. I used to see Hindi movies and read books and stories, say of Rabindranath Tagore, wherein you will always have women sitting and serving a man. If he eats, he is doing her a favour by eating. If he wants to please her, he will say, "Ma, I am hungry," and I used to think—are these real? When I got my own children I had the same problem again. They tell you so many things about being a mother but is it all real? Am I feeling these things because I have been told about them? I was able to really go beyond what I was told and I think this really was what took me to these writers.

Pall: Social archetypes regarding the status and behaviour of women have seeped into the life of the Indian people and girls are advised to imitate them. This phenomenon is exhibited in almost all your novels. With the growth in industrialization and women seeking independence how much relevant it is in your opinion to follow these archetypes in the present scenario?

SD: I think any archetype should be looked at very suspiciously. All these mythological stereotypes that we have now and what people keep telling you about Sita, Savitri and Draupadi—how do we know who these women are? They are creations made for a certain purpose. I am not saying that there is nothing real about them. They are very real. Our *Mahabharata* is a wonderfully real book. But the men were the main characters in these myths and the women were kind of props. They filled certain places which were important for women to fill. So if women are expected to behave like that today, it's very false because today's world is an altogether different world. Also we are individual human beings. We have come to this world with some unique qualities. The qualities that I have nobody else has and the quality you have nobody else has. Then why should we try to be somebody else? To me again feminism comes to the same point that I have to explore my full potential. Every human being whether it's a man or a woman, is not just a man or a woman. Men are often suppressed and not allowed to do something because it is unmanly. Mahesh Dattani, a playwright in Bangalore has written a play about a boy who wants to become a dancer and everybody laughs at him. They look upon it as a womanly activity. Both the sexes have been suppressed. Apart from gender restrictions there are millions of other restrictions. The mythological stereotypes have been used to put women in that place. I think it's very important to recognise that. We may be told that this is how a woman should be—look at Sita—docile, passive, long suffering, enduring. But why should one endure injustice? According to me no human being should endure injustice. Why should one put up with this? These things make life more comfortable for men. To have a Sita who listens to everything makes life very comfortable for you. I can admire certain qualities of Sita but I don't have to admire all her qualities. As an Indian a woman who has been brought up on these myths. I can still read Sita's story and get tears in my eyes, but that does not mean that I want to be like her. I would see Sita's story this way—I have to learn from that. I should not be like that. I will see Draupadi's story and I say I should not be like that. When she wants to marry Arjuna and they tell her to marry all the five she should have said no. Of course it was not possible for her. I recognise that. But today if it is possible for me I should learn to say no. So for me these things are imposed on women. Men are also conditioned by social archetypes—like men are supposed to be certain things—the protectors, the manly, the mature image, they are all part of men. But women are much more conditioned because being in a subordinate position, being the dependent gender, it has been more important for them to follow the path. It is very hard for them to break away since they are economically dependent on man. In a family woman never had any power. So she just had to be what she was expected to be. For me this whole thing was very important because the day I got married, I realized I cannot play any of those roles expected of me. I can be myself. I cannot be a good daughter-in-law, a devoted wife. I will be a good wife in my own way. I will be a good mother in my own way. So I learnt to shed the role through my own life and I think that is how it happens to many of us. It doesn't come through books.

Pall: What according to you is the major challenge for today's educated Indian women in their family life? In "A Wall is Safer" and "I Want," you have exhibited the feminine characteristic of self-abnegation. In "I Want," the female protagonist accepts the marriage proposal as she has no other choice, whereas in "A Wall is Safer" the protagonist shuns her career for the sake of her husband and moves with him from a metropolitan city to a remote area. However in contrast to this "It was a Nightingale" depicts the protagonist pursuing her career and independence despite her husband's reluctance. What do you think is the ideal way for the educated working women who want to take both the work and family together? What could be a substitute for self-abnegation for women which could help them to assert their individuality and existence without inducing in them a feeling of guilt?

SD: That is a very hard question because I cannot answer for other people. But let me correct you in one thing that in "A Wall is Safer," she is not self-abnegating. She is very conscious and aware of what she is doing. That's what she says: I have done this of my own choice. She has not obliterated herself. She has done it because it is the best choice for her family. And there is a difference between taking a choice, knowing that you are doing it and knowing why you are doing it and going into something passively, feeling that you have no choice and you are pushed into it. That is the kind of thing a lot of women have to do. Women of an earlier generation said that whatever is good for the family is good for us. It's not like that now. Nevertheless women would rather not have a divided family nor would men. If the man is earning more, which is more often true, the choice is simple. The woman gives up her job. But if the woman is earning more, it's going to be a hard choice because I do not know how the man will be able to take it. I keep saying unless men change there can be no real change. In the last 20 years women have changed enormously in this country but the men have not changed at all. That is why our problem has still continued. Women also need to get rid of guilt. To me it is the biggest problem working, middle-class, educated women are facing because whatever you do, you feel guilty. You sit at home without working you are guilty because you are wasting your education, you are not earning money. I was not earning money because I was not qualified to get a job and my son was born within a year of my marriage. So there was no question of my working and I was enormously guilty that I was not earning any money. Today when I look back I am very glad that I didn't go to work because I was able to give my children all my time. But at that time I could not think in that way. I think whatever we do we have a sense of guilt. What is important is to know what we are doing and why. In "A Wall is Safer," she knows what she is doing. In "It was a Nightingale," the woman is a little stronger. It all depends on your own strength. So it's very hard to give a general answer for everybody as circumstances, personalities and choices are different. I think it's important to know what you are doing and why you are doing it. Whether you want to give importance to your career or your husband's. Most of the time economics decides these things.

Pall: You have portrayed girl child in all your novels. Through Saru in *The Dark Holds No Terrors*, Indu in *Roots and Shadows*, Kalpana in *The Binding Vine* and Madhu in *Small Remedies* you have exhibited the Indian style of upbringing a girl-child. Do you think that social conditioning is responsible for setting limits on women's liberty, as you have exhibited in most of your novels.

SD: Well certainly it does matter how you are brought up. Madhu, for example, is brought up by her father. So there is nobody to tell her that you shouldn't do this. She grows up as a much freer child. Saru is constantly put in her place by her mother. So she grows up with a feeling of resentment and anger as if she has lost something. Certainly it matters how girls are brought up. It's mothers who are far more important than the father, because it is the mother who tells you what it is to be a woman. The father is always 'the other'. It is the mother you are going to be one day. So either you rebel and say I do not want to be like my mother or you take her as a role model. I have seen some very busy career women whose daughters say that they don't want to be like that. They just want to get married. That is one element of rebellion. So I think if you do not have a sympathetic mother it makes you rebel or if you have sympathetic mother, you continue to be what your mother was. Take for example Mira in *The Binding Vine*. She writes of her mother, "Why do you want to repeat your history when you are so despaired of your own?" I think this kind of continued history has to stop somewhere.

Some women would go the other way and say that I want my daughter to have all the freedom, I didn't have. Others would feel it's safer for their daughters if they put restrictions around them (not because they want to crush their daughters). To me awareness of these things is very important and may be writing can create this awareness. Because when we live our life we don't analyse our circumstances ourselves, we just live. It's only in writing that one stands at a distance and sees it more clearly. I think a reader is also able to see herself more clearly.

Pall: So, do you think that literature can generate revolutions?

SD: It cannot. Definitely cannot. But it can help people sometimes to see their lives more clearly. I don't think literature can change the world. Nor does one write to change the world. I am not writing to change the world or to make the world a better place for women. I am just writing what is in me and what comes out. But if by reading my work somebody gets a better awareness of his or her own life, I think it's a great thing. It is possible that these things do happen but it is not earthshaking.

Pall: Mother-daughter relationship has been drawn in a different perspective in your fiction. A sense of estrangement between the mother and the daughter can be seen in your stories like "Madhu," "Why a Robin?" and "My Beloved Charioteer" and novels like *The Dark Holds No Terrors*, *The Binding Vine* and *Small Remedies*. *The Dark Holds No Terrors* also exposes the deliberate cruelty of mothers inflicted on their girl child. This bold and sensitive illustration of mother-daughter relationship is still new in Indian English fiction and it is also different from the stereotyped image of mother-daughter relationship. Would you like to comment on it?

SD: That's very true. I remember I had gone for a three-day seminar on my work in a Madras college and some girls asked me, "Why are your mothers so unloving?" I thought about it and it struck me that they are neither unloving nor stereotypical. Now no relationship can be completely loving and supportive. It is a myth that mothers are always loving. Like I said, I had to learn about motherhood through my own experience. I knew that when I became a mother, I was the same person. So you can have angry, hot-headed, gentle, docile, and stupid mothers. It depends on the kind of person you are and your relationship with your child depends upon the kind of persons you and your child are. This is where people go wrong; when they find that their relationship is not stereotypical, they are puzzled. And certainly people expect the mother-daughter relationship to be completely loving. Very little has been written about it in literature. When I was working on a talk about myths and stereotypes, I realised that in our myths and epics there are no stories of mothers-daughters, only of mothers and sons. So traditionally a mother means a mother of a son. Until women started writing, nobody wrote the truth about the mother-daughter relationship. It required the women to write about this. When a man writes about mother-daughter relationship it is entirely different. So this has broken the stereotypes in one way. I remember after reading *The Dark Holds No Terrors*, a professor in a University wrote me a long letter saying that my book reminded her of her own relationship with her mother. And she said that she was so glad that I did not make it come all right in the end and that there was no reconciliation as it would have been very unnatural. "I never had one with my mother," she said, "My mother died unreconciled to me." So these things do happen. I don't call it cruel either. The mother in *The Dark Holds No Terrors* is not very normal. But in *The Binding Vine*, Urmi's mother is a very normal mother. She has her problems, she has her weaknesses, after her husband's death she becomes dependent and it is Urmi, who is looking after her. This is a very normal relationship. And there is always resentment between you and your mother. It expresses itself in little complaints and grievances. These are all very normal relationships. And that does not deny the blood tie. *The Dark*

Holds No Terrors presents a very highly abnormal situation. The mother is completely wrapped up in her son and it is the death of her son that completely destroys her equanimity. That's not very normal. That is why Saru suffers so much because of her mother's rejection. Now Savitribai and Munni are another very interesting mother-daughter relationship. And again it's not stereotypical. But again the circumstances are so unusual. So every relationship depends upon the circumstances and on who you are. What kind of a person you are. And I never see that any relationship is the same throughout the world. Every mother and daughter relationship in the world is not the same. There are different kinds of mothers and daughters; depending upon what kind of a person you and your mother are, your relationship takes a particular pattern. I see people as human beings first. And I see them as mothers, wives and daughters, next. We are born as human beings. All these come later. So we try to play these roles, but we don't always succeed because it's not possible for us.

Pall: You have portrayed mothers like Shakutai and Mira in *The Binding Vine* for whom motherhood is not the outcome of a mutual understanding, rather it is imposed on them. But there are also mothers in your fiction who refuse to be the "breeding animals" like the female protagonist in "The Death of a Child." Do you agree with the feminists who assert that the women should have a full control on their womb?

SD: If you are in a marriage and if you have a good relationship with your husband then I think he also has some say in the matter, though I think the woman's right is more important because she is going to bear and deliver the child. But it will be very cruel to say that the man has no say in this matter. Especially if it is the child of two people who have a good understanding and a good relationship then I would say that it would be wrong that the woman has 100% control over her womb. I wouldn't give him control over womb but certainly he should have a say in the decision. But for the women like Shakutai, whose husband is a waster and who really does not want children because it is too difficult to bring up children with no money and no place to live in, such a person I would say can take a unilateral decision. I hate generalizations. I can never generalize; that's why I would make a terrible theorist because theories believe in generalization. I would make a terrible academic because I don't believe in laying down rules. I believe there is no such thing as a general rule. Each human being is different, each relationship is different and the way we work our relations depends upon who we are and the way we live.

Pall: So it should be a mutual decision?

SD: Depending upon the relationship. But certainly not in a bad relationship where woman does not want it, where she is forced to bear a child. Like in *The Binding Vine*, Urmi's friend Vanaa wants a child (a son) and her husband says, "No stop now." So she can't have a child. You cannot call it a cruelty. Though Urmi calls it a cruelty because she knows that Vanaa is not happy with the decision. But one cannot call it a grave wrong.

Pall: "A Day like Any Other" and "The Sweet Antidote" are the stories which exhibit the women accepting their husband's sexual relationship with other women. In these two stories infidelity is not treated with contempt by the wives. In "The Sweet Antidote," the wife persuades her husband to have physical relationship with the maid in order to ensure a perfect domestic life. Whereas in another of your stories, "The Shadow," the man refuses to accept the illegitimate girl-child born to his wife and in this way never forgives his repenting wife. Do you think two different patterns have been set for males and females when we talk of infidelity?

SD: I think "The Sweet Antidote" was a bit of a joke. I wouldn't take it seriously. I sometimes wonder why I wrote it. I was writing a lot then and this was not one of my serious stories. In fact I had almost forgotten it until I saw it in your questionnaire. But "The Shadow" and "A Day like Any Other" are serious writings. "A Day like Any Other" was certainly more serious than that because in it I was pursuing this thought that this woman weighs all that she has against a momentary infidelity. I think it requires a lot of maturity which I gave that woman which I doubt I would now to say that it doesn't matter but I think for woman and man it matters a lot. A man's feelings about infidelity are much stronger for two reasons:

1. In our society a woman is supposed to be more chaste. A man can have affairs and get away with it.
2. For a man his children should be his own. To know that a woman has not been sexually loyal to him implies doubt about his own children.

As Marx said, it has its beginnings in the idea that my property should go to my children. So in these stories men react much more strongly. Above all it is very deeply ingrained belief in all societies, especially in our society, that a woman should be chaste. She should not look at any other man. Even second marriages are banned for women in many communities. They even had Sati, so that no man should have access to that woman's body afterwards. These are all dreadful, the extremes of these feelings. Women's objections do not find ways of being expressed. How do you express your objections? Now, of course marriages are breaking up because if a woman has economic independence she can certainly refuse to stay with a man who has not been faithful to her. But in what other ways can she rebel? Maybe in the bedroom at night, she might refuse to sleep with him—little acts of rebellion which a woman could do. But they didn't mean much. But certainly if a woman infringed the rules she could be severely punished. So I think different moral codes for men and women continue even today. The woman is supposed to be very moral. You have to be so careful about your moral conduct, especially if you are in public life. Men can get away with much more. It's wrong, but there it is!

Pall: Almost all the women in your major novels like *The Dark Holds No Terrors*, *That Long Silence*, *The Binding Vine*, *Roots and Shadows*, *If I Die Today*, and stories like "An Antidote to Boredom" have a male friend, a confidant and sometimes a lover. In *That Long Silence*, Jaya goes to meet Kamat in the absence of her husband and Indu in *Roots and Shadows* establishes even sexual relationship with Naren. This relationship enables your women to put their marriage within a perspective and review it. Thinkers like Sartre and Bertrand Russell have supported the idea of extramarital affairs as it helps people to understand themselves in a better way. Your fiction seems to advocate such relationships. Would you like to offer any comments on that?

SD: I don't think I would specifically call it an extra-marital affair. But I have seen marriages to be kind of restrictive. In a marital relationship—I cannot speak of a man but I can certainly speak of the woman—much of the woman has to remain unexpressed. It is expected of women that certain things are not to be done or not to be said or you have to be a certain kind of person. So the real 'you' remains unexpressed. Whenever I see women talking about their past, when they were children, before marriage, there is a kind of delight in remembering that person because that is the real you and after marriage, motherhood, and wifehood, take away certain aspects of you. It's not that it is deliberately done. It just happens that way, that as a wife you conform to a certain model. As a mother, parts of you remain unexpressed and I also feel the women in India also have a lot of relationships with their own sex, like female friends, cousins, in-laws. You do not have the same access to a male friendship, especially after marriage. I think that sometimes in relationships with the other sex certain parts of you come alive. A relationship with a male without this burden of sex and marriage seems a very good relationship to me. That is how I think and that is how I have written about these kinds of relationships whether it is Naren in

Roots and Shadows, Bhaskar in *The Binding Vine*, Kamat in *That Long Silence*. One needs those relationships. Jaya is very much aware that with Mohan she is Mohan's wife but with Kamat she is many things. She is that kid Jaya, a rebellious kid, she is a writer, she is a frustrated person who cannot write what she wants to. She can be angry with Kamat. With Mohan she cannot be angry because he does not like it. So it gives you a freedom to be yourself. I don't necessarily feel that it has to be an affair. Some relationships may move on to that but I think that would make a marriage an uneasy one. To me more than anything else it's the cheating aspect of these affairs that troubles me. It may not trouble women like Indu. She has sex with Naren and it means nothing to her. Like in "A Day like Any Other," the protagonist thinks that her husband may have had an affair with a girl but in their relationship it means nothing. But not everybody can think that way. I think that kind of a relationship is very rich. Like Urmi has Vanaa in *The Binding Vine* which is a very good relationship but at the same time with Bhaskar there is something more, although the minute she realizes he is interested in her as a woman, she withdraws.

Pall: So you mean to say that women as friend to males are more open and they become themselves?

SD: Yes, with a particular person—it may be a man, it may be a woman. But sometimes with the family we are not completely ourselves. Like I said, we are continuously restricted by our roles. I am so much the wife and mother here that I may not be able to express myself, my whole self. It's very rare with a marriage partner. If with a marriage partner you are able to do that it's a wonderful marriage. There is nothing like that, because then there is a freedom of friendship and the intimacy of marriage both combined. But often it is not possible. So it seems to me that a husband cannot be a friend most of the time.

Pall: Besides gender discrimination you have also presented the plight of women subjected to rape not only in the society but also within the family frame. Your stories "It was Dark," "The Intrusion" and novels *The Dark Holds No Terrors*, *The Binding Vine* and *Roots and Shadows* depict the trauma of forced sex on women. You are the first novelist to expose the protector as an aggressor in the family. What was the source behind this kind of writing?

SD: I don't know whether I am the first novelist to write on this theme. I would be surprised if I am, because it's a theme which cries loudly to be written about. When I first wrote this story "Intrusion," I never thought I was going to write about rape or about rape in the family. When I wrote "Intrusion," it came to me as a story of a honeymooning couple. That was how it presented itself to me—as the first night of a couple who had not met before. Of course for all Indian men, marriage is a marriage. As soon as you get married you go to bed together but for most girls there is a sense of fear because their bodies have been so private until now. For women sex is not such a strong instinct as it is for men, even biologically or physiologically. So for women, there is a lot of withdrawal, nervousness and fear of exposing their body or letting men have control on their body. But the men never see that and that was how the story came to me that the man is completely unaware of her feelings. I sent it to *Femina* and I rang up the editor, Vimala Patil, a few days later. I was quite nervous and I said, "Are you going to use it?" She said, "Which story—the story about rape?" I was so surprised as I never thought of it as a story of rape at all. Then I realized that of course it is rape. Nobody talked about marital rape in those days. These are all terms which are common now but they were not so common then. These things came to me out of what I saw around me and I never felt inhibitive because rape is for me the grossest violation of trust between two people. Whether it is someone in the family or your husband or any other man who commits a rape, it destroys the trust between men and women. It's also the greatest violence because it is not only a woman's body but it is her mind and feeling of her right to have a control on her body which is gone. So when I wrote "It Was Dark," the story of a child being raped, I read a news item in a newspaper one day, about a 14 year old school girl who was lost and found two or three days later. That was all. I thought, supposing the girl had been raped. What would have happened to her? What about her mother? It is not only the child—but also the parents are equally violated. For the mother it is even more personal feelings because she remembers her own marriage and how she was reluctant to sleep with her husband and how her mother told her not to deny him. 'You have to please him and go along with whatever he says.' That is what a lot of mothers must have told their daughters in those days. For the mother it was like a repetition of this thing in her own marriage. It's worse, more ghastly when it is an unknown person. But a known person is not much better, even if it is the husband. Like Mira, for example, her feelings are so strong about not wanting to sleep with her husband and she wants to say no, but she can't because it is her own husband. To me this is the most ugly and glaring spot in a man-woman relationship. It's really very disturbing.

Pall: Husband-wife relationship has been taken as a major theme in most of your stories and all the novels. You have exposed the exploitative trends of the patriarchal society in which man plays the dominating role. The basic instincts of men towards women have not changed. Here I am reminded of Virginia Woolf who believes that progress of both men and women is required to lead a balanced and fulfilled life and also asserts that the potential of women should be developed in a proper direction. Your fiction agrees with the ideology of Virginia Woolf but you also advise your protagonists to believe in themselves and accept the responsibilities of their own life. This offers a new solution and remedy to the fear of losing oneself in the dark labyrinthine passages of the inner and the outer world. Can we conclude that you have expounded a new way for women to survive in this patriarchal society and reshaped the women's ideology towards their life and freedom?

SD: I wish I could agree. It sounds such a big thing. Actually, what I've been doing is exploring my own way towards understanding these things because in each character and story, I learn a little more. It's not that I have all the knowledge. No way. I am just exploring and understanding myself a little bit each time. Certainly I agree with Virginia Woolf that both men and women have to progress because you cannot have men standing outside and women saying that we want this. It doesn't work that way. It should be not a question of what I want. It should be a question of both working together to make a better world. Self-awareness right from *The Dark Holds No Terrors*, is most important to me, because this is what women have lacked. We have not been told to know ourselves at all. We have been told to accept what has been told to us about ourselves. To me that has been extremely disturbing. Long back in 1975, somebody asked me to write about women's position in India. I wrote that 'know thyself' is one of the tenets of Hindu philosophy. But 'know thyself' is only for men and not for women. Women should never know themselves. According to Hindu philosophy or any other philosophy, you only have to know and understand men. You are not important at all. You are just an instrument. To me that was really the most disturbing thing. Even today when people say your novels are open ended, some people say it's not real feminism because Jaya goes back to her marriage. To me that is not important. To me Jaya knows herself and she can live her life better. Knowledge is so important. It's like opening your eyes which makes you see the world. It's like the sun. You can see the world more clearly. What you do with it, with all that knowledge, is a different matter. But without that knowledge you cannot do anything with your life. No education and money, nothing can help you to live a better life. I think it's more important to know yourself. To me that's the first step that you have to know yourself, you have to know what you are. Without that knowledge you cannot survive. You cannot live at all. You are not living a full life. You are just surviving. Once you have knowledge, the possibilities are endless.

Pall: The novel *The Dark Holds No Terrors* is an extended form of your story "The Liberated Woman." What made you develop the story in the novel form?

SD: I wrote this story when I was very ill. I was in bed for six months and this idea came to me and I just had to write the story and it was very difficult to sit up in bed but I wrote and rewrote it. I wrote it about 17 to 18 times before I got finally the form which it is now in. Even then I knew it was a bad story. I wrote it for the short story competitions of *Femina*. The idea had been nagging me for a long time. Anyway, I wrote it and sent it and got a prize. But I knew it was not a good story. I was quite ashamed of it really. It was very embarrassing for me even to read that story. And I didn't understand why I was so displeased with it. Finally I understood that the whole perspective in which I had presented it was wrong. And then I realized that it's too big a theme for a story. It had to be a novel. To bring all that in the story was very contrived. So I thought I had to write a novel about this. It took me five years to complete it. Before that I wrote *Roots and Shadows* because I didn't know how I was going to write a novel. It was really hard to write that novel. I had this woman, I had her husband and I had this peculiar relationship they had. I began writing and the brother came to me, the mother came to me, the teacher with whom she talks, fortunately he receded and became unimportant, because that was a big flaw in my story somehow. I had written the story through the teacher's point of view because I didn't want to make it a sob story. I thought if I narrate it through the woman's point of view, it would become one of those 'I confess' kind of stories. I didn't want that. So I used the man's point of view to make it a little distanced. But it didn't work. Luckily he vanished from my novel, he had just a small role. It took me nearly five years to complete it. But I knew it was a theme for a novel. I also knew that it was going to be a very tough novel to write. And it was.

Pall: But it's a very good novel?

SD: Well it is a good novel. I don't say that of all my novels. I am very surprised the way I wrote it in one go. Except the end which gave me a lot of trouble, the novel gave me a lot of pleasure.

Pall: Jaya in *That Long Silence* acknowledges her weaknesses and follies as a writer. She accepts that it was her fear of failure as a writer that kept her away from her profession and not the responsibilities towards her family. Do you think that the present Indian women are hesitant in developing their true potential? Has Jaya been portrayed as a representative of average Indian woman who is silent and submissive?

SD: None of my women are representatives of anyone; they are just themselves. I am not writing about representatives. I hate generalizations, symbolism, and representatives. Each woman is individually herself. Jaya is herself. But it is true that for a lot of us fear of failure keeps us away and I think it's very true that for a lot of women your fear of stepping out of your home, creating problems within the family and outside, keep you back. And it's very easy to say that I have no time. A lot of the writing came from my own life because I found time to work. I never waited for time to come to me. I made it possible. I had lots of problems, with children, no money, bad health, and all sorts of problems, but I kept working. It seemed to me that it's always possible to do that, and if you don't do that you are finding excuses. I don't think that Jaya is a representative but of course there must be Jaya around. I think more than anything else it's a kind of amateurism in women to which I object. Especially among writers I have seen women quite happy to be writing little things and not prepared to take that big leap from being an amateur writer to being a professional. To be a professional you have to give a lot of yourself. That is where the problem lies, really, because you have to be ruthless. Like Jaya begins by saying you have to be ruthless. You cannot have it all. So you have to give it 100% commitment. Now that is where women really falter. And for that there are a lot of reasons, we are soft, brain-washed, our families come first, genuinely we want to give our children more attention. The solution is not to have children and marriage but that is not possible. For most Indian women to live alone is a very hard life. So each one of us is trying to find our own way. There can be no generalization. We all are trying to find it in different ways. We all have to make compromises. To me it is important that I would never compromise on my professional excellence that I should give my best. I am not saying that I am an excellent writer, but I would give my best to my writing. I would not compromise, or say I have no time. But the family and children are facts which most of us have to take into account. We cannot say 'I don't care what happens to my family, I am going to write.' It is not possible.

Pall: Your latest novel *Small Remedies* exhibits a mature vision. In the novel the female protagonists like Savitribai Indorekar, Madhu, and Leela lead an independent life and have an independent thinking in the novel. Does it mean that you have given a final shape to the female protagonists of your novels who were relentlessly searching for their lost self-identity?

SD: I don't think so. I certainly hope that there is a mature vision because I certainly hope that I am more mature than what I was ten years ago. Otherwise just getting grey hair and becoming old is such a waste of time! But it gave me a lot of satisfaction because Savitribai has been in my mind for ten years now. It's not that the novel just happened now. More than 10 years I have been wanting to write this novel about Savitribai. What kept me back was that I did not have enough knowledge of music. That kept pushing it back and I wrote *The Binding Vine* and *A Matter of Time* and then Savitribai really came to the foreground and said that you cannot push me aside any more. I had to read a lot. Earlier, I had Indu who doesn't even want to admit that she is doing any writing, there was Jaya who writes rubbish and finds excuses for it, there was Mira who writes but never gets it published. Finally there is Savitribai who gloriously says that my work comes first. Maybe I was moving all the way towards Savitribai. One doesn't know, one doesn't analyse one's work and one should not either, but possibly these were the people who helped me to finally reach Savitribai. I would not say it is a final statement. But here is a woman who is not contemporary. It is interesting that the woman of 50 years ago is the really independent woman. As far as Madhu's independence is concerned, she was brought up differently. She is an orphan and she has to work for her living and is brought up by a doctor, and a different kind of person. All these things made her what she was. Now, Leela is a person who has also been in my mind for a very long time. I lived in Parel for many years. Parel is the hot bed of trade unionism in Bombay. We stayed in KEM Hospital Quarters. My husband was a doctor there. And just opposite the hospital there is a place called Kamgar Maidan. All the communist party meetings used to be held there. We used to see these meetings going on. Soon after that the Shiv-Sena came and there was a lot of conflict. It was a kind of happening time and all that penetrated into my mind. And then I saw a lot of women who were communist party members at that time. Not from near, I read about some of them—Ahilyabai Rangnekar. I have also seen the kind of social activism which was common at particular point of time, especially in Maharashtra. There were very socially committed women. So Leela had really entered my mind quite sometime back and I only feel sorry that she was marginalised by Savitribai because to me that again was a very fascinating character and a very true character. There are a lot of women who have lived lives like that. Durgabai Deshmukh was there. Probably Durgabai Deshmukh was in my mind when I wrote about Leela. They all belong to a different era but they are greater achievers than we have today. They all came to me and I am so glad that I wrote about them, especially both Leela and Savitribai.

Pall: In "Rain," "A Man and a Woman" and "The Cruelty Game," you have mentioned and highlighted the issue of the remarriage of widows. Even in contemporary middle-class Indian society, remarriage of widows is not appreciated and promoted. Do you plan to develop a novel on this theme in future as this theme has not as yet been taken by you in any of your novels?

SD: I don't write according to themes. People come to me. I don't take up issues and I don't plan a novel—I am going to write this time about rape, this time about widows. No, that's not the way I write. That would be the dreadful way of writing. For me the people come first. Like Savitribai came to me first. Then I wrote about her. She, as a human being was more important to me and through her all other characters came. So that is how my novels work. They don't work through issues. It's the people who come to me and the people of course have their lives and their problems. So when I wrote these stories it was not to write about widow remarriage or whatever. I mean if I were to write about these issues I would write non-fiction. I don't think fiction is suited for issues. Certainly not. I can't write that kind of thing. It spoils a novel. I think the aesthetics of a novel sort of rules out anything which is like an issue. By chance I may write a novel in which a woman is a widow and it may be that all kinds of things happen to her. She may marry, she may not marry.

Pall: "The Inner Rooms," "The Last Enemy' and "Hear Me Sanjay" are excerpts from the *Mahabharata*. You have revealed lamenting Kunti and humiliated Amba. A different image of Kunti has been presented by you by removing her mask of endurance. What motivated you to treat these mythical characters as common women and analyze their situation, position, desires and feelings as ordinary beings and not as queens and princesses?

SD: Like I told you I always see people as human beings. I go beyond their roles and certainly I will go beyond their queenly roles. I mean if I can go beyond woman as a mother, woman as a wife and see the human beings behind. Certainly I would see Kunti not just as a mother. I always go beyond the role, behind the role, so it didn't matter to me. But I tell you what really happened was that I was reading Iravati Karve's *Yuganta*. In that she has talked about Bhishma and she has talked about Bhishma's cruelty to women and she said it was unequalled cruelty. So she has spoken of Amba, Ambika and Ambalika and I was thinking of it and I still remember I was sitting somewhere and suddenly Amba came to me and I thought I must write about it. It was not that I planned to write about these people. Amba just came into my mind and I had to write a story about her and I wrote that story. Afterwards I found it intriguing because I wrote about Duryodhana. I went beyond Duryodhana as a king, Duryodhana as a villain, Duryodhana when he is dying and what his thoughts were and I thought that story also came out good. I had been wanting to write Kunti's story for a long time and I had titled it first *Kuntivacha*. Then I wrote a story on Draupadi. People keep saying that Draupadi really caused the war. It is a story with one small episode where Draupadi finds these people conferring and they are going to send Krishna to Hastinapur after Abhimanyu's wedding to talk about peace. She asks: how can you talk about peace and accept five villages? How can you do that when Duryodhana has already said that he would not give you even a needle point of land. They all argue with her and Krishna promises her that they will do what she wants, etc. Afterwards she finds out that all this time they had been planning for war. It is really how things are in life, because women's wishes don't count. Why should Draupadi's wishes have counted so much that they should have gone to war for her sake? People go for war mainly for economic reasons. They don't go to war for a woman or because somebody pulled a woman's hair. To me it is total nonsense. These women have been given a certain kind of role to occupy in those myths and through the years they have become stereotypes. In the myth themselves, they may not be stereotypes, in fact they are not. Even Shakuntala, in the original *Mahabharata* is not the Shakuntala of Kalidasa. Through the centuries they have become stereotypes and we have accepted them as they are—that Kunti is a devoted mother, Draupadi is an angry woman, Gandhari blinded herself out of loyalty to her husband. You know, Iravati Karve says that she blinded herself not because she wanted to be a good wife, but because she was angry she was cheated. They brought her all the way from Kandhar, she comes to palace and finds that she has a blind husband. She gets absolutely furious and says, "I am going to punish him." A real devoted wife would have kept her eyes open and would have shown him the world. So I could see so much in Iravati Karve which I wanted to pursue. Iravati Karve was my inspiration, but I also always like to go beyond the roles and I never see human beings as they are presented to us. I like to have my own views. You can't tell me anything, I am going to find out myself. That is how it has always been with my life. So that is how it is in my writing also. I won't take anybody's word for anything.

Pall: Do you think that Hindu mythology has promoted the image of submissive woman in contemporary society? To what extent your sensitivity as an author has been influenced by your early exposure to Hindu mythology?

SD: Certainly Hindu mythology has a lot to answer for. What it has done to women is terrible. Hindu mythology has created through these stereotypes, and now movies are carrying them on. Movies are terrible because this idea we have of Sita and Savitri image really come to us now from the movies and no longer from the myths. How many people read the myths now? So you know it has been kind of taken over and either we have a Sita, a Savitri or we have that angry Devi which is the other side of the image and both are the terrible stereotypes for women to bear the burden. I was not much exposed to mythology as a child because I didn't grow up in a traditional family. But my father was a Sanskrit scholar, people used to come and talk. So it's whatever I picked up from some people's talk. I still remember my father talking one day when I was a child, saying that there are only two heroes in the *Mahabharata*—Bhishma and Abhimanyu—one old man and one boy. I never forgot that and then I read Iravati Karve and when she said Bhishma was a cruel man, it took me some time to accept this because I was so influenced by my father's words. The starting point was really my own pursuit of these things, my own interest, curiosity and desire to know more. Like I said, a desire to think for myself and not accept what was given to me. I was always very invasive in my thinking. It took me a long time to trust myself. Because you think there is something wrong with you when you think differently from others. I did not have the courage or confidence to think that my views were correct. It was the exploration I undertook as a writer which really helped to understand that these are my views and I have every right to express them.

Pall: "The Narayanpur Incident" is quite similar in theme to Raja Rao's *Kanthapura.* Though you have narrated it in the form of a children's story yet thematic similarity is visible in it. Would you like to offer any comments?

SD: Well, I never thought that. Yeah, I know. I am surprised because I never thought of it in that way at all. I hadn't read *Kanthapura*. I read it after I wrote "The Narayanpur Incident." My father wrote a history of the quit India movement in Karnataka and one day he was telling us about it. He was commissioned by a newspaper to write this history. They had asked people who had experiences of the movement to send them in. So my father had a lot of material. I asked him if I could take those papers. He said, "Take it. It's just lying in my loft." So we brought the box home. But I couldn't read the papers because they were all in Kannada. So my husband went through it for me and read out. And then I thought, let me write about this for children. So that was how it happened. It has nothing to do with *Kanthapura*. But I am surprised and pleased too because *Kanthapura* is a beautiful book.

Pall: Among your novels, which do you think is your best and why?

SD: The next one I hope. No, no one can answer this question. It is difficult because each one gives you its own pleasure, each one has its own flaws. I don't read my own work. Once I finish I don't go back. After reading the proofs and all, I am fed up. But I think *The Dark Holds No Terrors* in a way was to me, like I said, more satisfying because one way it was hardest to write, in other way it was more compact—sort of more intense than any other novel. It may be that. But of course *That Long Silence* was really the hardest to write. Because there was really no material there. It is just a woman's thoughts. And that was really in one way extremely hard to write. But I don't know which is the best. I hope the next one.

Pall: By which great writers have you been influenced and inspired? Which is your favourite book?

SD: I don't know which great writers I have been influenced by, because it's difficult to say. But I have read lots of early English writers—Jane Austen is favourite—I don't claim to have any influence of her but I think she is the finest writer ever. Of course I have read Dickens, Trollope, Gaskell, and all the Victorians. The Russian writers—*Anna Karenina* to me is one of the finest books. I have read *Crime and Punishment*. *Crime and Punishment* is another great book. *Crime and Punishment* has left a very lasting impression on me. I've read modern books like *To*

Kill a Mocking Bird which I think is one of the finest books. But I think that I would relate to any book with a very strong moral concern.

Pall: The traces of Buddhist philosophy are discernible in the thematic motifs of almost all your novels. In *The Dark Holds No Terrors*, a couplet from the Dhammapada has been quoted as:

> You are your own refuge;
> There is no other refuge.
> This refuge is hard to achieve.

Have you been consciously influenced by the Buddhist philosophy in your life?

SD: Well, there was a time when I was very deeply affected by Buddha's story, not by the Buddhist thought. For me, it has always been a powerful recurring symbol in my life. The idea of Buddha giving up everything and going in search of knowledge to me has been a kind of very important recurring symbol in my life. I don't claim to be a scholar and I'm not a Buddhist but to me it also has seemed to be a more reasonable philosophy by which to lead one's life rather than the Hindu philosophy which is too metaphysical and which is sort of unreasonable for most human beings, whereas Buddhism seems possible for all human beings. But maybe I was reading the *Dhammapada* at that time when I wrote *The Dark Holds No Terrors*. When I was writing *A Matter of Time*, I was reading *The Upanishads*. So they do appear much more in that. I think that's all. The connection is there. But they are part of me, certainly. I think Buddhism is certainly something which is part of me but so are the *Upanishads* because I do relate a lot to them. There are certain gems of thoughts in it. But I am not a scholar.

Pall: The inner determination of your protagonists, their resilience to transcend barriers or constraints, rational analysis of the cause of their unhappiness and above all their compassionate attitude towards everyone are quite similar to the Buddhist preachings. Sometimes these Buddhist principles are used to present the protagonists' journey towards self-actualization in a figurative manner, as symbolic motifs while at other times we feel that the tenets of Buddhist philosophy form the very basis of your argument. Do you think that the interpretation of your texts through Buddhist philosophy is justified?

SD: You know, once I finish writing a novel it's over for me and anybody is free to do what they want with it. I don't think about it. I don't take too much interest in it. Like if somebody makes a movie of my novel it wouldn't bother me. I wouldn't be excited. For me it's mine until I write it. Once it is published and gone it is not mine. So you are quite free to do what you want with it. It doesn't trouble me. It's quite O.K. Nor am I going to judge whether you are right or wrong. My business is to write. Each reader has his or her interpretation. That is how the connection between the writer and the reader always is. Each reader is going to see something different. I think that's perfectly natural.

Pall: When did you decide to choose writing as a career? What are the comments of your family regarding your works? Whom do you consider as the best judge of your writings within your family?

SD: I never took up writing as a career. Like I said, I just stumbled into it. I wanted to write and I wrote. It became a career because I am a very sincere person, and my commitment is a hundred percent, I mean, I know this is my life's work. Not that I consciously sat down one day and very solemnly told myself that this is my life's work. But it was something to which I gave myself more completely than I had ever done in my life before. I had been never interested in any other thing. I am not talking about my family. I am talking of work. I did my law, I did my B.A., I did this, I did that, and nothing interested me. My father was convinced I would never do anything in my life. But once I took up writing, I myself was surprised the way I gave myself to it, complete commitment. And hard work. I was a very lazy person but worked very hard over my writing. So I just stumbled into it. Found out it is the right thing for me and worked at it. I never called it a career, never had great ambitions, never had great dreams of becoming a great writer one day. Nothing like that. I just wanted to write, I wanted it to be published. I hoped to earn a little money, that's all. At home I am not a writer. My husband is always my first reader, but he doesn't judge. He is thankfully, totally, non-literary. So he just reads it and leaves it and doesn't comment on it at all. I don't know anybody who is the best judge. I think I am the best judge because when there is something bad or wrong I feel it myself. I am quite harsh on myself. It is true that one cannot be a judge of oneself but one can be a critic and I do try to be one. I am a fairly harsh self-critic. So, beyond that I've not given anybody that position. I never had somebody whom I can give my writing to, and get a feed-back. My readers ultimately are the best judge. As a writer, I want people to say my book is good. But that doesn't always happen. Somebody rings me up and says I have written a wonderful book and it makes my day for me. But one day you will get a reaction that it's a horrible book and it will spoil your day. So ultimately one has to become philosophical about it.

Pall: Your novels so realistically display the true facet of the Indian society. How do you select your themes?

SD: I don't select them. They come to me. The people, the characters come to me first. And through the characters, the themes evolve. People come to me as people; since they are people they have their lives and through the complexity of their lives, the themes evolve. Like Jaya and her husband came to me first and I knew they are people who grew up in a pre-independence or rather were born in pre-independence India. That's all. The themes always come out of the people.

Pall: Are you working on any new novel at present?

SD: Yes, I am. I've just started actually. After *Small Remedies*, I was really very tired. I've been working non-stop for nearly 25 years now. And along with work life goes on. So many things have happened in the last, especially in the last 10 years, which have been hard. So I was really very exhausted and I told myself that I am not going to write, but another has come. Only just begun. It's going to take a long time.

Bharati Mukherjee's *Desirable Daughters*: Cultural Perspectives

SARIKA PRADIPRAO AURADKAR
Pratibha Niketan College, Naded

Bharati Mukherjee was born in Kolkata in 1940 to an upper middle class Bengali Brahmin family, the elite caste of Hindu society. Her father was the head of a pharmaceutical firm. Her early childhood was spent in the few years before India's independence. She attended schools in both Britain and Switzerland, and then returned to India to attend Loretto School run by Irish nuns. She was taught to devalue Bengali culture, and it was not until later that she reconnected with her Hindu heritage. Mukherjee received from the University of Kolkata a B.A. in English in 1959 and an M.A. in English and Ancient Indian Culture in 1961. The same year, she came to the United States to study at Iowa writers' workshop. There she met and married Canadian writer Clark Blaise, with whom she later collaborated on two non-fiction works. Mukherjee's marriage to someone outside her culture changed her life and writing dramatically. She moved with her husband to his native Canada and encountered racism and alienation. She quickly became a vocal civil rights activist and the nature of her fiction changed irrevocably. In 1980 she decided that she could not survive as an outsider in Canada and moved with her family to the United States. She became an American citizen in 1988. Mukherjee has been a professor of English and creative writing at various universities in both Canada and the United States, including Columbia University in New York and the University of California at Berkeley. In 1988 she won the National Book Critics Circle Award for *The Middleman and Other Stories*.

Bharati Mukherjee has spent most of her career portraying the humiliation and pain often associated with third world people adapting to North American culture. She has developed an understated prose style and tells her story from many different cultural perspectives. Her protagonists are usually sensitive, lack a stable sense of personal and cultural identify, and are victimized by racism, sexism, or other forms of social oppression. In her fiction Mukherjee depicts problems faced by Indian and other third world immigrants who attempt to assimilate into North American lifestyles. Using an understated prose style replete with ironic developments and witty observation, Mukherjee focuses upon sensitive protagonists who lack a stable sense of personal and cultural identity and are victimized by other forms of social oppression.

In her first novel, *The Tiger's Daughter,* Mukherjee presents a satirical portrait of Indian society from the perspective of Tara Banerjee, a young expatriate. Mukherjee's second novel, *Wife* is a psychological study of Dimple, a young woman from Kolkata who settles in New York with her husband. Raised to be passive and dependent according to traditional Indian standards of feminity, Dimple lacks the inner resources to cope with the fear and alienation that she experiences in New York, and she gradually descends into psychotic violence. *Jasmine* is a tremendously interesting work, not simply because it foregrounds characters and situations and nationalities so often disguised or dismissed in the western tradition, but primarily because of Mukherjee's ironic nuance and sinewy revisionism. This is an important novel not only for what it says, but also for how it says it. Mukherjee's novel, *The Holder of the World* is historical romance framed in a science fiction staple, and it purports, in a surprise ending, to be relating the "true" history of a famous character in American literature. Mukherjee's novel *Leave It to Me*, has all her trademark preoccupations: exiles, émigrés and outsiders tirelessly reinventing themselves, as they shed old lives, old lovers, old selves, and an America reeling from violence and non-stop change, a country in which freedom has translated into rootlessness, possibility into dislocation. It has a heroine who is addicted to change, a supporting cast of eccentrics and a wildly manic plot.

Desirable Daughters reads like Mukherjee's sly response to the doctrinaire multiculturalists who demand that she writes about their own kind. She's done just that, with precision and mockery and strong reminders of dangers inherent in narrow cultural self-definition. Mukherjee begins the novel by telling the story "The Tree Bride" which has influence on the rest of the book. Jai Krishna Gangooly was a pleader at Dhaka High Court. A Bengali Brahmin, he was a staunch believer in Hindu culture. He had three daughters, Tara Lata, Parvati and Padma. The youngest named Tara Lata was five years old and he arranged her marriage.

> The youngest dressed in her bridal Sari, her little hands painted with red lac dye, her hair oiled and set. Her arms are heavy with dowry gold; bangles ring tiny arms from wrist to shoulder. Childish voices chant a song, hands clap, gold bracelets tinkle. I cannot imagine the loneliness of this child. A Bengali girl's happiest night is about to become her lifetime imprisonment. It seems all the sorrow of history, all that is unjust in society and cruel in religion has settled on her. (4)

Just before the wedding, however, the bridegroom's father increased his demands for the dowry. Refusing to be cowed into submission, Jai Krishna took his daughter into a deep forest and married her to a tree, and thus Tara became known as Tree Bride.

> Tara Lata is five year old and headed deep into the forest to marry a tree.—And so my history begins with a family wedding on the coldest, darkest night in Bengali month of Paush—December/January—in a district of the Bengal Presidency that lies east of Calcutta—now Kolkata—and South of Dacca—now Dhaka—as the English year of 1879 is about to shed its final two digits, although the Hindu years of 1285 still has four months to run, the Muslim year of 1297 has barely begun. (5)

Jai Krishna turned his back on the avaricious man who would have been Tara Lata's father-in-law if fate hadn't intervened. Jai

Krishna would see his daughter married to a tree, but Tara Lata's father-in-law would not get a single piece. Jai Krishna gave dowry only to a person who did not demand it. The novel *Desirable Daughters* is both lyrical and insightful, sharing observations about family that apply to almost all cultures. While the first twenty pages can seem somewhat plodding as the author relates the legend of Tara Lata, the 'Tree Bride' who became 'the least known martyr to Indian freedom,' the tale's meaning is integral to the journey that Tara, and all women, must make.

Tara Lata, a self-possessed and curious woman, exhibits a fervent quest for identity and space of her own. In fact, central to the theme of the novel is this quest of her. She has done what is quite unimaginable; she has divorced her brilliant, extremely rich and famous husband. Moreover, she frees her artistic son from school and chooses to live with her lover, without marrying him and thus proving herself to be her own guide. As an individual, she enforces her identity as a self-propelled woman by exerting her own will on decisions about her life.

> The only person I'd checked up on was Andy, and that was because Bish had bullied me into doing it. Bish, in fact, had offered to "take care"—his phrase—of the background check himself. We'd started the process of negotiation by e-mail with a terse, "I'm free to make a mess of my own life!" from me, then got stuck for a while on Bish's rejoinder, "You're not free to wreck our son's" and finally compromised with Bish. (48)

So she prefers to make her own tradition, to choose her own home and place rather than those given to her by her father or husband. She is one of those kinds of diasporic women who gladly renounce the security within the confines of the four walls to walk the path of freedom,, to explore their own method, and devise their own plans to go on in life.

Tara, the heroine of *Desirable Daughters*, is a bit of an Indian princess. When a strange young man shows up at her San Francisco house claiming to be a long lost nephew, she's suspicious of the way he carries his cigarettes, loose in his pockets, like the "Uppity Servants" in her Kolkata neighbourhood "who liked to smoke the same brand as their employers." Visiting her sister in New Jersey, she averts her eyes self-protectively from "the hideous mall scarred landscape." She dismisses the street crowds of Jackson Heights, thriving commercial centre of Indian life in New York city, as "the hungering classes. They look to her like a bunch of documented felons." But give her a break—she's 36, divorced, a single mom, and drop by drop, to paraphrase Chekhov, she's wringing the snob out of herself.

> When I left Bish (let us be clear on this) after a decade of marriage, it was because the promise of life as an American wife was not being fulfilled. I wanted to drive, but where would I go? I wanted to work, but would people think that Bish Chatterjee couldn't support his wife? (82)

This novel hyper-alertly charts the making of a consciousness, the ebbs and eddies of the elusive mental processes by which a daughter of privilege learns to observe without flinching the world she lives in and the world she came from.

> It's good to rediscover my roots, but not if they rise up and strangle me. I wanted to be persuaded by cool logic. My sister couldn't be both a child denying monster and an angel; Chris couldn't be a victim and a villain; my father our protector and destroyer. (138)

Tara is the youngest of three beautiful sisters in an affluent family of Bengali Hindu Brahmins, raised in 1960s Kolkata. Like fairytale princesses, all three girls share the same birthday. At nineteen Tara dutifully entered an arranged marriage, wholly innocent of the facts of sexual anatomy. Within a few years her brilliant husband, Bishwapriya Chatterjee, Ph.D. from Stanford, has parlayed his inventions into a global telecommunications empire. Tara becomes a billionaire's wife, living in a gated community in Silicon Valley.

> I reached for his hand. "Bish" I said, "it doesn't have to be." You are a blind but blameless man. I wanted to know, but could not ask, where are you getting all this stuff? Up in San Francisco we get rumours of domestic discord in Silicon Valley. (266)

Bish (his American nickname means poison in Bengali, another cross-cultural misunderstanding) is so busy expanding his

Mughal like empire that his humanity suffers. Working fifteen hours a day, at home he relapses into the role of a traditionally demanding Indian husband, threatening his dreamy, artistic son Rabi. To save her son from his father's crushing contempt; Tara flees the gated community and moves to San Francisco, where she takes a volunteer job at a local public school and a live-in lover, ex-member of biker gang turned peaceful Zen adept. He's a nice enough guy but she likes him for the wrong reasons: the thought of his violent past gives her a thrill.

She has never bothered to turn back and examine her life but has just been talking all goody things with her sisters and parents over telephone. It is only after that incident that she reconsiders her assumptions about her family and begins her quest for reality. It is through this quest only that she finds her true identity. When she realizes how things were covered up in her family, how her sister still denied the fact of her having a child outside wedlock,

> I couldn't distinguish Muslims from Hindus any more. I wasn't even one hundred percent sure of Bengalis. I felt as though I were lost inside a Salman Rushdie novel, a one-firm identity smashed by hammer blows, melted down and re-emerging as something wondrous, or grotesque. (195)

She realizes the pernicious intentions of somebody behind Chris Day's arrival at her new home, but finds nobody to support her in her search to know the truth. Her lover deserts her for her going to the police, her son gets irritated; but despite all this, she takes it upon herself to find out the reality. Till now, there was a conflict going on in her mind between her need to adhere to her family's old traditions and desires to be an active part of the contemporary American culture. However, she realizes at last that she does not have the traditions that she thought supported her, but she goes on in her efforts.

Parvati, the middle sister, marries and remains in Mumbai, the wife of a wealthy, traditional Bengali businessman. Her life revolves around her two sons, visiting in-laws and her aging parents, devout Hindus who are in ill health. The oldest sister,

Padma, is the elusive sibling who left for the bright lights of New York in her early 20s. Padma, whose beauty and intelligence are matched only by her ambition, puts on a happy face for sisterly phone calls and occasional visits, but she keeps the truth of what has happened to her since leaving India a secret. Family secrets, of course, are never kept, and when a young man drops into Tara's life and claims to be an unacknowledged relative, the family Tara thought she knew begins to unravel before her frightened eyes.

> "Love" is slippery word when both partners bring their own definition. Love to Bish, is the residence of providing for parents and family,—Love is having fun with someone, more fun with that person than with anyone else, over a longer haul.—"Love" is my childhood and adolescence (although we didn't have an "adolescence" and we were never "teenagers") was indistinguishable from duty and obedience. (27)

The marriage that takes Tara to America gives her an undreamed-of independence and longing for more than just trips to the shopping mall. Her search for identity leads her back through childhood memories against the backdrop of scenes from India's history, which gives a rich portrait of what it means to grow up female in a society that has little regard for women. Moreover, the things Tara discovers about her family's past assist her in opening up to a wider world, and in this process, her personal evolution comes about from dealing with something thrust upon her from the outside in the form of the false Chris Day, as much as her own decisions and actions. The point is that though she is not completely free of her long ingrained prejudices regarding cast or religion, she is trying gradually to break out of these mindsets and come to terms with the reality with an American mind. That is why some of her actions seem apparently contradictory. She is appalled at her sister's doubtful adultery, finds herself unable to slap her son; calls her husband by his name only after divorce, yet she is quite comfortable while mentioning her lovers and knowing her son being a gay, preferring western clothes and food.

In *Desirable Daughters*, three Lear-like sisters born in a wealthy Kolkata family are faced with the realities of living in modern-day India and American societies. Although Padma, Parvati and Tara have obeyed their ancestral teachings and adhered to the laws of arranged marriage, their everyday rebellions are tenderly charted. The grand themes of secrets and lies in families are explored with subtlety and humour. Mukherjee does not shy away from portraying her characters as three-dimensional human beings with frailties, needs and desires. Tara, the youngest and the rebel of the family, is divorced. In San Francisco, a mysterious stranger enters her life, claiming to be the son of her older sister Padma. Tara, the sophisticated valley denizen, is suddenly caught in a mysterious web of deceit, she is faced with the fact that she really does not know her sisters. Could her sister have had a child out of wedlock? Were her parents instrumental in keeping the entire affair secret? Is she the only one who does not know?

At this point, Mukherjee changes gears. Obsessed with finding the truth, Tara relies on memory to piece together the past. Suddenly, innocent events take on mysterious hues. The thoroughly modern Tara explores the nature of familial relationships and learns that, even in the closest of relationships, humans are often true only to themselves. Even in our tell-all society, where the spilling of guts is commonplace. One really never knows the entire truth. Truth, like everything else, has nuances and layers, and is inevitably cliché ridden.

In researching her personal past, Tara discovers connections to history. She finds there are no coincidences, only convergences. Tara is searching for the pattern that connects "human memory and mathematical certainty." She seeks information about her heritage. She's trying to figure out what a 5 year old child, married to a tree in the late 19th century, could have to do to become a vibrant, independent woman of the 21st century. The novel tells three stories as it moves back and forth in time and over several continents. There's the story of Tara and her ex-husband as they try to reconcile; the story of Tara and her newly conceived child and the relationship with her new ob-gyn, Dr. Victoria Treadwell Khanna, and the history of the title character.

It appears to be merely a coincidence that the doctor's husband taught computer engineering to Tara's husband at Stanford University. Tara soon learns, however, that she bears a telling historical relationship to her gynaecologist who, in turn, passes on a cache of "moldering papers" that detail the history of the Treadwell family and its connection to Tara Lata Gangooly, the tree bride. The bulk of the novel slowly uncovers the modern-day Tara's connection to the woman who was a freedom fighter in India.

> The Tree Bride, the aged virgin who did not leave her father's house until the British dragged her off to jail, the least known martyr to Indian freedom, is the quiet center of every story. Each generation of women in my family has discovered in her something new. Even in far flung California, the Tree Bride speaks again. I've come back to India this time for something more than rest and shopping and these gin and lime-filled evenings with my mirror self. I'm like a pilgrim following the course of the Ganges all the way to its source. (289)

This includes a swashbuckling tale of piracy and mutiny on the high seas, a mute orphan and a colonialist with a hidden past. The years of World War Second detail Britain's involvement with India and the Tree Bride's clashes with established regime.

> The desk is littered with placards. QUIT INDIA, JAI HIND, JAI MA KALI, JAI BHARAT MATA, SHAME! BRITISH DEVIL, GO HOME. BANDE MATARAM! INDIA FOR INDIANS. Some of the placards are blood splattered. In the hall outside this room and in the inner courtyard, rows of the wounded are being tended by housewives, schoolgirls, and widows. . . . There are two surgeons in town, one Hindu, one Muslim, but both happen to be in the British Jail, awaiting exile to the Andaman Islands. (307)

Bharati Mukherjee was born in 1940, which means that she was witness to colonial brutality. They lived on a large street along which there were regular funeral processions of teenage martyrs. They were carried in rope cots, all strewn with flowers, everyone shouting "Quit India!" There was constant domestic brutality all around—extreme verbal, physical abuse of women, which Mukherjee witnessed, and a lot of it ritualized.

Mukherjee's characters are exiles caught between two cultures, Indian and American, as well as between tradition and the pull of modern life. There is no better example of this than Tara Chatterjee, the central character in Mukherjee's novel, *Desirable Daughters*. In this spellbinding and suspenseful tale, Tara is one of the three sisters who came of age in Kolkata, the daughters of a well-off tea merchant. The only sister to succumb to an arranged marriage, she moved her husband, Bish, to California, where he became the boy wonder of Silicon Valley and the head of a powerful technology company.

Tara smoothly assimilated into American culture, but constantly cast glances over her shoulder at her deeply rooted family history in India. Tired of Bish's constant absence, she filed for divorce and eventually moved to San Francisco with her son Rabi, where she is just another single working mom albeit one with an exotic history. What unfolded in *Desirable Daughters* was the beginning of a riveting mystery tied to Tara's family's past and the vast history and turmoil of India's fight for freedom.

In the final pages of *Desirable Daughters*, Tara stands in San Francisco street watching her house go up in flames. Along with her teenage son, Rabi and ex-husband, Bish, she was lucky to be alive after barely escaping what turned out to be a bomb set to kill. Throughout the novel, Mukherjee uses these marginal plotlines to propel Tara into a re-examination of her life. She may be as comfortable in jeans as in a Silk Sari, but she cannot discard the demands of her deeply ingrained Indian upbringing. She is also a believer in ghosts, visions, rituals, Hindu cosmology and above all, coincidence. By way of Tara's discoveries, the author creates a palpable and personal history of British colonial rule in India.

Smart and unstoppable, Tara, who's 36 but feels older, had been researching the Tree Bridge of Mishtigunj when the bomb blast left her own life in shambles. Reunited with Bish, who was severely injured saving her from the fire, she is scarred and pregnant. Mukherjee, moving back and forth between cultures and across continents, weaves an enchanting and disturbing story that is as much a mystery as it is a history lesson. The Tree Bride delves deep into the complex story of India's fight for freedom from the British Raj. As Charles Dickens did with Victorian England, Mukherjee unspools her story with a beguiling use of humour, detail, and colour. She grasps the complex points of history and whittles them into a compelling, if sometimes confusing, story. Mukherjee is a master at creating magical, mysterious characters that resound with spiritual healing for both the dead and the living.

Mukherjee examines "the stubborn potency of myth in the face of overwhelming change" in the lives of the three desirable daughters. Tara struggles to unravel the secrecy surrounding her past, to discover the truth behind her sisters' prevarications and fragmented stories. Plot recapitulation would only spoil the novel's many surprises. *Desirable Daughters* confirms Mukherjee's place as a complex writer with a keen eye for the subtleties of Indo-American life and a superb gift for characterization.

NOTE

Bharati Mukherjee. 2002. *Desirable Daughters*. Thea, USA.

The Gaze of a Subaltern and the Voice of a Reinvented Mythic Figure in Mahasweta Devi's "Draupadi"

LATA CHATURVEDI
Banaras Hindu University, Varanasi

As a social activist with an acute sense of Indian history, Mahasweta Devi has interrogated into the intersection of politics, gender and class. She is incessantly engaged in portraying the inner lives of the tribal communities and landless labourers in her novels, short stories and plays. Her powerful and haunting tales of exploitation and struggle offer us a rich site of feminist discourse. In this paper I will be reading 'Draupadi' the story that first appeared in *Agnigarbha* (*Womb of Fire*), a collection of loosely connected short political narratives. In the Introduction, Mahasweta makes her objective clear: "Life is not mathematics and the human being is not made for the sake of politics. I want a change in the present social system and do not believe in mere party politics."[1] Here an attempt will be made to explore into Devi's venture of rewriting an episode from the great epic, the *Mahabharata*. As a feminist response to the myth of Draupadi, she reinvents a cultural history and shows how this deconstructs the representation of women in cultures, images, stereotypes and archetypes. Significantly enough, the politics of interpretation has most often been the politics of gender.

The force of the story lies in its grounding in the subaltern's body, the female body which is only exploited. In the reinvented mythic image of Draupadi, the body of Draupadi figures forth the unutterable ugliness and cruelty as she articulates a truth that speaks of her situation. The relationship between the tribal and classical characters of Draupadi, the gaze and voice of the subaltern Dopadi at the close of the story, the reading of Senanayak's proper name Arijit and Dopadi's unusual employment of the term 'counter' are some of the focal points of my paper.

Dopadi becomes the medium through which the nature of women's exploitation within the patriarchal structure of family and society is explored. As Gayatri Chakravorty Spivak in "A Literary Representation of the Subaltern" says that Mahasweta Devi has always been 'gripped by the individual in history.' She writes of what may be called, 'history imagined into fiction.' (95)[2] The plausibility of Draupadi is that she could have existed as a subaltern in a specific historical moment imagined and tested by other assumptions. The term subaltern is used to denote the category of people who are subordinate in terms of class, caste, age gender and office.

In her trenchant, powerful and satiric fiction she has carved a niche for herself as a long time champion for the political, social and economic advancement of the tribals whom she characterizes as "suffering spectators of the India that is travelling towards the last century."[3] She has a penchant for interweaving myth and history with the prevalent condition of tribal lives and shows how their lives are being exploited by society. In an Interview in April 1983, she told Samik Bandapadhyaya: "A writer should document his own time and history. The socio-economic history of human development has always fascinated me. . . . So I chose to resurrect older periods in history in their immediate physicality, as if they were nothing less than contemporary." In 'Draupadi,' she has reinvented the mythic figure of Draupadi to highlight a legacy of the exploitation and subjugation of tribal people and erode the foundation on which the patriarchal society stands.

The protagonist Dopadi is a gendered subaltern who is disposed of, discarded, rejected and humiliated. As Jasbir Jain observes, "Gender continues to govern the individual's interaction with society and gender is both a social and cultural construct"[4] (54). As a tribal she is subjected to double "jeopardy."

"Draupadi" is perhaps one of Mahasweta Devi's most widely known stories that has been reprinted and translated in several collections. Like most of her works, it s set among the tribal communities in Bengal. Draupadi or the aboriginal Dopdi (as her name appears in dialect) is a rebel, hunted down by the government in their attempt to subjugate these groups. The government callously employs all forces available to them like kidnapping, murder, and rape, and a tribal death in custody is invariably known as accident. But Dopdi is not so easily tamed. After continuous days of rape and abuse, deprived of food and water, the story ends with a magnificent final scene in which she musters up the courage to face her abusers naked and bloody, but fiercely strong, hiding an awesome rebellion in her starved belly.

This indeed is a potent and disturbing story that requires a perceptive and moderately serious-minded reader. The seriousness of her purpose while writing the story stands in stark contrast to the simple language used by the writer. For instance; "Now Dopdi spreads her arms, raised her face to the sky, turns towards the forest, and ululates with the force of her entire being. Once, twice, three times. At the third burst the birds in the trees at the outskirt of the forest awake and flap their wings. The echo of the call travels for. (34)[5] Devi's language perhaps must have been very hard to translate. That's why the English intentionally startles the reader into an awareness that there are words and world beyond the English translation.

Devi's stories are remarkable for the fact that she never indulges in sentimentality. The hard life story of the subaltern, who is oppressed by her master/mistress, is conveyed convincingly, as the rape, the most heinous violence by the authorizers of the state. Whenever there is war, there is the rape and abuse of women. Right from the Trojan War to the Middle East conflict, this has been a tactic of war. Rape is the worst female degradation that can happen to a woman for it at once strips her off honour and humanity. Devi's narrative reminds one of Saadat Hasan Manto's story "Open It" where a young girl is raped by young men of her community. But unlike Manto, in "Draupadi" the unveiling of cloths highlights immense female power. Though, both the writers employ the stripping off of dress to create a dramatic climax. But they convey contrasting ideas about the sexual violence and degradation of women.

In Spivak's question "Can the Subaltern Speak?" the encouragement for the efforts of the subaltern studies group led by Ranjit Guha is implied. But she also criticizes them. As Ranjit Guha has appropriated Gramsci's term 'subaltern' (the economically dispossessed) in order to locate and re-establish a voice or collective locus of agency in India in the post-colonial scene. Subalterns should be allowed to speak for themselves.[6] A subaltern like the tribal Draupadi speaks out and reclaims a cultural identity that reinscribes her oppressed position in society.

In Devi's text Draupadi / Dopadi Mejhen, is a tribal revolutionary for whom her sexuality becomes the means of a harsh indictment of an exploitative social system. After being gang-raped in custody, she quickly turns the terrible wounds of her breasts into a counter offensive. Devi has chosen her from the plethora of renewed images of mythic women whom she recreates. The tribal Draupadi is the "object" of her feelings, instead of simply being viewed as the "other" and portrayed as the object of male desire. Many feminist writers have employed different textual strategies to restore women to their rightful place in literature. The feminist response to myths forms a vital focus of critical distance. Highlighting the significance of recasting the past tradition and creating a new history for women, Adrienne Rich observes: "Re-vision, the act of looking back, of seeing with fresh eyes, of entering an old text from a new critical direction—is for women more than a chapter in cultural history, it is an act of survival."[7]

Nabaneeta Dev Sen, another Bengali writer has rewritten many epic tales. In a series of stories she reinvents the epic women like Amba, Kaushalya, Sita, Surpanaka and Shakuntala. Most of the time, the epic women are used as pawns to prepare the grounds for the heroic deeds.

Mahasweta Devi, while rewriting the episode from the *Mahabharata* grants Dopadi the freedom of speech. In the epic Draupadi serves as a singular example of polyandry, a scarcely found marriage system in the Indian society. She becomes the wife of the five sons of Pandu. In the patriarchal context Draupadi becomes singular whereas her husbands are pluralized. The story questions this singularity because Dopdi is placed first in a comradely activist monogamous marriage and later in a situation of multiple rape. The classical character of Draupadi is used as a pawn to pave the way for heroic deeds. As a wife among husbands, she only highlights the male glory. Like Sita in the *Ramayana* and Helen in the Trojan War, she is shown to be the cause of the crucial battle. Her eldest husband Yudhishtir is on the verge of losing her in the game of dice. When Duryodhana, the enemy chief begins to pull her saree, she prays to Lord Krishna to save her honour. As divine miracle she sees herself to be infinitely clothed and consequently therefore, she cannot be publically stripped off.

The reconstructed mythic figure of Draupadi foregrounds a tribal named Dopadi, who was not entitled a heroic name. The pious name was given to her by the Brahmin mistress. The aboriginal name signifies the mark of her distance form the upper rung of the ladder. The onset of the story clearly puts things in proper perspective:

> "An exchange between two medallion uniforms.
>
> First Medallion: What's this, a tribal called Dopdi? The list of names I brought has nothing like it! . . .
>
> Second: Draupadi Mejhen. Born the year her mother threshed rice at Surja Sahu (killed)'s at Bakuli. Surja Sahu's wife gave her the name.
>
> Second: Most notorious female. Long wanted in many. (25)

The entire action of the story revolves around the search for Dopdi until she is apprehended. The last disastrous scene finds her in a situation when she becomes a hapless victim of the most atrocious sexual cruelty. Devi offers one of the most terrifying and stark critique of the dominant cultural perceptions. The story inhabits the space of the 'subaltern' that has feminism inscribed within it. Devi works actively to move the subaltern Draupadi into hegemony and she, in turn, is pushed towards another episteme that results in an awakening of a reinvented mythic figure in the gendered subaltern. Unlike the classical Draupadi, the tribal woman, does not seek the benign help of the Almighty, she discovers an ingenious way to counter sexual battering because of her moral strength. She is brought to the fore as a figure of refusal as she blatantly explodes the Hindu traditional imagination of the female.

The tribal Draupadi loves her husband "Dulna more than her blood." (25) When we first see her, she is thinking of washing her hair. She is so tactful that she never responds when she hears her own name being called. She "has seen in the panchayat office just today the notice for the reward in her name" (27). The reinvented mythic figure of Draupadi adores her ancestors. "Dopdi's blood was the pure-unadulterated black blood of Champabhumi. From Champa to Bakuli the blood could have been contaminated; Dopdi felt proud of her forefathers. They stood guard over their women's blood in black armour" (31).

It is fit to remember that the classical Draupadi's honour could not be saved by the elderly Bhiṣhma Pitamah. Here we come across the reconstructed mythic figure who leaves an indelible mark on the minds of the readers.

> Draupadi sits up as soon as she hears 'move!' and asks, 'where do you want me to go?'
>
> Draupadi fires her red eyes on the tent, says, come, I'll go.
>
> Draupadi stands up. She pours the water down on the ground. Tears her piece of cloth with her teeth.
>
> . . . The commotion is as if the alarm had sounded in a prison. Senanayak walks out surprised and sees Draupadi, naked, walking towards him in the bright sunlight with her head high. The nervous guards trail behind. (35-36)

When Draupadi stands finally fixed and naked in front of the police officer, "thigh and pubic hair matted with dry blood. Two breasts, two wounds" (36). Even after being gang-raped in custody, her indomitable spirit remains intact. It seems as if a phoenix like Draupadi dies in the rape and a new figure comes out of the ashes. Significantly enough, her weakness becomes her greatest strength.

> "Draupadi" comes closer. Stands with her hand on her hip, laughs and says. "The object of your search, Dopdi Mejhen. You asked them to make me up, don't you want to see how they made me?"
>
> Draupadi's black body comes even closer. . . . Her ravaged lips bleed as she begins laughing. Draupadi wipes the blood on her palm and says in a voice that is as terrifying, sky splitting, and sharp as her ululation, what's the use of clothes? You can strip me, but how can you clothe me again? Are you a man? . . . What more can you do? Come on, Kounter me—Come on, Kounter me?
>
> Draupadi pushes Senanayak with her two mangled breasts, and for the first time Senanayak is afraid to stand before an unarmed target, terribly afraid? (37)

After undergoing the third degree in violence, she musters up courage to speak if not for herself, at least for her comrades. A subaltern like the tribal Draupadi speaks out and reclaims a cultural identity that re-inscribes her oppressed position in the patriarchal society.

Spivak's essay "Can the Subaltern Speak"? perhaps best exemplifies Devi's concern for the processes that invite postcolonial studies to ironically re-inscribe, co-opt and rehearse neocolonial imperatives of political domination, economic exploitation and cultural erasure. Draupadi's political/sexual enemy is Senanayak. It is not for nothing that he is named Arijit, one who is victorious over the enemy. It is his voice that gives Draupadi the courage to speak if not for herself, at least for her comrades. With the entry of this subaltern at the close of the story, her gaze and voice, the army officer is baffled and outwitted. Despite the fact that she does not know English, she uses the English word 'Kounter' in an ingenious way. In her Introduction, Spivak argues, "In 'Draupadi' what is represented as an erotic object is transformed into an object of torture and revenge where the line between (hetro)sexuality and gender violence begins to waver." (7)[8]

After being gang-raped in custody, she emerges as a terrifying super object. Mahasweta Devi perhaps never conceived of the modern story as a refutation of the ancient. One must agree with Spivak when she says 'Dopdi is (as heroic as) Draupadi.

She is also what Draupadi—written into the patriarchal and authoritative sacred text as proof of male power—could not be. Dopdi is at once a palimpsest and a contradiction" (11).

In her interview 'Telling History,' Gayatri Chakravorty Spivak observes that Draupadi was a fighter: "She fought in the end in a woman's way—Senanayak was afraid in front of a woman's body" (18). It is not for nothing that Mahasweta Devi, declares in unequivocal terms: "By just making them non-existents they do not exist for her, all this, male stuff, they are trying to do this, by mass raping, by gang raping also, you just cannot destroy a woman's spirit, she does not recognize their existence, they are nonexistent for her." (19)[9]

And this is precisely what makes the gaze of a subaltern her counter offensive. This reinvented mythic figure of Draupadi will always be one of the memorable creations of Mahasweta Devi's cultural activism. The invincible spirit of the reconstructed Dopdi has secured a place for itself in the annals of subaltern literature.

NOTES

1. Mahasweta Devi, *Agnigarbha* (Calcutta, 1978), p. 8.
2. Mahasweta Devi, *Imaginary Maps*, Trans. Gayatri Chakravorty Spivak (Thema, Calcutta, 1993).
3. Gayatri Chakravorty Spivak, "A Literary Representation of the Subaltern," *Subaltern Studies*, V (New Delhi, O.U.P. 1987).
4. Jasbir Jain, *Writing Women across Cultures* (New Delhi and Jaipur: Rawat, 2002).
5 Mahasweta Devi, "Draupadi" in *Breast Stories* (Calcutta: Seagull, 2002).
6 http:/postcolonialweb.org/poldiscourse/spivak/spivak2.html
7 Maggie Humm, *Feminist Criticism: Women as contemporary critics* (Great Britain: The Harvester Press, 1986), p. 186.
8 "Telling History," Gayatri Chakravorty Spivak, Interview of Mahasweta Devi, *Chotti Munda and His Arrow*, trans. and intro. Spivak (Calcutta: Seagull,, 2002), pp. 18-19.

Mahasweta Devi's Feminist Rewriting/Righting of the Great War in *After Kurukshetra*

LATA CHATURVEDI
B.H.U., Varanasi

This paper intends to read the stories written by Mahasweta Devi entitled *After Kurukshetra* that take us to the unexpected and startling episodes of the conventional epic saga, the *Mahabharata*. She makes us perceive the great war from the eyes of subalterns—marginalized, dispossessed and dalit women.

The term subaltern which has an ultimate military etymology is derived from the work of the Italian Marxist Antonio Gramsci, who used it to designate new elite social classes and groupings like the proletariat. Spivak employed the term to expand its signification to include groups more downgraded than these for instance, tribals or scheduled castes, untouchab es and, within all those groups of women. Here Mahasweta Devi ventures to rewrite the saga of the ancient epic as it is seen through the eyes of the subaltern: the women and the underclass, panchakanya the five women, Nishadin and Sauvali. The rewritten stories offer us a feminist version of the re-interpreted and re-invented heterogeneous classical text like the *Mahabharata*.

At the outset of the story "The Five Women," Mahasweta Devi puts things in perspective when we come to know that after the dharmayudha, the battiefield is set ablaze with funeral pyres. "As the pyres burn, a crowd of women huddled in the distance cries out in grief."

> These women are not of the rajavritta, women of royalty, nor are they servants or attendants. These women are from the families of the hundreds of foot soldiers—padatiks—from various other little

> kingdoms. They had been slaughtered every day, in their thousands, their function being to protect the chariot-mounted heroes. They were issued no armour. So they died in large number. (1)

They were brought to become Uttara's companions. Abhimanyu's pregnant widow, Uttara who has been "withering away in the cruel heat of grief." They introduce themselves before Subhadra: "I'm Godduni. This is Gomati holding my hand. That's Yamuna, with the red spot between her brows that one standing there with a finger on her chin is Vitasta. And this is Vipasha, Vitasa's little sister" (4).

The war had brought their world to the brink of a complete disaster and had caused unimaginable havoc and suffering to the lives of women. The epical women characters castigate the wanton waste and inhumanity of war. Kurukshetra, as depicted by Mahasweta Devi is not the glorifying Dharmayudha of the popular culture but rather a cold-blooded and callous power game sacrificing innumerable innocent human lives. Kunti begins to observe her "son's arrogance in victory with the distant gaze of a self-exiled onlooker" (7) once she chooses to ask Draupadi: "Panchali, be quiet now. You have borne endless injustice and humiliation. It was to avenge that humiliation that the entire Kaurava clan has been destroyed." (7) But significantly enough, Draupadi only "keeps herself cloaked in a veil of silence" (8). Subhadra, on the other hand, drives home one of the other cruel realities of war when she laments that 'sons are dead, their fathers are alive. Daughters-in-law have lost their husbands, while their mothers-in-law are still married." (8)

Mahasweta Devi in her powerful way presents a stark contrast between the royal women and their peasant counterparts. The shadowy existences of the royal widows resonate in the 'chambers of silence" (17). It is surprising to note: "Everything happens outside the women's quarters, here, Pujas, ceremonial sacrifices, Yagnas. There, the world is full of bustle and activity. Here, you white-clad widows float around like shadowy ghosts. We wonder, won't you ever laugh, talk loudly, run outside on restless feet? No!" (17) Subhadra intervenes telling them that "Rajavritta widow must follow the example. Set by Arya Kunti.

In *ihlok*, in this world of ours, widows have no right to happiness" (17).

Contrary to this, when we look at the Lokavritta way of life we find that despite the fact that these women's husbands/ soldiers died in "the king's war," no 'Divyalok' is assured for them as heaven is the privilege only for the rajavritta. Their view of the war does not ascribe the dharmayudha status to it. This is made manifest in the following observation: "Brother kills brother, uncle kills nephew, shishya kills guru. It may be your idea of dharma, it's not ours" (23).

The five women's articulation/speech, lively movements and habits stand in stark contrast to the royal queen's existence as mute/shadowy ghosts "shrouded in silence" (23). They are acutely aware of the fact: "If we don't go . . . the fields will lie fallow, the cattle will be uncared for. Once we return, all of us together will perform the necessary funeral ritual for our dead. Then the elders will arrange marriages, we need husbands, we need children. . . . We will . . . create life. That's what Nature teaches us" (22).

As the member of royalty, Subhadra somehow fails to sense the silence that has began to suffocate Uttara, her daughter-in-law who was widowed in her early youth. Although Subhadra's mind gets turbulent, she continues to be a "concerned mother" (18) when she says, "Just don't upset my daughter-in-law Subhadra's heart, like that of any woman, feels close to bursting with those words. The five women exchange glances. Shake their heads, sigh, and turn away" (18).

Here Mahasweta Devi seems to foreground the reality that the *Lokavritta* (the folk way of life) and *Rajavritta* (the life of the rulers) stand in stark contrast to each other. The resilience of the five widows of ordinary farmers and artisans pressed into the royal service is strikingly differentiated from the effete royalty of the Pandava queens. The grief of the pregnant, sorrowing Uttara is touched with a masterly stroke because Panchakanya ("the five women") do not remain widows, life must go on and if they do not bear children, cultivate the fields, grind the grain, society will collapse. That's why they prefer to leave the palace and seek out new husbands. These vibrant and strong-willed women are capable of managing their lives with meaningful and joyous spirits. The portrayal of the plight of these women reaches high watermark as they "seem to think as one. They are so close that they seem to understand each other without words, speak to one another with their eyes alone. They look, they understand" (18).

Mahasweta Devi deftly touches upon what perhaps remained away from Ved Vyasa's grandiloquent imagination. She purposively brings to the fore three classes of women—women from the royalty, women from the Pandava peasantry and women from the Kauravas. And their typical portrayal signifies the effect of war on the subaltern or subproletariat, especially the women. Through the different women who appear to have their stories told—Uttara and Subhadra in the first instance, the Pandava's mother Kunti and Nisadin, in the second and Souvali, the dasi-wife of Dhritarashtra in the last tale—all of these are victimised. In 'The Five Women' Kunti quite sharply asks Draupadi—who is incessantly condemning the Kauravas—whether she has ever looked at the Kaurava women—husband- and son-less: "But place your hand upon your heart and tell me—have you not been avenged in full? The Kaurava men are all dead. Have you ever looked at the bereft Kaurava women, who have lost their husbands and sons? Are they responsible, tell me? Try to feel a little compassion, a little pity. A little affection for them, you will see how it will soften your heart" (7-8). Draupadi, in her response gets herself further cloaked in a 'veil of silence.'

The next story "Kunti and the Nishadin" brings face-to-face the killer of a tribal woman and her five sons with that women's daughter-in-law when Kunti is eking out her last days in the forest. Just as those tribals were put in the house of lac to be burnt alive, Kunti is trapped in a forest fire with Gandhari and Dhritarashtra. Kunti unleashes her "burden of unspoken thoughts and feelings" (26). As she reflects: "Life in the Rajavritta was so different. Mother of the Pandavas. Wife of Pandu. The role of daughter-in-law, the role of queen, the role of mother, playing these hundreds of roles, where was the space, the time to be her true self? All that while amazingly—she never felt that anything was hers, hers alone" (26).

At this chosen moment in her life she chooses to look outside the life of rajavritta and decides to speak to a dasi: "How could they? Her life had been the rajavritta, the gods, serving the brahmans, . . . Had she ever spoken to a dasi? Had she developed any genuine bond with Hidimba? Life outside the rajavritta had not touched her at all." (27).

A candid confession gushes forth from her heart, as she begins to compare herself with the truly pious and dutiful character of Gandhari: "I am not truly pious and dutiful like Gandhari. I lack the courage that comes from dharma. I was overwhelmed to find my sons alive after the battle of Kurukshetra. But Draupadi and Uttara were devastated at the death of the r sons. I could not console them. Gandhari did." (28)

Slowly she begins to realize: "No, I have none of Gandhari's true piety and righteousness. When, before Krishna, she mourned the dead, was it only her dead sons and grandsons, the countless widows, she lamented over. . . She was cursing war and bloodshed on behalf of all the women in this world." (28) Significantly enough, at this juncture she tries to come to terms with her guilt over her unacknowledged and disowned son Karna, her first-born who was abandoned for fear of public shame.

The royalty has turned her to be treacherous and cunning. Despite the fact that she never visited Karna to hold him to her bosom to offer her long locked up affection, she does see him for the sake of her sons, Pandavas, and pleads to him to leave Kauravas and join hands with Pandavas. "Only the wars of the victorious are known as dharmayudha. The wars of the vanquished are never called thus. Knowing this . . . Karna said . . . he could not abandon Duryodhana. Apart from Arjuna, he would not harm any of the other Pandavas—you will still have five sons left alive." (32) This gives Kunti a great consolation that Karna regards himself as one of her sons. The bitter memory of leaving him at birth keeps gnawing at her heart.

In her desperate bid of feminist rewriting/ righting of the tale, Mahasweta Devi's eloquent voice can be heard when she makes Kunti encounter Nishadin who goes to the extent of reminding a crime, the murder of a family of Nisad forest dwellers which she has complacently forgotten. For her, Kunti's confession is futile because she spells out clearly: "The rajvritta folk and the Lokavritta folk have different values, different ideas of right and wrong. If a young nishad girl makes love to the boy of her choice and get pregnant, we celebrate it with a wedding" (36). She calls this to be a nature's law. "Nature abhors waste. We honour life, when a man and woman come together, they create a new life" (36). She wonders why Kunti has not been able to come to terms with "the gravest sin."

"But to the people of the Lokavritta, to sacrifice or harm innocents in one's own self-interest is the most unpardonable sin, you are guilty of that sin." (36) Kunti being a member of the royalty does not hesitate causing six innocent forest tribals to be burnt alive to serve her own interest to give an irrefutable proof of six people (the Pandavas and their mother Kunti) burnt to death. The Rajavritta and Janavritta life is again brought to the fore with contrasting notes.

> The Nishadin said with pride: "We don't deny the demands of life. If we are widowed and we have the right to remarry. Those who wish to can marry again. We did so, we have husbands, children."
>
> "What will you . . .?"
>
> "No. An eye for an eye, a tooth for a tooth, that's the way of the rajvritta. That's what Kurukshetra was all about. The Lokavritta ways are different." (38)

When Kunti asks for forgiveness, Nishadin, whose mother-in-law along with her five sons was burnt alive, bursts out in agony. "To beg forgiveness is typical of the rajavritta. We don't understand such things." (39)

The last story 'Souvali' centres around the story of Dhritarashtra's dasi-putra, Souvalya better known as Yuvutsu in *Mahabharata*. He is the son of a prostitute who was brought in to serve as dasi when Gandhari was carrying a child. Souvali got pregnant and she gave birth to a half-royal offspring. His mother fumes and frets against the royal name Yuvutsu that was given to him by the royally. As she says, "Today they had to grant you the first right. You are Dhritarashtra's son. If they left you out, they would have gone against dharma." "Give the boy a name and that's the end of all responsibility" (43).

The slave child/ dasiputra is startled when he is asked to perform the last rites of his father, tarpan. He wonders: "Never went near him, never called him 'father,' and today I did the tarpan for him" (43).

Souvalya was taken away from his mother to join Gurukul because this was the tradition in the royalty. As he avers: "They'd taunt me. Say that only dasiputras suffered such unmanly needs, cried for their mothers. It's true it's in the janavritta, amongst the common people, that we are in touch with our natural emotions. Tenderness, caring, compassion, romance, love, anger, jealousy. But in the rajvritta, you know how they keep such natural emotions strictly in check. And that's their downfall. It's always been power, greed, arrogance and enmity that's caused the ruin of the rajavritta' (47).

As a deliberate act of defiance, Souvali refuses to offer death rites to Dhritarashtra because he was only her son's father and not her wedded husband. When she compares and contrasts between her earlier status as a dasi in the royal household and a free woman residing on the outskirts of the town amongst the common people, she finds enough reasons to rejoice and to feast on sweets while living in a place of her own free will. "It feels good to have defiled the dead Dhritarashtra. In the royal household, the other dasis would be roaming around in white widow clothing eating only the prescribed meager fare." (48) "I was nothing but a dasi in the royal household here, amongst the common people. I'm a free woman." (49)

At the twilight of her life, after undergoing multiple experiential realities, she has explored certain true fragments underlying the royalty and the under class. As a concerned mother, she is highly anxious about her son as she reflects while eating; "When will Souvalya realize? That even the Pandavas will never accept him as one of their own?" (49)

In this way, Mahasweta Devi heralds her blue-print of revolt as a story teller par-excellence. This could be viewed as a clarion call to all the feminist thinkers who have chosen for reinterpretation and re-invention of the classical myths and characters as their mode of survival.

Works Cited

Mahasweta Devi, *After Kurukshetra: Three Stories*. Kolkata: Seagull Books. Trans. Anjum Katyal. 2005.

Fresh Retellings of the *Mahabharata*, Review by Pradip Bhattacharya, http:/www.boloji.com/bookreviews/ 065.htm

A Journey to Selfhood: Manju Kapur's *A Married Woman*

PUSHPA MOHANDAS
Z.G. College, University of Calicut

In a male-dominated society, woman is expected to be an ideal wife, a mother, a home-maker with multifarious roles in the family. According to Indian tradition, a woman must defer to her husband in every possible respect. She must acquiesce to her husband's demands. At every stage of her life, she is dependent on her father, husband or son. The Indian woman is often seen to be passive and accepting her given role. Exposure to reformist movements, economic independence and the impact of the Western feminist movement brought about a significant change in the attitude and position of woman in India. A few women began to voice their feelings freely through their writings. Fiction became a powerful form of literary expression of their struggle to establish their identity and individuality. In the late 1960s and 1970s, issues which were taboo earlier were boldly though subtly taken up by women writers. The women writers of the late 1980s openly brought out the question of female sexuality. Woman was seen as a living human being who was neither superhuman nor a weakling and who looked for something beyond sex in marriage. Woman stepped out of the rigid sex roles assigned to them traditionally and struggled to achieve a racial, social and economic equality with men. The traditional standard equation has been radically altered.

Fiction by women writers constitutes a major part of Indian English literature. They portray women who struggle to establish their identity and individuality by waging a desperate battle against the existing social order. These women fiction writers, in their writing provide insights, a wealth of understanding and a platform for discussion. The new ideology is reflected not only in the various political, economic and social movements but also in the literature that has been written during the last few decades, especially in the post-Independence Indian feminist writers like Nayantara Sahgal, Shashi Deshpande, Shoba De, Arundhathi Roy, Anita Desai, Manju Kapur and Jhumpa Lahiri. Nayantara Sahgal lashes out at those who regard women as property and discourage individuality in them:

> When I heard someone remark "we never allow our daughters to go out" or "I can't do that, my husband would not like it", it sounded a very peculiar, alien jargon. As if, I thought, women were property not persons. (qtd. Dass 220)

This awakening among women writers has helped them to project a woman who is undergoing a change, trying to establish her identity. Shashi Deshpande portrays modern, educated and career-oriented middle class women, sensitive to the changing time and situations. They seek change within the cultural norms. Her women are caught in a flux between responsibility to oneself and the traditional role of a wife. But rather than revolt and challenge their victimization, they compromise for the sake of domestic harmony. Nayantara Sahgal shows the need for a new morality in which women will be treated as equal to men. She is a champion of individual freedom. Her women refuse to be an acquiescent, suffering and sacrificing lot. Anita Desai is different in that she makes a psychological exploration of her women protagonists who are lonely and sensitive. They are hypersensitive and highly individualistic. In their existential struggle, they suffer intensely but refuse to be crushed. Arundhathi Roy's novel *The God of Small Things*. (1997) deals with the insult and abuse the women of society are subjected to. It is also a crusade against male chauvinism. Manju Kapur, like Roy, experiments with new themes such as gratification of sex from women's point of view along with the politics of the day. Feminism and contemporary history go hand in hand to give a new dimension to their fiction.

Their novels are a bold step ahead on man-woman relationship from the viewpoint of a woman.

In her debut novel *Difficult Daughters* (1998), which won her the most acclaimed commonwealth prize for the best first book, Manju Kapur shows women in search of their own space.. Her second novel, *A Married Woman* (2002), is about what happens when old customs lose their power and the woman no longer believes that her life should be determined in a narrow fashion. The protagonist of the novel Astha Vadera, undergoes profound changes against the backdrop of an India that is also evolving. Manju Kapur's preoccupation with the female revolt against deep-rooted family values and the institution of marriage is seen in *A Married Woman.* In depicting the inner subtlety of a woman's mind, Kapur displays a mature understanding of the female psyche. She has thus joined the growing number of women writers from India on whom the image of the suffering but stoic woman eventually breaking traditional boundaries has had a significant impact.

In *A Married Woman*, Kapur characterizes Astha with sympathy and insight, highlighting her youthful innocence and her transformation into a woman who understands that she must struggle to achieve her desires. Astha, the daughter of middle-class Indian parents marries Hemant, a foreign-returned M.B.A and a bank employee from a good family because it is expected of her. Her married life is filled with promises, privileges and prosperity. Hemant sets up a manufacturing factory for producing televisions. He does well and the marriage falls into the usual pattern. They have two children, a girl and a boy. Hemant's official assignments prevent him from spending much time with his family. Astha's job as a teacher divides her time between her family and school. Astha begins to find marital life oppressive and feels suffocated in the routine responsibilities as a wife and mother. She becomes more restless because of her insensitive, indifferent husband who makes her feel worthless. She believes in freedom, equality and her right to her own individuality. Hemant denies her all these things. Within a few years of her marriage, she realizes, "this boat could not be rocked" (99). She had

had a good life so far because nothing was questioned. Kapoor beautifully depicts the power struggle that emerges to mar the couple's relationship.

As we delve into Astha's adult life, we find a free spirit trapped in a suffocating traditional society whose restrictions make us doubt whether we have entered the 21st century. Astha receives a callous treatment from her own people, even her mother who hands over the money received from the sale of her plot to Hemant. Astha is not happy about it, "Really, Ma, don't you think women can be responsible for their own investment?" (97). After her mother's departure, when Hemant discloses what he intends to do with the money, Astha says, "But I was wondering whether I could also have a say in what you do with it" (98). Hemant is furious and goes ahead with his business deals without having the slightest concern for Astha's wish. She sinks more and more into loneliness. Being an educated lady, she yearns for independence of thought and action. She turns to writing poems and painting. Hemant does nothing to encourage her; on the contrary, he finds fault with her poems. His disinterestedness in her achievements deprives her of her happiness. She receives a further jolt when she learns that their Goan trip had materialized with the help of the huge amount of money that her painting bought and because it was off-season. She had wanted to develop as a visual artist and rent a proper studio with the money. While Hemant indulges the children by buying them expensive dishes, he refuses to buy Astha, the little antique silver box she had fancied and which cost much lesser than the dishes. Such lack of concern for her creates havoc in her life.

Kapur depicts the gripping political situation with the same fervour and graphic detail as she describes Astha's actions and inner conflicts. Religious tension between Hindus and Muslims mirrors Astha's frustrations. Although her marriage seems far less violent than the political and religious tensions, it is in reality no less oppressive or damaging. Astha wanted to involve herself in the Hindu-Muslim conflicts taking place in Ayodhya, "there are too many people like me in this country who are not paying attention to what is happening", (116) she says, to which

Hemant retorts, "Please, keep to what you know best, the home, children, teaching. All this doesn't suit you" (116). He wanted her to stay at home and look after the children. Aijaz Akhtar khan, a history lecturer, noted theatre activist and founder of The Street Theatre Group, is invited to the school where Astha teaches, to conduct a summer workshop on theatre. He assigns Astha to unearth the historical details about Ram Janambhumi—Babri Masjid. Aijaz improvises on Astha's findings on the sensational issue as "Fact, Fiction and You". Astha fails to see the repercussions or sequel to the staging of such a play. She finds satisfaction in her artistic achievement. He applauds her and she finds him a man with a mission. The desire to cause awareness among the public costs Aijaz his life. To add to the shock of Aijaz's death, Astha is stunned by Hemant's reaction to the incident. He finds fault with her for meddling in things that did not concern her. "This kind of thing happens all the time," he says, "I don't see why you are wasting your tears." (139) Astha stares at her husband in revulsion. She cannot understand how anyone can be so indifferent to as ghastly an incident as the burning alive of a whole theatre group in a van.

There are long processions, strikes, dharnas and slogans which however take the shape of propaganda and signify how religious issues can be sensitized. Astha joins the demonstrations. Her active involvement in demonstrations led by the Sampradayakta Mukti Manch is an eye-opener to people like Hemant who sympathise but are silent spectators of those fundamentalists who create chaos in the name of religion. Kapur tries to awaken the intellectuals of this country who hesitate to voice their truth, when she writes: "Is this the message for the citizens of this country, live in fear, do not raise your voices, for they will be stifled by fire, murder and violence" (140).

Astha's association with Sampradayakta Mukti Manch provides her with a platform to expose her talent in painting. Just as she found in Aijaz, an admirer of her writing and painting skills, she finds in Pipeelika, his young widow, an admirer of her oratorical skills. Hemant's lack of concern and absence of creativity had disappointed Astha. His disinterestedness in her achievements deprives her of a married woman's delight. She feels terribly exploited. The tensions surface from time to time as paralyzing migraines. Marriage proves a terrible experience for Astha. She laments that women have no choice except to surrender and accept.

Astha's dejected self finds solace in Pipeelika, the young widow of Aijaz. They have many common interests. A rapport is quickly established between Astha and Pip. Astha finds in her a comrade in her lesbian love. Through this relationship, Astha realizes that true union in love means the union of not only two bodies but also their souls, their feelings and ideologies. Manju Kapur is the first Indian feminist to introduce lesbian love as an important topic of discussion. Woman-woman bonding helps us not only to understand the significance of the self-in-community, it also reveals the complexity of women's experience of caring. The logical outcome of this bonding is the rejection of the earlier stress on the equality of sexes. It upholds the significance of the female qualities. The concept of woman's bonding leads us to see the new female who achieves great heights without emulating the male. Mother-daughter relationship and woman-woman dyad are significant components of the new paradigm. Through the intimacy which is knowledge, woman's bonding becomes a vehicle of self-definition. She has the courage to be herself. This new Indian woman can be discerned in Indian fiction to an extent. For the new woman, the deeper meaning of life is realized when her emotional and spiritual needs get recognition instead of the socially accepted ones of security, comfort and respectability. Literature, by reflecting the new woman helps her to overcome the sense of isolation which has been one of the main instruments of her oppression in a patriarchal society.

Kapur explores in *A Married Woman*, the positioning of women in the context of sexual orientation. The lesbian relationship that develops between Astha and Pip fills Astha's life with fresh air, joy and vibrant health. She no longer feels worthless or unwanted. Her migraines no longer trouble her. She finds freedom in her relation with Pip and also in voicing her opinions on politics. She is able to freely pursue her passion for painting and to assert her rights with the new-found strength infused in her by Pip. The relationship serves as an eye-opener to her. She realizes that marriage is not just sex but also togetherness and respect for each other. With encouragement from Pip, Astha organizes an exhibition of her paintings and becomes independent economically. She feels loved and strong through Pip. She expresses her happiness in the jottings in her diary: "Maybe this is what good marriages are like. To be able to express what comes into your head and know it will be understood as you meant it" (260).

Kapur is conscious of the challenges of a man-woman relationship in the present world and wants us to take notice of the complete compatibility and rapport between two women, the emotional and physical bonding between them. The two, Astha and Pip, mirror each other equally. Astha, who had begun to feel like a sex machine for her husband and who had lost self-worth, rediscovers herself through Pip's desire. She is made to feel beautiful and wanted by her partner. From a commodity or a machine, she transforms into a human being with a sense of dignity, self-confidence and self-esteem. She is once again a healthy vibrant individual. She is confident of her creative powers. Astha's bonding with Pip is not a choice exercised by a woman who would take the initiative to start and sustain a lesbian relationship. It could be interpreted as an act arising from resentment of her particular situation: "When she was with Hemant, she felt like a woman of straw, her inner life dead, with a man who noticed nothing" (287).

Kapur tries to justify Astha's lesbian love with Pip in an interview with Ira Pandey: "This relationship suggested itself to me as an interesting means of making Astha mature and change. An affair with a man would have been the classic cliché and so I ruled it out and tried out a same sex affair. I don't know how successful I have been nor is this based on any real life relationship. It is as I said a writer's experiment with a plot."

A Married Woman contributes issues to the lesbian discourse that is being generated almost shyly in India. Astha and Pip share tender moments together but the relationship is not allowed to travel the trajectory. Astha feels morally responsible and emotionally attached to her children. Even when she is with Pip, she wonders about them. For Astha and Kapur, family means the traditional heterosexual union. Astha prioritises her family over Pip. She offers clichéd arguments for her inability to join Pip in a lasting, exclusive relationship. Her commitment to heterosexuality is reinforced by her steadfastness in continuing with her marriage irrespective of her meaningless existence. She enjoys but is not prepared to acknowledge her relationship with Pip. She cannot forsake her family and children. Even when she sounds as an advocate of women's rights, Kapur keeps the values of Indian middle class families intact. Astha is disinterested and distressed but she won't go for a divorce. She has lesbian love with Pip but looks to her husband for security and comfort. She protests against her husband's dominance, challenges the social taboos and social norms but gives in ultimately. She makes a compromise realizing that it is the only course open to her to save her marriage. She has voluntarily made the choice and it makes a difference. Kapur shows the new woman as a product of the inevitable transformation taking place in society.

In Kapur's novels, the new woman refuses to play second fiddle to her husband. They refuse to have their moments choreographed by certain implicit cultural rules. They grapple with significant issues like motherhood, mothering, marriage and marginalization, women in several roles as wife, sister and friend and above all as human beings. Thematically the novel, *A Married Woman*, like Kiran Desai's *Hullabaloo in the Guava Orchard* and Arundhati Roy's *God of Small Things* belongs to the genre of the bildungsroman as the protagonist passes through a phase of growth, self-discovery, alienation and a conflict of generations which leads her from innocence to knowledge, from immaturity to a certain amount of understanding of human motives, whims and fancies. Towards the end of the novel, we find Pip leaving for Illinois to pursue her Ph.D. This comes as a blessing to Astha. The novel ends with Astha changing her dress and brushing her teeth and getting into her side of the bed. She wants to sleep so that she could forget all that is unusual.

The Indian woman as depicted in *A Married Woman* is representative of the transitory phase of Indian society, torn asunder by the traditional values, the country's heritage and the modern, liberal values imbibed from the West. Man-woman equation has been re-defined. The protagonist in the novel differs from others in that she aspires, attempts and strives to be her true self. The 'glorified' woman is replaced by the 'real' woman. Kapur portrays a woman who has become aware of the biased attitude of her husband and stands for the modern emancipated woman, asserting her individuality by challenging the taboos and destructive social norms.

Works cited

Kapur, Manju. *A Married Woman*. New Delhi: IndiaInk, 2002.

Bhongle, Rangarao. *Native Responses to Contemporary Indian English Novel*. New Delhi: Atlantic, 2003.

Das, Bijay Kumar. *Postmodern Indian English Literature*. Delhi: Atlantic, 2003.

Dass, Veena Noble. *Feminism and Literature*. New Delhi: Prestige, 1995.

Pandey, Ira. Interview with Manju Kapur. *The Hindu*, January 5, 2003.

Ray, Mohit K. and Rama Kundu. *Studies in Women Writers in English*. Delhi: Atlantic, 2005.

Singh, Anita. *Indian English Novel in the Nineties and After: A Study of the Text and its Context*. Delhi: Adhyaya, 2004.

Girish Karnad's *Naga-Mandala*: A Sociological Study

LUCKY GUPTA
T.R. (P.G.) College, Aligarh

Dramatic creations of India have had a rich haul of great talents like Bhasa and Kalidasa. Even the languages that do not possess great texts, their available narrative literature reveals prominent theatre properties. Post-Independence era witnessed the awareness of creative writers on socio-political manifestations. The early state of decolonized India was to stabilize its political power but simultaneously the literary manifesto was to represent socio-political dimensions of imperial authority. The award winning dramatist Girish Karnad is one of the frontline playwrights in contemporary Indian theatre along with Mohan Rakesh, Badal Sircar, Mahesh Dattani and Vijay Tendulkar. Born in May 19, 1938 in Matheran, Maharashtra, Girish Karnad has become one of India's brightest stars earning international praise as a playwright, poet, actor, director, critic and translator. For four decades, Karnad has continued to compose top-notch plays, often using history and mythology to tackle contemporary themes, focusing on the significance of Indian theatre. Karnad reveals: "The basic concern of Indian theatre in the post-independence period has been to try to define its 'Indianness.'"[1]

In 1992 Karnataka Sahitya Akademi Awarded play, *Naga-Mandala*, is his most creative work based on two Kannada folk tales which he heard from A.K. Ramanujan. Apart from the various characteristics of traditional Indian theatre, the play presents a picture of the society in which woman is subjected to all sorts of invidious discriminations. The present paper is focused to reveal woman's understanding of the reality and highlights her subjugated position and her helpless state to defend her 'identity' and 'self' in the traditional society of India. The discussions are also focused towards the marginality of woman in Indian society. She is either ill treated or elevated at the heights of Gods and Goddesses. In the 'introduction' to the play, Karnad reveals: "The position of Rani in the story of *Naga-Mandala* . . . can be seen as a metaphor for the situation of a young girl in the bosom of a joint family where she sees her husband only in two unconnected roles—as a stranger during the day and as a lover at night. . . . The empty house Rani is locked in could be the family she is married into." (17)

The play begins with the Prologue in which one is taken to the inner sanctum of a ruined temple. The idol is broken and therefore cannot be identified. In the prologue, Karnad reveals that man is a bundle of weaknesses, but he is either not aware about them or doesn't want to get rid of them: "I may be dead within the next-few hours. . . . A mendicant told me: 'You must keep awake at least one whole night this month, if you can do that, you will live. If not, you will die on the last night of the month.'" (22)

The man, talking to the spectators, pledges that if he survives that night, he will have nothing more to do with themes, plots or stories:

> I asked the mendicant what I had done to deserve this fate and he said, 'You have written plays. You have staged them. You have caused so many good people, who came trusting you to fall asleep twisted in miserable chairs, that all the mass of sleep has turned against you and become the curse of death.' (23)

Suddenly the man perceives the naked flames conversing as they enter the temple. The flame transforms and assumes female voices. They come from different houses to exchange their views on the present social scenario. The flame discovers that most of the people are engaged in the worldly pleasure and are asleep to the spiritual thrust of man. Flame First comes from the house of a miserly fellow who retires to bed early to save 'Kusbi Oil' spending on lamp. Flame Third reveals that she is forced to witness lasciviousness of the master who needs light to feast his eyes on the limbs of his wife to make the rest of him to react. Flame Fourth comes from a house in which the old mother has died neglected. She had bed sores and the house stank with phlegm, pus and urine. Now the master and mistress have the freedom to pass their nights in voluptuous pleasures. The new flame has a different story. The old mistress had a doubt lurking in her mind that her husband has illicit relations with some young woman. In fact the old mistress had a story and a song impressioned in her mind, both the story and the song simmering to be free. Therefore the story transforms into a young woman and song becomes a sari. However the story comes to the temple and desires to be heard by somebody. The man offers to hear the story if he will be kept awake all the night. Thus the prologue explores the aberrations of man and woman to convey the message that 'men' in general are slaves of passion and are asleep to the hard realities of life.

Act one begins with the story addressing the audience: "A young girl. Her name . . . It does not matter. But she was an only daughter, so her parents called her Rani, Queen." (27) The story is the narrator in the play and plays the same role which Bhagavata in *Hayavadana* plays. The story also intervenes at several other places and tries to establish a communion with the audience. Thus both the story and the man involve the spectators in the play. The story continues to tell that Rani is the Queen of long tresses. Her beauty can be felt even by blind Kurudavva:

> Ayyo! How beautiful you are? Ears like hibicus, skin like young mango leaves. Lips like roll of silk. How can that Appanna gallivant around leaving such loveliness wasting away at home? (32)

Rani's doting father finds her a suitable match Appanna (any man). But Appanna ill-treats her and keeps her under lock and key. Even Kappanna, Kurudavva's son, is astonished at viewing it, 'Mother, what does it mean when a man locks his wife in?' (30)

On the other hand Appanna spends his night with a concubine and comes home only for lunch. Rani's image of an ideal marriage shatters and she faces the reality. Her 'self' is broken and she finds no one to support her in her solitary cell. Being locked has a great impact on Rani's psyche. She starts living in the dreams and tries to seek the fulfillment of her desires in the daydreams. Her parents appear in the dreams and console her: 'Don't worry', they promise her 'we won't let you go away again ever!" (28) The harsh reality of her isolation shatters the veil from her ivory image of a married life and the dreams assume strange shapes:

> In the morning, the stag with the golden antlers comes to the door. He calls out to Rani. She refuses to go. 'I am not a stag', he explains, 'I am a prince.' (28)

In utter despondency, Rani meets the prince of her dreams and talks to herself, then breaks into sobs realizing the harshness of truth.

If bolt comes from the blue, the help also sometimes comes from the unexpected quarter. Kurudavva, who is the friend of her husband's mother, visits her. She is distressed to see her pathetic plight. She is passionately touched to see Rani 'locked up like a caged bird.' Therefore she provides Rani a root which has the magical quality of igniting love in the heart of the man that eats it as it has been tested on her own husband. Kurudavva says: "Grind it into a nice paste and feed it to your husband and watch the results. Once he smells you, he won't go sniffing after that bitch. He will make you a wife instantly." (34)

Generally, the cynics of feminism declare that women are the enemies of woman. But this is due to the fact that women are urged for their survival to absorb, observe and propagate patriarchal culture as aptly argued by Srilata Batliwala in her brilliant article, "Why do women oppress women."[2] But contrary to it, Karnad in this play creates Kurudavva's character who understands the oppression of a woman and tries to support Rani in her strife against the patriarchal mind-set.

Further Rani prepares the paste and pours it into the curry. She is flustered when the curry turns blood red. Rani gets horrified and she goes out and pours the entire curry into the ant-hill in the premises where King Cobra lives. The charm works. Naga, the king cobra living in the ant-hill consumes the curry and falls in love with Rani at once. Naga enters Rani's house at night in the shape of Appanna and at this juncture Act First ends.

Act Two presents the love story of Rani and Naga. The cobra continues to visit her every night. He assuages the hurt feelings of Rani by making little inquiries. Rani is confused. Appanna of the day is totally different from Appanna of the night. The former is cold and cruel while the latter is warm and loving. She fails to make out how the man changes so completely. She is in a dilemma. She does not believe her senses: "His visit last night I assumed I must have dreamt that. I am certainly not dreaming now, which means I am going mad. Spending the whole day by myself is rotting my brain." (42)

The actual Appanna has brought a dog to keep blind Kurudavva away from his wife. Naga kills the dog since it creates disturbance in Rani's sleep in the daytime. Naga explains to Rani that the spirit of love pervades the whole universe. Even animals and plants do it:

> Frogs croaking in pelting rain, tortoises singing soundlessly in the dark, foxes, crabs, ants, rattles, sharks, swallows—even the geese! The female begins to smell like the wet earth. And stung by her smell, the king Cobra starts searching for his queen. The tiger bellows for his mate. . . . Within everything that sprouts, grows, stretches, creaks and blooms—everywhere, those who come together, cling, fall apart lazily! It is there and there and there, everywhere. (45)

Consequently, Rani becomes pregnant. Naga asks her to hide her pregnancy as long as she can. The actual husband is now upset. Appanna drags her to the village court where the village elders order her to prove her chastity by taking the ordeal of red hot iron, while Appanna conniving at the extra-marital relation with his concubine and his inhuman treatment of his wife. This juxtaposition of innocent Rani and Appanna, the blatant male culprit, exposes gender-biased value system of the patriarchal society. This play can be compared with Vijay Tendulkar's *Silence! The Court is in the Session,* where the protagonist, Leela Benare, an emancipated woman, is entangled in the relationship with Prof. Damle. In Tendulkar's play also, Damle's crime is connived at whereas Benare is accused of indecent behaviour.

The question arises whether Rani is a chaste woman in spite of getting a child from the lover snake. Even Ahilya was outcast for a similar offence. Hardy has tackled this question judiciously in his novel *Tess of the D'Urbervilles*. Tess becomes the victim of the prurient employer. The world changed overnight for her. None but Tess holds herself guilty so much so that nature seems to revile at her: "The midnight airs and gusts, moaning amongst and tightly wrapped buds and bark of the winter twigs, were formulate of bitter reproach. . . . She looked upon herself as a figure of guilt intruding into the haunts of Innocence."[3] But the innocent girl thinks: "Was once lost always lost really true of chastity? She would ask herself. She might prove it false if she could veil bygones. The recuperative power which pervades organic nature was surely not denied to maidenhood alone."[4]

But the Indian Rani is caught in the steel frame-work of social ethics so strongly that she cannot rise above ingrained moral values. It is therefore natural for Rani to suffer. Rani confesses swearing by king cobra: "Yes, my husband is this king Cobra. Except for these two, I have not touched any one of the male sex . . . if I lie let the Cobra bite me." (58)

The Naga realizing her predicament advises Rani to hold King Cobra instead of a red hot iron bar. As soon as Rani plunges her hand in the ant-hill and pulls out the cobra, the cobra spreads its hood like an umbrella over her head and does not bite her. The crowd is enchanted by this miracle and elevates Rani to the position of a Goddess. This fragment of the play explores Karnad's "Indianness" of Indian Theatre through the presentation of the true character of Indian society.

However Appanna believes at heart that he has been tricked into accepting the paternity of someone else's child. He is distraught: "What am I to do? Is the whole world against me? Have I sinned so much that even nature should laugh at me? I know I haven't slept with my wife. . . . Let any miracle declare her a goddess. But I know! What sense am I to make of my life if that's worth nothing?" (60)

On the other hand, Naga is also disconcerted. He is also unable to bear the pain of being separated from Rani. He reveals: "Rani! My Queen! The fragrance of my night! The blossom of my dream. In another man's arm? . . . Someone must die. Someone has to die." (61) The Naga who is now unable to fulfill his love commits suicide and dies like a true lover and finds place in the tresses of Rani's hair.

Thus, the conclusion of the play is used by the playwright to anticipate the spectators or the man's objection to the unconvincing ending of the fairytale, "they lived happily ever after." (64) It can be established that Girish Karnad presents a comprehensive and all-embracing Indian social milieu. The sociological picture of the Indian woman is not idyllic, poetic or one-sided but realistic and truthful. The attention is also focused on the marginalized position of the woman in the Indian society as well as 'her' elevated heights in the traditional patriarchal society.

NOTES

1. Girish Karnad, "Introduction", *Three Plays* (Oxford University Press, 1994), p. 17.
2. Srilata Batliwala "Why do women oppress women?" *The Hindu*, Sunday Magazine, 2 May 1992, III.
3. Thomas Hardy, *Tess of the D'Urbervilles* (Rupa Paperback, 2002).
4. *Ibid.*